THE NATIONAL HEALTH SERVICE

A POLITICAL HISTORY

NEW EDITION

Charles Webster

OXFORD
UNIVERSITY PRESS

OXFORD
UNIVERSITY PRESS

Great Clarendon Street, Oxford OX2 6DP

Oxford University Press is a department of the University of Oxford.
It furthers the University's objective of excellence in research, scholarship,
and education by publishing worldwide in

Oxford New York

Auckland Cape Town Dar es Salaam Hong Kong Karachi Kuala Lumpur
Madrid Melbourne Mexico City Nairobi New Delhi Shanghai Taipei Toronto

With offices in

Argentina Austria Brazil Chile Czech Republic France Greece
Guatemala Hungary Italy Japan South Korea Poland Portugal
Singapore Switzerland Thailand Turkey Ukraine Vietnam

Oxford is a registered trade mark of Oxford University Press
in the UK and in certain other countries

Published in the United States
by Oxford University Press Inc., New York

First edition published 1998
Second edition published 2002

British Library Cataloguing in Publication Data

Data available

Library of Congress Cataloging in Publication Data

Webster, Charles, 1936–
The National Health Service : a political history / Charles
Webster.
p. cm.
Includes bibliographical references and index.
1. National Health Service (Great Britain)–History. 2. Medical
care–Great Britain–History. 3. Public health–Great Britain–
History. I. Title.
RA413.5.G7W43 1998 362.1'0941–dc21 97-47054

ISBN 0-19-925110-X

7 9 10 8 6

Typeset by SNP Best-set Typesetter Ltd., Hong Kong
Printed in Great Britain
on acid-free paper by
Biddles Ltd., King's Lynn, Norfolk

For Carol

PREFACE TO THE SECOND EDITION

This book was conceived towards the end of a long period of Conservative government. A change of administration occurred just before the book was completed. The second edition is produced in very different circumstances from the first. Labour is now the settled party of government. Five years of New Labour administration has brought about a transformation in the NHS. Labour's programme of modernisation and more recent commitment to higher spending are a response to the mounting crisis of confidence that I highlighted in the Conclusions to my first edition. A second edition taking account of the period ending February 2002 will hopefully reinforce the value of this book. The NHS was a live political issue at the date of the first edition. Since then the health service has moved to the top of the domestic political agenda. Future policy and indeed the very survival of the NHS are now recognised as matters of great national urgency. As politicians embark on yet further major policy reviews, they appreciate more that ever before that the past record is crucial to the resolution of the crisis that they currently confront.

Alterations and additions to the text are particularly designed to provide a guide to the thinking and policies of New Labour and also a general context for current policy exchanges. My book remains one of very few to survey the entire history of the NHS. In view of the deep-rooted character of the problems facing the NHS, this long-term perspective possesses an obvious utility. This study is of course only one among many sources containing an assessment of recent events. There is now a new and welcome convergence between the policy and historical literature. Reflecting this change of perspective, politicians and policy analysts now reach instinctively for historical justification of their conclusions. Consequently, more than ever before in the life of the NHS, history plays an operational role in the policy process. The National Health Service therefore constitutes an ideal territory for establishing the constructive value of contemporary history.

In addition to those thanked in the preface to the first edition, I would like to express warm gratitude for contributions of various kinds from my following friends and colleagues, Tony Cowper, Basiro Davey, Derek Gillard, Avner Offer, Allyson Pollock, Mike Rayner, Jon Sussex, also Ivon Asquith, Ruth Parr and colleagues at OUP.

C.W.

All Souls College
February 2002

PREFACE TO THE FIRST EDITION

This historical review of the National Health Service, timed to coincide with the fiftieth anniversary, requires no special explanation. The tendency for lapses in the collective memory, even about quite recent events, together with a multiplicity of ill-founded myths about the more distant past, argue for the utility of a fresh examination of the history of the NHS as a whole. This book makes no pretence to deal with all aspects of health care during the period under consideration, nor to give more than a limited insight into medical advances. It concentrates on points involving political controversy and central issues of policy-making, hopefully in an accessible manner, with the aim of explaining why the health service was established and the steps by which it has reached the internal market structure favoured in the 1990s. This political subject matter is sufficiently complex, important, and topical to merit concentrated attention, but I have also tried to convey an impression of the health service as a humane activity. The first chapter, Creation and Consolidation, characterizes the health service during the inter-war period, followed by an account of preparations for a comprehensive health service during the Second World War and under the post-war Labour government, and finally of the first phase of the NHS ending in 1964. The second chapter, Planning and Reorganization, takes the history of the health service from the onset of the first Wilson administration in 1964 to the end of the Callaghan administration in 1979. The third chapter, Continuous Revolution, deals with the long period of Conservative government from 1979 to 1997, ending with a brief sequel on the first few months of the Blair New Labour administration.

The three chapters represent reasonably natural divisions, but since each embraces a group of administrations, both Labour and Conservative, essential details relating to changes of government and rotation of English health ministers are included as an Appendix. For reasons that will be evident in the text, in the interests of economy of treatment, in some cases the period divisions adopted for the chapters are not exactly observed. This is particularly the case in the treatment of the hospital services in Chapter 2, where no counterpart is included in the third chapter.

It is obviously impracticable in the limited space available to provide a comparative history of the health service in the four parts of the United Kingdom. For most purposes the account can be taken as referring to Great Britain as a whole, and more approximately to the UK, but sometimes this is not the case. Accordingly, at some points reference will be made to separate developments in Scotland and Wales, either in the text or in the notes. In accordance with the style of the relevant OUP series, annotations have been kept to a minimum; these relate mainly to primary sources. It is not practicable in the notes to refer to the voluminous relevant secondary literature, but a short guide to further reading provides selective introduction to these sources. On the same account it is not practicable to engage in interpretative debate, but it is hoped that the present survey will provide a fresh historian's insight into topics considered elsewhere with great intelligence by my social-science colleagues. Apart from one case relating to NHS expenditure, the text has not been altered in proof to take account of changes occurring after the date of this preface. The White Papers on the future of the NHS, published in December 1997, are therefore not described, although some comments are offered about their likely contents. At many points, the following text refects information generously provided by colleagues associated with the health service or government more generally. The author would also like to acknowledge generous assistance given in various capacities by Virginia Berridge, Jane Brown, Sir Henry Chadwick, Stephen Cretney, Professor Rees Davies, Kevin Fiddler, Andrew Glyn, Sir George Godber, Deborah McGovern, Richard Ponman, Mavis Porter, Norma Potter, and Carol Webster. Finally, I would like to thank Hilary Walford, George Miller, and colleagues at OUP for their encouragement and most effective support.

C.W.

All Souls College
July 1997

CONTENTS

LIST OF FIGURES

LIST OF TABLES

ABBREVIATIONS

Aegis	Aid for the Elderly in Government Institutions
AHA	Area Health Authority
AIDS	Acquired immune deficiency syndrome
BMA	British Medical Association
BSE	bovine spongiform encephalopathy
CHC	Community Health Council
CHI	Commission for Health Improvement
CHSC	Central Health Services Council
COI	Central Office of Information
CPC	Conservative Political Centre
CPRS	Central Policy Review Staff
DHA	District Health Authority
DHSS	Department of Health and Social Security
EU	European Union
FHSA	Family Health Service Authority
FPC	Family Practitioner Committee
FPS	Family Practitioner Services
GDP	Gross Domestic Product
HC Debates	House of Commons Debates
HIV	Human immunodeficiency virus
HCHS	Hospital and Community Health Services
HMC	Hospital Management Committee
HMO	Health Maintenance Organization
HMSO	Her Majesty's Stationery Office
ICRF	Imperial Cancer Research Fund
IHSM	Institute of Health Services Management
IMF	International Monetary Fund
LEA	Local Education Authority
LHA	Local Health Authority
Mencap	National Association of Parents of Backward Children
Mind	National Association for Mental Health
MOH	Medical Officer of Health

NAHAT	National Association of Health Authorities and Trusts
NBPI	National Board for Prices and Incomes
NHI	National Health Insurance
NHS	National Health Service
NICE	National Institute for Clinical Excellence
NIESR	National Institute of Economic and Social Research
NPHT	Nuffield Provincial Hospitals Trust
NSRS	Nuffield Social Reconstruction Survey
OECD	Organization for Economic Cooperation and Development
OHE	Office of Health Economics
PALS	Patient Advocacy and Liaison Service
PCG	Primary Care Group
PCT	Primary Care Trust
PEP	Political and Economic Planning
PESC	Public Expenditure Survey Committee
PFI	Private Finance Initiative
PRO	Public Record Office
RAWP	Resource Allocation Working Party
RCOG	Royal College of Obstetricians and Gynaecologists
RHA	Regional Health Authority
RHB	Regional Hospital Board
SDP	Social Democratic Party
SHHD	Scottish Home and Health Department
TUC	Trades Union Council
vCJD	variant Creutzfeldt-Jakob Disease
Webster	Charles Webster, *The Health Services since the War*, i. *Problems of Health Care: The National Health Service before 1957* (London: HMSO, 1988); ii. *Government and Health Care: The British National Health Service 1958–1979* (London: The Stationery Office, 1996).
WHO	World Health Organization

I

CREATION AND CONSOLIDATION

> We ought to take a pride in the fact that, despite our financial and economic anxieties, we are still able to do the most civilised thing in the world—put the welfare of the sick in front of every other consideration.[1]

At the time of its establishment in 1948 the National Health Service was recognised as a remarkable experiment in health care. Alone among its capitalist partners, the United Kingdom offered comprehensive health care to its entire population. On the basis of finance from general taxation, all of its services were free at point of use. This huge public service was recognised by outsiders as the outstanding example of 'socialised medicine' in the western world. Aneurin Bevan, architect of the new service, adopted the most ambitious remit for his creation, which he was apt to call 'the most civilised achievement of modern Government'.

On the basis of its unusual characteristics, from the moment of its inception, the NHS came under the national and international spotlight. Particular interest attaches to the conspicuously political character of the UK health service. To a greater degree than elsewhere, funding and policy became the province of the politician and the civil servant. Everywhere else health care was subject to political intervention, but the UK was unusual in the extent to which politicians assumed command and took over the levers of control for the entire health care system. This was an awesome responsibility. In some respects Bevan's mission was accomplished. Over the course of time the NHS consolidated its position and developed into a prestigious national institution. The high standing of the NHS in the eyes of the public, consistently displayed over a long period, is of course primarily a testimony to the consistent record of achievement of a dedicated health care workforce.

The historical record suggests a less generous estimate of the contribution of governments, politicians and bureaucrats. Notwithstanding their habitual claim that the NHS is granted the highest priority, in practice it has been mismanaged, neglected and starved of resources. Thereby the work of the NHS workforce has been seriously handicapped and services have fallen short of the standards taken for granted elsewhere. In response to growing public alarm and the sense of crisis that has overtaken the NHS, health issues have steadily moved up the political agenda until they now occupy the front line of British politics. The troubled history of the political stewardship over the health service constitutes the central subject matter of this book. A closer look at the controversies surrounding the origins of the health service enables us better to understand how easily Bevan's great dream was translated into disappointing reality.

Flawed Inheritance

It would be an error to regard the NHS as a spontaneous creation. The very scale and complexity of the formative process testify to the substantial scale of existing health services. In common with other advanced Western economies, the UK experienced a steady expansion in its health services. As a consequence of a long process of accretion, by the outset of the Second World War voluntary agencies and public authorities had built up a formidable array of services at least nominally covering the basic medical needs of all sections of the population. From the mid-nineteenth century, direct state intervention in health care had steadily increased. Following a pattern common to other European states, the UK accumulated a large body of legislation addressed to the control of public health, the regulation of the health-care professions, and the provision of services to many different client groups. Through the mechanisms of the poor law, public health, education, and health insurance, central and local government between them provided and financed an ever-increasing range of health services, until by 1939 a few of the more affluent and most progressive local authorities were within sight of providing a comprehensive health service.

Expansion of the public sector reduced the role of voluntary agencies, but the voluntary sector retained its importance. It even proved capable of generating resources sufficient for the rebuilding of some major hospitals. Indeed, in the course of the inter-war period, many new voluntary bodies were established in response to the escalating problems of poverty and ill health associated with the economic depression.

The process of incremental growth operating over the course of more than a century has sometimes fostered the impression that by the start of the Second World War a comprehensive health service was so near to accomplishment that its final institution represented an inevitability. Any such construction tends to overlook the shortcomings of the health-care system and underestimate the obstacles to further change. The path to the NHS was by no means an inevitable and logical progression. There was no smooth process of evolutionary change and a noticeable absence of consensus over most basic aspects of health-care policy. Informed opinion was indeed united over the merit of maintaining decent standards of health, but this was little more than a commonplace of civilized society, for the most part a vacuous assertion, since its denial was inconceivable.

In practice any step towards translation of pious sentiments regarding health care into practicable objectives was liable to expose clashes of ideological loyalty and stir up conflict between affected vested interests. Consequently, the transition from the haphazard assemblage of pre-war health services to the NHS was characterized by protracted and intense dispute, during the entire course of which the final outcome remained in doubt. It was perhaps inevitable that the publicly-funded health services would continue to expand, but throughout the Second World War the scale and character of this reform remained an entirely unsettled question.

Chaos and Depression

Despite the high status of the great teaching hospitals, continuing successes in medical research, and some impressive initiatives undertaken by local government, during the inter-war period it was impossible to disguise the overall sense of disquiet about the state of the UK health services. By comparison with many other advanced

Western economies, including the white dominions, the UK's health services were falling behind, and these deficiencies showed up in the international league tables of health indices. An embarrassing gulf opened up between the aspirations of enlightened planners and realities on the ground. Whereas the important Dawson Report of 1920 had looked forward to the creation of a coordinated system of comprehensive health centres situated in garden-city environments, the greater part of the population continued to live in conditions of Dickensian squalor. These slum-dwellers were denied the basic amenities of civilized life and of course they lacked access to health services of even a decent minimum standard, let alone the advantage of the new forms of treatment made possible by advances in medical science. Social investigations amply testified to the damaging consequences of poverty, ill health, and inadequate sources of social support. The worst affected were working-class women. As dependants, they were even excluded from meagre National Health Insurance (NHI) medical provisions. They lacked the material resources adequately to support their families and were therefore forced to deny themselves medical assistance or even an adequate diet. Their adversity was compounded by the absence of access to family-planning services.

Although there occurred a series of marginal improvements in health services, throughout the inter-war period there was a palpable sense of crisis, even panic, about the lethargic pace of improvement and the absence of effective leadership from the health departments. Even the big rationalization attempted through the Local Government Act of 1929 was unsuccessful in instilling confidence. Commenting on this development, W. A. Robson complained about the continuing 'multiplication of health authorities and the disintegration of function'. With respect to the health services as a whole, he regretted the continuing 'waste, inefficiency, chaos, and worst of all, a failure to envisage the health of the community at different ages and different stages'. This latter criticism was aimed at the bewildering range of agencies supplying health care, which deprived any individual of continuity of treatment. Robson called for application of the principles of integration, unification, and simplification in the organization of health care to guarantee the protection of the health of all members of the community 'from womb to grave'.[2]

Improving economic conditions in the late 1930s failed to reduce the sense of alarm. Writing in 1937, the chief author of the Dawson Report expressed concern that health care was being damaged by the isolation and widening administrative division between services. He particularly regretted that there existed two rival hospital systems, the public sector and the voluntary hospitals, 'duplicating and even conflicting, without machinery in existence for coordinating their activities'.[3] The recently formed and influential social-science pressure group, Political and Economic Planning (PEP), the body that produced the only comprehensive review of the British health services undertaken before the Second World War, complained about lack of unity in the two hospital systems; the 1,000 voluntary hospitals were 'self-governing institutions, jealous of their independence and only loosely associated with each other', while the 3,000 public hospitals were distributed between hundreds of separate local authorities only remotely regulated by the health departments.[4] As witnessed by the wartime surveys of hospital facilities, any area was likely to illustrate the chaos of the situation, as, for instance, when the South Wales surveyors discovered that in their area ninety-three hospitals were being provided by forty-six local authorities. Functioning entirely independently of the local authorities and of one another, there were also forty-eight voluntary hospitals. With some understatement, the surveyors concluded that 'the integration of all these hospitals would have many advantages'.[5]

Even within any one local authority, health functions were distributed between many committees, operating without coordination and therefore liable to dangerous lapses, as witnessed by a notorious typhoid outbreak that occurred in Croydon in 1937. Adding further to the confusion of the situation, a further entirely independent entity was the cumbersome NHI administration, established in 1911, the main function of which was supplying minimum financial relief during sickness and 'panel-doctor' services for the low paid on the basis of weekly deductions of income for the so-called 'health stamp'.

World War and Planning for Reconstruction

It took a second world war to shatter the inertia of the established regime. In anticipation of likely air-raid casualties amounting to at least 300,000, with remarkable speed and efficiency an Emergency Medical Service was set in place. PEP pointed out that 'the bombing plane, by transforming the nature of warfare, has forced on us a transformation of our medical services'.[6] The *Luftwaffe* achieved in months what had defeated politicians and planners for at least two decades. For the purposes of war, all hospitals were coordinated together under the civil defence regional administration. This regional organization supervised the training and distribution of professional personnel and the modernization of hospitals; it also organized for the first time a regional blood transfusion service, a national public health laboratory service, and regional specialist facilities for services as diverse as rehabilitation, fractures, plastic surgery, neurology, and psychiatry. The need for emergency action to introduce these services was itself a reflection of the backwardness of facilities for specialist treatment. It was self-evident to planners that the nation's capacity to engage in warfare with ramifications affecting the entire population was likely to be handicapped by its inability to exploit the capacities of medical advance. Just before the war the Director General of the Emergency Medical Service complained that his initial surveys had confirmed the 'low standard of hospital accommodation in the country as a whole'; even the prestigious teaching centres were 'structurally unsafe or woefully antiquated' and therefore unable to meet the needs of the emergency services.[7] Although the Emergency Medical Service was allocated the resources to transform the acute and casualty services, as the wartime regional surveys indicated, many parts of the old system were left untouched by its activities. Indeed, the successes of the Emergency Medical Service were dependent on its appropriation of the better hospital facilities of all types, with the result that the plight of large numbers of vulnerable and long-stay patients became even worse; these most deprived members of the community were exposed to humiliating conditions arguably little better than the concentration camp.

The Emergency Medical Service and related support services

demonstrated the remarkable capacity to make up for lost ground and prepare for a bombing catastrophe on a scale that mercifully failed to materialize. So impressive was this great constructive enterprise that PEP in common with many others called for the immediate conversion of the Emergency Hospital Scheme into a National Hospital Service.[8] This obsession with ambitious schemes for peacetime reconstruction reflected a spirit of euphoria that took hold of the intelligentsia during the darkest days of the war. Although the main energies of the nation were absorbed in the desperate struggle for survival, 'post-war reconstruction' was pursued with the greatest seriousness as a task of complementary importance. The outburst of planning activity in the fields of health and welfare at this time prompted Richard Titmuss to draw attention to the paradox that 'when human lives are cheapest, the desire to preserve life and health is at its highest'.[9]

The Emergency Medical Service and general cry for radical change emanating from many different groups of planners forced the health departments to accept the need for a substantial measure of reform to meet the needs of a future peacetime situation. As a first step, the Minister of Health promised that after the war the government would establish a comprehensive hospital service. It was envisaged that existing local authorities would undertake planning, but the actual service would involve a partnership between the public and voluntary sectors. As a concession to advanced thinking, it was agreed that the new service would be designed on the basis of areas substantially larger than existing local authorities.[10] Any intention to limit post-war changes to the hospital service was soon undermined by Sir William Beveridge, whose audacious scheme for reconstructing social security included as a prior 'assumption *B*' that a 'national health service for prevention and comprehensive treatment' would be available to all members of the community.[11] In fact Beveridge was merely the most eloquent and strategically best-placed exponent of this call for radical overhaul of the health services. Directly parallel to the Beveridge Report, a group of Fabians outlined a similar ambitious scheme for the reconstruction of social security, also assuming the establishment of a comprehensive state medical service.[12] Reflecting opinion at the grass roots, the Nuffield Social Reconstruction

Survey recorded widespread demand for the replacement of the panel system by a comprehensive state medical service.[13]

Although the government was divided over its response to Beveridge, his report both reflected and released a tide of expectation that could not be stemmed. Indicative of the high level of anxiety concerning the defectiveness of the existing system, the idea of a national health service evoked spontaneous and passionate support from all sections of the community. Beveridge became the convenient focus for more determined agitation for a new health service for the entire population, capable of supplying the most modern forms of treatment and care without the humiliation and stigma associated with established agencies of charity, the poor law, or public health.

The fresh spirit of solidarity and altruism associated with war has perhaps contributed subsequently to a spurious impression that such an obviously desirable objective as an efficient health service represented a readily achievable objective. While the relevant interest groups spontaneously subscribed to this aspiration, it was immediately evident that they would pursue without compromise their totally divergent and incompatible ideas about realizing the objective of modernization. Accordingly, the interest groups responded to Beveridge by retreating to their entrenched positions. The bitter jealousies that wrecked the pathetically limited pre-war efforts at reform resurfaced during the Second World War and precluded the prospect of achieving consensus over the shape of the new health service.

Preparations for reform took place in an atmosphere of noisy conflict. This was not merely a temporary perturbation among negotiating parties. The polarization of attitudes experienced at this time was deeply damaging and it cast a long shadow over the future NHS. This episode reflects badly on all the parties. The planners were inflexible in their thinking, wedded to out-of-date conceptions of local administration, and misguided about the character and power of opposition forces, especially within the medical profession. The latter persisted with constructions of the future entirely determined and shaped by their financial self-interest and ideologies rooted in the distant past.

The main running in the wartime negotiations was made by the

Ministry of Health and the local-government associations, a long-standing and comfortable partnership which represented the biggest power block on account of the importance of the former as the main agent of policy-making and the latter as the dominant provider of services. They envisaged that a comprehensive health service would be established by further extending the powers of existing local authorities, with the formation of joint bodies to overcome difficulties associated with the small size of existing local-government entities. This formula represented minimum interference with the established policy regime within the Ministry of Health. It was expected that voluntary hospitals would continue in some kind of partnership with the municipal sector, but it was anticipated that this would be a temporary device, since the voluntary hospitals would prove incapable of sustaining themselves. The radicalism of the new plan centred on primary care; general practitioners were to be employed directly by local authorities, thereby losing the autonomy associated with their status as independent contractors under the NHI system.[14] It was also assumed that as quickly as feasible general practitioners would be assembled into groups to work alongside other local-authority staff in purpose-built health centres.

Notwithstanding its limitations, the above plan at least represented a significant step towards objectives that had defeated generations of public-health planners. At least since the Royal Sanitary Commission Report of 1871, reformers such as Sir John Simon, author of the classic *English Sanitary Institutions* (1891), or Sidney and Beatrice Webb, through the medium of the Minority Report of the Poor Law Commissioners (1909), had attached high priority to the goal of unifying all state-provided health services in any one natural area of administration under a single agency of local government. The proposals of the Coalition Government, first formulated in 1943, were the first officially sanctioned scheme to approximate to this objective. This plan aimed to assemble all publicly funded health services under some forty bodies constituted from single local authorities or combinations of them. Voluntary hospitals constituted the only stumbling block to complete integration.

The bureaucrats completely miscalculated about the acceptability of their scheme. Ironically, their own earlier dismissal of the Dawson Report on account of its oversimplifications and lack of political realism now became the basis for the attack on the official scheme. From the traditionalist camp, neither the voluntary hospitals nor the general practitioners were willing to contemplate being swallowed up by the unified system. The voluntary hospitals sought guarantees to prevent local government exercising a stranglehold over the public subsidies they were promised, while their staffs resented the prospect of being reduced to the rank of public-health employees. General medical practitioners insisted on continuing separate administration of their service and retention of their status as independent contractors.

In the spring of 1943 the government embarked on confidential discussions on its provisional plan; in modified form, this scheme was then described in a long, diffuse, and confusing White Paper, *A National Health Service*, issued in February 1944.[15] The government's proposals were heavily criticized, especially by medical organizations and the voluntary hospital lobby. In an effort to conciliate these interests, in 1945 a further White Paper was drafted by the Conservative caretaker administration. The agent of appeasement was Henry U. Willink, the Conservative Minister of Health. The details of Willink's scheme were circulated to all members of the medical profession, but the White Paper was never released on account of Conservative ministers' estimate of its likely unpopularity and vulnerability to criticism.[16]

The mature proposals emerging in 1945 under Willink, after more than four years of wartime preparation and debate, entailed reversal of many characteristics of the scheme originally promulgated within the Ministry of Health. It was now suggested that local government would retain direct control only of the services that it had traditionally administered. For the purposes of planning over wider areas, it was proposed to establish area planning bodies and regional planning councils, which were conceived as a forum for joint effort by local authorities, voluntary hospitals, and the medical profession. It was anticipated that regional councils based on the areas of influence of university medical schools would take on the crucial task of advising the minister on the development of hospital specialities and the appointment of all consultants and specialists. The joint authorities of local government of the earlier proposal were scrapped and replaced by area planning bodies, which would assume statutory responsibility for producing a plan for the whole health service for each group of local authorities. In order to satisfy voluntary hospital sensitivities about direct relations with local authorities, it was agreed that disbursements from the local rates would be transferred through the medium of specially established area 'clearing houses', while hospital-planning would be largely devolved to hospital-planning groups working in direct collaboration with the regional councils. General medical practitioners were promised continuity of their existing arrangements for employment through a proposal to replace existing Insurance Committees by new 'local committees', fulfilling similar functions. Accordingly, general practitioners would remain as independent contractors; their payment would continue on the basis of capitation rather than salary; private practice would continue to be permitted. Health centres would survive as an option, but without affecting the contractual situation of general practitioners, and such health centres were to be regarded as a limited and 'controlled experiment' overseen by the central department. Having failed to produce a scheme acceptable to the professions, the government abandoned its earlier proposals for controlling the distribution of general practitioners in the interests of improving services in depressed areas. Previous government proposals had envisaged the establishment of a Central Medical Board to regulate the distribution of general practitioners and operate other professional controls. In response to an antagonistic response to this form of 'central direction', this proposal was now dropped. A final important concession to general practitioners was the government's agreement to allow the continuation of the established custom of the sale and purchase of goodwill.

The above proposals represented a major retreat from the 1944 White Paper. In particular, the long-established goal of unified administration under local government was now abandoned. The new proposals not only froze local-government participation at its current level, but also made local authorities subservient to area and regional planning bodies in which non-elected representatives would exercise a substantial voice. Local authorities were even threatened with the prospect of intrusion by non-elected professionals and other outsiders into their statutory health committees.

By this stage the health scheme was on the verge of becoming a particularly unhappy compromise, incapable of commanding support from any group, and offensive to all. Even some of the experts within the Ministry of Health regretted many of these concessions, which among other things had resulted in the 'abandonment of the cardinal principle of combining planning and execution in the same hands, but also the creation of a planning and administrative system of almost unworkable complexity'.[17] The local-authority associations recognized that departures from the original scheme had fundamentally eroded their power to plan and control the new health service. The medical profession and the voluntary hospitals knew that they had gained ground, but were hungry for yet further concessions.

In summary, negotiations conducted during the Second World War resulted in substantial capitulation to the medical and voluntary hospital lobbies, but at the cost of alienating Labour and local government. The bureaucrats were divided among themselves, but the majority of the planners sided with local government, which exposed them to bitter attack, especially from the British Medical Association (BMA). The objective of translating the Beveridge 'assumption *B*' into reality was no nearer realization in 1945 than it had been in 1942.

Labour in Power

The landslide victory obtained by Labour in the summer of 1945 presented an opportunity for decisive leadership on social policy; indeed Labour was pledged to an ambitious welfare-state programme. Labour had long been committed to establishing a comprehensive health service and this pledge was reaffirmed in its policy document *National Service for Health*, published in April 1943, coinciding with the launch of the Coalition Government's similar plan. Within the Coalition, Labour ministers tried to force the pace of health-service reform. After the collapse of the 1943 plan, Labour only reluctantly accepted the 1944 White Paper and it was distrustful of all further modifications, which it viewed as an erosion of the uneasy compromises embodied in the White Paper.

At the outset of the Attlee administration it was uncertain whether Labour would abide by the 1944 White Paper, or revert to the more radical alternative embodied in its own policy document or the Coalition's original plan. The uncertainty was increased by the appointment of Aneurin Bevan as Minister of Health. An ex-miner from South Wales, Bevan was notorious as a backbench irritant and leftist political maverick. This untried hand and the youngest member of Attlee's Cabinet was now given control over one of the largest departments in Whitehall; in this capacity he assumed power over housing and health, two of the biggest and most difficult undertakings for the post-war administration and fundamental to the maintenance of its credibility. Collapse of the government's housing and health reconstruction programmes after the First World War provided a doleful reminder of the pitfalls of Bevan's assignment.

Bevan quickly dispelled doubts about his abilities for decisive and constructive action. Civil servants understood that the Ministry of Health was now headed by a figure of much greater political stature than his recent predecessors. Bevan immediately gained the confidence of junior staff engaged in the health-service planning operation, one of whom recorded her impression that the new minister 'really cared about the way in which the people lived.'[18] This charisma and general capacity to inspire confidence was vital for the ambitious mission upon which Bevan was embarking. At all levels within the health service and among the population at large, Bevan tried and succeeded to a substantial degree in stimulating the belief that the new health service was a bold advance in which the UK was showing the way forward for civilization as a whole. Helpfully, Bevan's charismatic qualities were complemented by the more mundane gifts required to steer his programme through delicate negotiations both within the Cabinet and with outside interests. His pragmatism, common sense, and instinctive regard for the practical solution enabled his ambitious plan for transforming the health service to be realized in the remarkably short space of three years. Bevan therefore succeeded in dispelling the pessimism generated by many years of futile wrangling about the future of the health service, and he launched the new service on a new note of optimism.

At the outset of this great constructive enterprise, Bevan's gifts were not appreciated by senior officials within his department. The latter were firmly wedded to the Willink compromises and they were clearly determined to forge ahead with legislation on this basis. They were particularly protective of the independent status of the voluntary hospitals. Bevan's inclination to personal initiative was treated as an irritating diversion. The Permanent Secretary warned him that it was 'a pity to discard a plan which gives us much, if not all, of what we want, which is practically ready, and which would have a very large measure of agreement in its passage'.[19]

Bevan ignored this advice. To the chagrin of his senior officials, on the crucial question of the hospital service he struck out in an entirely fresh direction, which placed the emphasis on the scarcely considered alternative of nationalization. Perhaps within a couple of weeks of his appointment, he was already considering a scheme for bringing all hospitals under a single public authority controlled by the minister. Indeed these early deliberations about nationalization even considered adopting a regionalized and nationalized system for unification of all health services, except perhaps for the independent contractors.

Once Bevan had reached his conclusion, he moved quickly to regain the initiative in policy-making, much to the disconcertment of his own senior officials and the outside negotiators, especially the medical profession. During the war the profession had successfully cultivated a regime of continuous negotiation to the point where, by a process of attrition, it had successfully wrenched policy-making out of the hands of the government and effectively annexed it under its own control. Bevan declined the invitation to adopt the subordinate status imposed on his predecessor. He immediately re-established the minister's supremacy in policy-making, acting with remarkably little reference to outside interests, Whitehall departments, or even his own senior officials or ministerial colleagues. By disentangling himself from these impediments, Bevan broke out of the regime of interminable negotiations and tentative policy documents. With the aid of his little group of immediate advisers, within a few weeks Bevan had drawn up a firm plan; with little alteration this was translated into legislation within the space of a year.

Bevan's key proposal for a nationalized and regionalized hospital service was tried out on Cabinet colleagues on 11 and 18 October 1945, followed by discussion of his proposals for the abolition of the sale and purchase of medical practices on 3 December, and finally detailed consideration of the whole NHS scheme on 20 December 1945, 8 January and 8 March 1946. Considering the importance of the issues under consideration, these ministerial deliberations were little more than cursory, except on the sole issue of hospital nationalization, where Herbert Morrison led an abortive rearguard action in favour of the municipal alternative. These discussions paved the way for publication on 21 March 1946 of the National Health Service Bill and a White Paper containing an outline of the proposed legislation.[20] Although there had been many press leaks concerning Bevan's ideas over the previous six months, it was not until this date that his full intentions became evident. Owing to determined leadership from Bevan and only weak obstruction from an ineffective opposition in parliament, with remarkably little amendment the NHS legislation passed into law on 6 November 1946. With a similar lack of difficulty the Scottish health service legislation was set in place in 1947.

The New Plan for Health

Bevan's mature proposals represented a mixture of audacity and prudence. In some respects they were slightly less radical than the scheme originally contemplated in 1943. Unification of all health services under a single system of administration was regarded as impracticable and was abandoned in favour of the tripartite scheme already implicit in the plan inherited from the caretaker administration. The decision to adopt different forms of administration for hospitals, public health, and independent-contractor services represented a concession to the local authorities and the independent contractors, who were promised continuity of their existing forms of administration, which of course also possessed the additional advantage of saving planners from wrestling with big administrative changes on too many fronts simultaneously. However, this complex administrative system, the details of which are indicated in Fig. 1.1, risked creating a series of parallel, unequal, incompatible, and unintegrated health services, a danger counteracted by promises of active intervention on the part of the minister and high expectations concerning the role of the complicated central consultative machinery inherited from Willink's scheme. Although, like the new school system, the NHS was commonly called 'tripartite', in practice it was considerably more complicated than this.

The dominant and most original feature of Bevan's scheme lay in its proposals concerning the nationalization and regionalization of the hospital service. Although neither of these ideas had previously been regarded as practicable by the department on account of their known contentiousness, both attracted firm advocates among the experts. Indeed, regionalization of health administration and regional local government had been widely canvassed during the Second World War. This trend of thinking about local administration was consistent with advanced ideas about medical organization, especially among the hospital medical specialities, where many expert groups produced schemes for future development premised on the assumption of moves towards regionalization. With these aspirations in mind, R. C. Wofinden aptly summarized the medical case for regionalization:

> It was significant that in all these plans for future health services the key word was 'regionalisation' generally with the university medical school acting as focal point. There are obvious advantages in regional organisation. It allows economy of buildings, staff, and equipment, and enables the staff, by providing more clinical material, to become more proficient in their specialty Further, well-equipped centres are available for training and research purposes. Modern transport arrangements have provided a satisfactory answer to the original criticisms against regionalisation . . . There must be some co-operation to perfect services on a wider scale and to do away with narrow parochial boundaries which so often prevent individuals from obtaining treatment merely because they do not reside within the appropriate area. Regionalisation would appear to be the answer.[21]

These conclusions, written shortly before Bevan's plan was unveiled, indicated receptivity among leading hospital planners to the form of regionalization embodied in Bevan's new scheme. However, despite close harmony of attitudes, neither Wolfinden, nor other leaders of consultant opinion, seemed to appreciate that Bevan also was considering nationalization as a serious proposition.

The idea of using the Emergency Hospital Service as a springboard for the nationalization of hospitals had occasionally been canvassed during the Second World War in both England and Scotland, but this idea had been rejected in all the major planning documents. Although Labour favoured evolution towards a municipalized hospital service, its policy statements were careful to avoid offence to the voluntary sector.

There is virtually no direct evidence about the course of Bevan's thinking, but it is quite likely that his solution grew out of consideration of post-war reconstruction as a whole, especially with respect to his joint responsibility for housing and health. During the war there had been mounting concern about the ability of local government to take on all of the tasks of reconstruction lying within its traditional ambit, especially on account of the massive task of rebuilding and rehousing, and with the prospect of ambitious plans for the expansion of services such as education and health. Local government had been further handicapped by the government's decision to defer consideration of both local-government reorganization and the overhaul of the rate system of local taxation. Although the antiquated system of local government had performed creditably during the war, there was little confidence in its ability to take on all the tasks envisaged for the post-war period. Advocates of local-government reform singled out the health services for illustrating the weakness of the existing local-government system. In particular, the creation of a modern, integrated hospital system seemed beyond the capacities and purse of local government. Reflecting this conclusion, in January 1945 *The Economist* called for the creation of 'the new Medical Service on a national basis, wholly financed from national resources and embracing part or all of the health services which form so large a part of the local authorities' total expenditure'. It was pointed out that the nationalization alternative was less objectionable to the medical profession and perhaps even palatable to the voluntary hospitals, whereas both were vehemently antagonistic to any form of local-government control of their services.[22]

Although nationalization and regionalization were recognized as radical concepts, Bevan was not alone in favouring these alternatives. He was indeed aligning himself with a distinct body of expert opinion. These conclusions also fitted in with his own reservations about the capacities of local government and his ideas about the modernization of medical institutions. By emphasizing the scale and cost of the opportunities offered by housing and other developments remaining within local-government control, he calculated that local government would at least be reconciled to being relieved of the responsibility for the new health service and to the sacrifice of the major part of its traditional health-service functions. Since the voluntary hospitals were no longer financially viable and would be completely dependent on public subsidy, a change in their status was inevitable. Bevan calculated that the voluntary sector would regard nationalization as infinitely preferable to municipalization.

Bevan urged that the nationalized and regionalized scheme was an essential prerequisite for social and geographical equality: to 'achieve as nearly as possible a uniform standard of service for all', or to ensure that an 'equally good service is available everywhere'.[23] Also, to universalize the rudimentary specialist and consultant services, or reconstruction of the bomb-damaged and obsolete hospital stock, required a new system of organization transcending the limitations of local-government boundaries, and it needed resources on a scale beyond the competence of the rate system, even given the most generous level of the standard subsidies available from exchequer sources.

Nationalization permitted escape from the limitations of local-government divisions and made possible the full integration of all types of hospital. The system could be designed afresh, 'starting again with a clean slate'.[24] The minister's administrative agents were the regional boards (soon called Regional Hospital Boards (RHBs)), which exercised control over 'natural hospital regions'. The final proposals identified fourteen of these natural regions in England and Wales (London and the Home Counties being split segmentally into four regions, with Wales constituting a single region), and five in Scotland. It was envisaged that the regions would be responsible for the application of government policy, overall strategic planning, budgetary control, and some specific duties such as determining the development of specialities and consultant appointments. Bevan's scheme envisaged the maximum degree of delegation to local administrative bodies (initially called District Committees, soon renamed Hospital Management Committees (HMCs)), which would be concerned with the day-to-day management of groups of hospitals for each 'natural hospital district'—defined initially as an 'area able to support a general hospital or combined group of hospitals big enough to employ a full specialist staff for all normal needs'. It was anticipated that a characteristic local hospital group would contain about 1,000 beds. Geographical division was not in practice attained, since it was found more convenient to delegate mental and mental-handicap hospitals to specially designated HMCs. These constituted about one-third of the HMCs. Many of the remaining HMCs administered considerably fewer than the 1,000 beds originally anticipated. Half of these general HMCs contained fewer than 1,000 beds, while fifty possessed fewer than 500. At the local level the hospital system was therefore considerably more fragmented than originally intended.

In line with latest medical thinking, the 'natural hospital regions' were defined with respect to the catchments and spheres of influence of the major teaching hospitals—single undergraduate teaching hospitals outside London, or groups of these hospitals in the metropolitan regions. The only major point of disagreement between Bevan and his Scottish colleague related to the teaching hospitals. At first, in England and Wales it was proposed to exempt the teaching hospitals from state control, whereas in Scotland their nationalization was favoured from the outset. Bevan quickly changed his mind; the teaching hospitals were nationalized, but it was agreed to preserve their independent administration; each was granted its own Board of Governors, providing direct links with the central department, thereby avoiding subservience to the regional board. As indicated by Fig. 1.1, this represented a major complication of the 'tripartite' arrangement, and it was subversive to the unified regional conception, as, for instance, expressed by experts such as Wofinden, cited above. Scotland integrated the teaching hospitals into the regional structure from the outset. This constituted the main administrative difference between the health services north and south of the border.

Nationalization of municipal hospitals left for consideration the fate of the small and miscellaneous rump of remaining local-authority-administered health services. After briefly considering their assimilation into the regional system, Bevan elected to leave these services in the hands of local government. Local Health Authorities (LHAs) were constituted from existing county councils and county boroughs. This was a helpful concession to local government, and it also made sense, since many of the services were self-contained, related to the local-authority welfare services, or to the School Health Service administered by Local Education Authorities (LEAs). It was therefore agreed to leave the Medical Officer of Health (MOH) in charge of such functions as maternity and child welfare, domiciliary midwifery, health visiting, home nursing, home helps, care and aftercare services, vaccination and immunization, and other activities connected with public health and health education. Local authorities also retained control of the large ambulance service, and they were promised an important new function, the provision and maintenance of health centres, which it was hoped would 'be developed as fast and as widely as possible'.[25] These health centres were intended to house not only local-authority staff, but also the independent contractors.

Bevan reaffirmed his predecessor's compromises concerning the separate administration of independent-contractor services. At the local level it was agreed to administer the services provided by general medical practitioners, general dental practitioners, opticians, and pharmacists, by committees (soon called Executive Councils) that were essentially renamed Insurance Committees inherited from the panel system. The Executive Councils followed the geographical pattern of the LHAs, except that in eight cases county towns were assimilated with their surrounding county areas. The main features of Bevan's modified tripartite scheme are summarized in Fig. 1.1.

Labour revived the proposal for a central committee to control the distribution of medical practices (soon called Medical Practices Committee), which had featured in the 1944 White Paper, but had

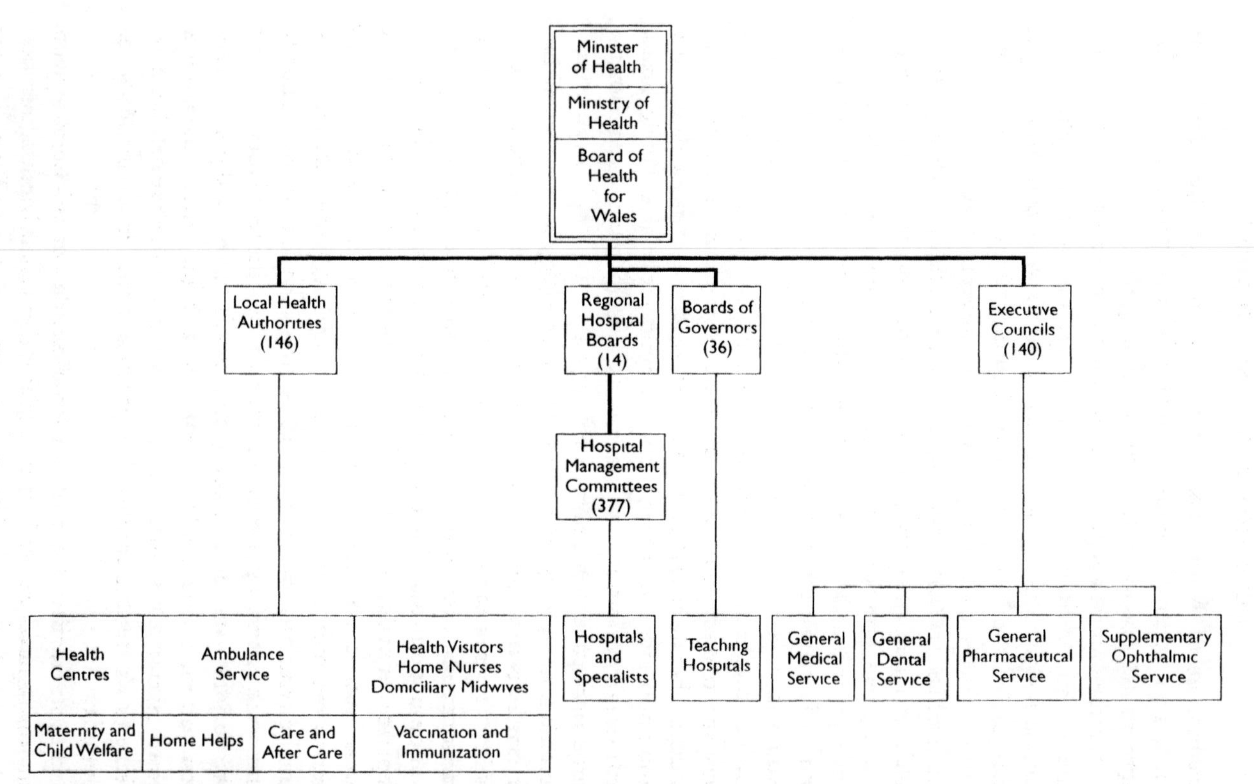

Figure 1.1. The National Health Service in England and Wales, 1948

been scrapped by Willink at the insistence of the BMA. The Medical Practices Committee possessed additional importance, since its controls on distribution would undermine the system of selling the value of practices, to which the profession was attached and had successfully defended in negotiations with Willink.

Consistent with the aspirations of the Beveridge Report, from the date of the earliest planning documents it had been assumed that the new health service would be universal (available to all), comprehensive (including all services, both preventive and curative), and free (involving no payment at the point of delivery). These three important ideas were carried over into Bevan's scheme without demur. However, there was much ambiguity about these principles and some of this opacity persisted into the Bevan proposals.

The BMA had opposed universality of the new service on account of undermining opportunities for private practice among general practitioners, but Willink had held on to this idea, and the BMA had given way on account of many other gains in its negotiations. The principle of universality was therefore no longer in dispute when Bevan assumed office.

The comprehensive principle was accepted by all concerned, but reservations existed on many fronts: owing to the special character of the services involved, there was opposition to infringing upon the independence of the Board of Control by ending the separate administration of the mental health services. On account of the shortage of trained practitioners, during the early planning stages there was hesitation about attempting to provide comprehensive dental and ophthalmic services. Some marginal services such as the children's service were divided between government departments and were candidates for rationalization, but the case for inclusion in the NHS was not regarded as compelling. Finally, many other services, such as the School Health Service and the occupational health services, fell under other government departments which were unwilling to contemplate their assimilation into the NHS. Bevan ended these uncertainties: the mental health services were included, but the Board of Control was allowed to continue with a more limited remit; comprehensive dental and ophthalmic services were included, but there were uncertainties about the final form these services would take; to avoid controversy with other government departments, such functions as the school and occupational health services remained outside the NHS.

The issue of charging for services was especially sensitive, rousing passions and fears among the people about exploitation by unscrupulous practitioners and purveyors of patent remedies, means-testing, unaffordable doctors' bills, and other humiliations connected with charity and the poor law. The 1944 White Paper contained the assurance that the 'new service will be free to all, apart from possible charges when certain appliances are provided . . . the costs of the new health service will be borne partly from central funds, partly from local rates and partly from the contributions of the public under any scheme of social insurance which may be brought into operation'.[26]

In explaining the sources of finance for his scheme to colleagues, Bevan repeated almost exactly the 1944 White Paper statement quoted above.[27] As indicated by Table 1.1, the proposal for nationalization of hospitals brought about a sharp change in the balance of contributions from the three sources of funding. The new system extinguished the small but unquantifiable contribution from voluntary sources, and also sharply reduced the share from local-authority rates. The effect was to transfer virtually the whole

TABLE 1.1. *The cost of the health service, England and Wales, 1938–1945* (£m.)

Sources of funding	1938/9 (actual)	1944 (estimate)	1945 (estimate)
Social-security contributions	11.2	35.7	35.7
Central taxation	3.0	48.3	103.3
Local taxation	40.3	48.0	6.0
Voluntary sources[a]	11.5	—	—
TOTAL	66.0	132.0	145.0

[a] It was assumed that the voluntary contribution would decline after the Second World War, but the extent of this reduction was uncertain

Sources: Ministry of Health, Department of Health for Scotland, *A National Health Service*, Cmd 6502 (London: HMSO, 1944); Bevan, 'Proposals for a National Health Service', CP(45)339, 13 Dec 1945, PRO CAB 129/5

burden of financing the health service to central taxation, of which the social-security contribution was part. Bevan's memoranda were strangely lacking in precision about estimates of costs or justification for changes in funding arrangements, but he urged that, since there were uniform rates of insurance contribution, it was essential to guarantee an equal quality of treatment for all, something attainable only by transfer of the burden of the service to the exchequer.[28] Elsewhere Bevan justified this new balance as being consistent with socialist commitments to progressive taxation and related redistributional objectives. The promise of a free service was a principle to which Bevan became irrevocably attached, as indicated in the bold declaration comprising the first page of the leaflet, *The New National Health Service*, distributed to all homes at the outset of the new service:

> It will provide you with all medical, dental, and nursing care. Everyone—rich or poor, man, woman or child—can use it or any part of it. There are no charges, except for a few special items. There are no insurance qualifications But it is not a charity. You are all paying for it, mainly as taxpayers, and it will relieve your money worries in time of illness.

Such unambiguous assurances concerning absence of direct charges reflect the sensitivity of this issue among the public, for whom this reassurance constituted one of the greatest attractions and a major source of relief from anxiety. On the basis of his experience in overseeing the introduction of the new service, Sir George Godber confirms that freedom from charges and doctors' bills was for the population and the professions alike 'the most satisfying thing about the Health Service'.[29]

As already indicated, Bevan went further than his predecessors in promising a scheme involving an explicit egalitarian commitment and a first-class standard of treatment, thereby implying emancipation from the preoccupation with the 'minimum' or subsistence standards that had characterized earlier welfare proposals. Bevan's model was therefore the private wing of the voluntary hospital rather than the poor-law infirmary—hence his frequent promises to eliminate the second-class types of treatment and to 'generalize' or 'universalize' the best standards of treatment and care, and thereby 'place this country in the forefront of all countries of the world' in its medical services.[30] The Attlee administration somewhat casually fell into line with Bevan's proposal, without any real sense of the momentous scale of the financial commitments that would be entailed in establishing services on the ambitious scale envisaged in Bevan's health plan.

Renewed Confrontation

Although Bevan's scheme was implemented almost as originally conceived, this outcome was far from certain in 1946. On account of its unambiguous rejection of the discredited pre-war system and the prospect of building still further on the already substantial improvements experienced during the Second World War, the public was overwhelmingly supportive of the new scheme. The media were also generally appreciative. Even organs not particularly sympathetic to Labour such as *The Times* and *The Economist*, although expressing reservations, also accepted that, with respect to the crucial issue of hospital organization, Bevan's solution was superior to any previous alternative. Indeed *The Economist* even suggested that Bevan had succeeded in proving that, contrary to the assertions of the great Lord Dawson, it was possible to combine 'socialism in its administration with individualism in its practice'.[31]

The high expectations and euphoria concerning the new health service among the public and the media contrast with the predominantly sceptical response among many medico-politicians. Among the power-brokers there was dissatisfaction both with the policy and with Bevan's way of doing business. Bevan was in no doubt about the potential controversiality of his proposals. At the outset he warned Cabinet colleagues that there would be an outcry from both the voluntary hospitals and the local authorities. He was less certain about the response of the medical profession, but on the whole he believed that they would be satisfied that the new service would offer them a 'square deal'. On this basis he thought that the 'profession would be solidly behind it'.[32]

The above construction turned out to be entirely at odds with events. The voluntary hospitals and the local authorities lamented their losses, but neither mounted sustained opposition against Bevan's proposals. Only the medical profession, and more particularly the powerful BMA, elected to fight and succeeded in driving its thorn deeply into Bevan's flesh.

Most of the major negotiating parties could decently bury their pride and become reconciled to Bevan's scheme. The voluntary hospitals were relieved to have escaped control by local government; they took comfort from the high degree of independence granted to teaching hospitals and the prospect that they would be granted a substantial voice in hospital management at all levels. In general the new hospital system was modelled more on the voluntary pattern than on its municipal competitor. The local authorities were dissatisfied, but, since most of the large authorities were Labour controlled, they were disinclined to disrupt a scheme that was clearly greatly to the advantage of their constituents.

From the outset of negotiations it was evident that the medical profession comprised an uneasy alliance of diverse interests. Bevan's scheme finally disrupted the unity of this coalition. The consultant élite had long been favourable to regionalization and they were prepared to contemplate nationalization as a means to realize this objective. In addition, Bevan's scheme offered many other tangible benefits to hospital medical staff. The senior staff were rescued from their honorary status, whereby they gave their services without charge in voluntary hospitals in anticipation of compensatory returns from private patients, who were increasingly treated in the exclusive private wings of the same hospitals, the proliferation of which exercised a notorious distorting effect on the voluntary system in the twentieth century. Consultants were offered either full-time or part-time contracts. The latter enabled them to engage in private practice in return for a small reduction in salary; to facilitate this private practice, the pay beds of voluntary hospitals were carried over into the NHS. Consultants were also granted a generous system of distinction awards to compensate for any loss of private earnings and reward excellence in their professional accomplishments. Furthermore, hospital medical staff were promised involvement at all levels in the management structure. There was nothing in the Bevan scheme meriting militancy and non-cooperation on the part of consultant staff. The politically dominant element within the Royal Colleges therefore assumed the role of peacemakers.

The threat of non-cooperation stemmed from the general medical practitioners and general dental practitioners. The former dominated the BMA and they were mobilized by an aggressive and battle-hardened leadership. The responses of the BMA were conditioned by memories of its past failures extending back to at least 1911; its leaders were determined to reverse their earlier humiliations. They therefore entered into negotiation with maximum distrust and unwillingness to compromise. Employing techniques of megaphone diplomacy imitative of totalitarian regimes, the BMA set about shaping the new health service in accordance with its own policies. As already noted, by virtue of hard negotiation the representatives of the profession had effectively wrecked the plans framed by Coalition ministers and they had been particularly successful in securing concessions relating to general practice. By reversing some of these decisions, Bevan renewed fears that Labour was preparing to conscript general practitioners into becoming full-time salaried servants of a state medical service. The Bevan plan therefore stirred up all the fears traditionally associated with the threat of full-time salaried service under the MOH. No amount of disclaimers on the part of Bevan, or assurances concerning essential continuity with the panel system, were sufficient to alleviate these anxieties.

The BMA accordingly embarked on a campaign to expunge all features of Bevan's proposals identified as eroding the established employment conventions applying to independent contractors. Their targets of attack perhaps seem rather trivial from our later perspective, but at the time they were regarded as essential and non-negotiable demands; unless they were met in full, the whole profession seemed likely to boycott entry into the new service. The intransigence of the profession was confirmed regularly at representative meetings of the BMA and by three plebiscites of the entire profession.

The profession made four main demands: first, that the sale and purchase of goodwill associated with medical practices should be allowed to continue; secondly, that the basic salary component in remuneration should be eliminated and that payment should be entirely by capitation; thirdly, that the proposed controls over the distribution of general practitioners should be dismantled; and, finally, that the minister should not constitute the final point of appeal in the tribunal structure applying to general medical practitioners threatened with termination of their NHS contracts.

Final agreement over these demands was not reached until a few weeks before the new health service was due to commence. As late as February 1948 the parties were in a situation of stalemate and were trading insults. At this stage the profession voted eight to one absolutely to reject the NHS Act. With the help of mediation from the consultant leadership, the two sides retreated from their embattled positions and reached a reasonable compromise. The minister made no concession over the abolition of the sale and purchase of goodwill, but an enhanced package of compensation was confirmed. Dispensing with this old imposition was positively welcomed by a substantial section of the profession, especially younger entrants, for whom it entailed a substantial burden of debt. Bevan offered minor concessions with respect to the tribunal structure and the procedures of the Medical Practices Committee, but neither of these was likely in practice to impinge on the lives of the great majority of practitioners. Bevan's only significant concession related to the small basic salary component of remuneration, which was eliminated, except for a limited category of practitioners, for whom the terms of eligibility were strictly defined. Furthermore, Bevan promised and quickly introduced amending legislation to rule out the introduction of salaried service. With these concessions, opposition rapidly melted away in time for the new health service to be introduced in a spirit of harmony on 5 July 1948, the same 'Appointed Day' as other components in Labour's social-services reforms.

Appointed Day

Despite the late start in preparations and various delays along the way, the high level of dedication of the staff involved, both in the central departments and all the various employing bodies, meant that the lost ground was made up and the NHS was introduced with remarkable smoothness. As Sir George Godber recollects, 'there were forebodings of chaos on the Appointed Day but in the event, on 5 July 1948 services were given to patients just as they had been during the previous week'.[33] The introduction of the NHS entailed the creation of very few new medical services; the two main changes from the point of view of recipients were relief from direct charges and access to existing services for large groups who had previously been excluded. The change was more evident to staff, who transferred from a multiplicity of employers to the more uniform structure of the NHS employing authorities, with terms of employment and levels of remuneration being for the most part determined by a newly established Whitley Council structure.

Only when all the assembled elements had been brought together was the vast scale of the new health service fully evident. The employees and contractors of the new service amounted to about 500,000, which made the NHS the third largest non-military organization in Great Britain, being exceeded only by the British Transport Commission and the National Coal Board. The dominant group was the hospital staff of about 360,000, of whom about 150,000 were nurses and midwives. The 3,100 hospitals provided no fewer than 550,000 beds, of which nearly 200,000 were located in the mental-health services. By comparison, the LHA and Executive Council sectors were small-scale operations, employing or contracting 26,000 and 55,000 professional staff respectively.

The parts of this huge and disparate organization fell into place with remarkable speed and tranquillity. Helped by the charismatic leadership of Bevan, the staff of the various parts of the NHS soon achieved a sense of corporate unity and came to share Bevan's sense that they were part of a prestigious national service, capable of achieving in peacetime something like the feats of collective action and patriotic sacrifice recently witnessed in the special circumstances of total warfare. Echoing the sentiments of Bevan, Sir George Godber remarks on the 'odd euphoria about what had been done and a tendency to pride ourselves on having the finest health service in the world'.[34]

The most conspicuous feature of the new situation was the deluge of demand. It was also clear that short-term action to provide false teeth, spectacles, and hearing aids on a massive scale was merely the first step towards a hugely expensive long-term programme of modernization, the realistic execution of which would entail in perpetuity the commitment of resources on a scale way beyond any of the projections that had hitherto emanated from the health departments. Events, therefore, immediately exploded as fallacious any notion that the health service would be utilized sparingly, that it would represent a long-term economy, or even possibly become a self-liquidating expenditure commitment. Indeed, quite the opposite scare took hold. The sceptics suggested that the new health service constituted such a drain on resources that the economy would be wrecked and the nation thereby risked plunging into totalitarianism.[35]

Political Trustees

The establishment of the new health service is often thought to have marked the beginning of a long period of tranquillity, effectively removing the NHS from the province of political disagreement. With the emergence of this consensus over the virtues of the NHS, the political parties might have competed with one another to shower benefits on this favoured child of the welfare state. There certainly existed a greater measure of political agreement, giving expression to a great deal of vacuous rhetoric, but the politicians neither guaranteed the patrimony of the new health service, nor offered effective leadership over policies relating to health and health care. For the most part, the situation between 1948 and 1964 was characterized by resource starvation and policy neglect.

In his address to the medical profession, Bevan promised to devote himself to giving them 'all the facilities, resources, apparatus and help I can, and then to leave you alone as professional men and women to use your skills and judgement without hindrance'.[36] This objective was by no means easy to attain. Under the NHS legislation a high level of responsibility rested on the minister with respect to policy and finance. In particular, the standard achieved within the health service depended on the success of the Minister of Health's advocacy during each round of public expenditure negotiations. If a low threshold was set at the outset, it was likely to prove difficult subsequently to achieve the quantum leap to a higher threshold. Notwithstanding Bevan's high level of commitment and senior Cabinet position, it proved beyond his capacity to negotiate a stable mechanism for assuring the health service of an adequate flow of resources for all, or even the majority of its essential needs.

Bevan's negotiating position was weakened by the huge and unanticipated overspend on the new health service during its first two years. The bald facts are indicated in Table 1.2. This record looks particularly bleak against the wartime estimates listed in Table 1.1 and the financial memorandum to the NHS Bill, which confidently set the gross cost of the new service at £152 million. The unexpectedly large demand in all the independent-contractor services provided the main explanation for the rise in costs. This excess was stoutly defended by Bevan as a temporary perturbation and a reasonable cost of humanitarian relief directed mainly to the elderly and the poor. His explanation gained credibility when expenditure turned out to run exactly on course in the year 1950/1.

Neither Bevan nor his health service emerged unscathed from the overspending experience. Sceptics within the Labour Cabinet, headed by Morrison, exploited this issue to cause Bevan maximum political embarrassment, in the end precipitating his resignation from his new post as Minister of Labour and from the government in April 1951 over the Cabinet's decision to end the free service and impose health charges. This crisis was also more fundamentally damaging, since it supplied alarmists with ammunition concerning the potentially explosive costs of the new health service. This enabled the Treasury to trap Labour not only into introducing direct health-service charges, but also into imposing a ceiling on

TABLE 1.2. *The cost of the National Health Service, England and Wales, 1948–1951* (£m.)

Estimate	1948/9		1949/50	1950/1
	9 months	Annual rate		
Original	198.4	268.0	352.3	464.5
Final	275.9	373.0	449.2	465.0

Source: J S Ross, *The National Health Service in Great Britain* (London: Oxford University Press, 1952), 15

exchequer resources for the health service. This idea persisted for a decade. Throughout the 1950s convention determined that the contribution to the health service from direct taxation should be limited to about £400 million at 1950 prices; after allowing for inflation, all increases in expenditure above this level were expected to derive from such expedients as efficiency savings, cuts in fees to independent contractors, increased health-service charges, or increases in the National Health Service Contribution paid in connection with National Insurance. The latter was the post-1948 descendant of the 'health-stamp' deduction from pay made under the 1911 NHI scheme. The £400 million norm effectively became an arbitrarily imposed low baseline from which it was extremely difficult to escape. Thereby, even strongly justified bids for increased expenditure tended to be rejected on account of the need to keep NHS spending within its artificially constructed limits.

The brief overspending episode at the beginning of the NHS cast a long shadow, contributing to a seemingly indelible impression that the NHS constituted the bottomless pit for public expenditure. This construction was never supported by the evidence, and the 1950s provided a useful test case for its demolition. Indeed, even at the time of maximum alarm it was difficult to sustain a case for the excessive cost of the NHS. In 1952 the government set up an independent committee under the experienced Cambridge economist, Claude W. Guillebaud, to investigate this problem. In connection with this investigation the Guillebaud Committee commissioned an economic analysis undertaken by Brian Abel-Smith under the instruction of Professor R. M. Titmuss. No part of this powerful investigative process discovered evidence of waste within the NHS; the investigators were generally satisfied that the service was delivering a high quality of service in an economical manner. They were not even convinced of the need for health-service charges. They also urged that additional resources were required, particularly to support hospital modernization and the extension of community care.[37] These findings came as a shock and a disappointment to the government, which was expecting to use the Guillebaud Report as an instrument for imposing a regime of even tighter retrenchment on the new health service. Instead, the Guillebaud Report served the opposite purpose, while the Abel-

Smith and Titmuss investigation established itself as a classic defence of welfare-state expenditure. After this frustrating experience, no subsequent administration has dared to set up an independent inquiry into the cost of health care in the UK.

Taking the period from 1950 to 1964 as a whole, if current expenditure on the NHS is deflated using an NHS price index, it is seen that there was an average annual increase in expenditure of about 2.5 per cent, but with half of the increase being concentrated into the last five years. This pattern reflected the general course of public expenditure, itself affected by a rate of growth in the economy averaging at about 2.3 per cent during the 1950s, which is less than the growth rate in other comparable Western economies. During the lean years between the Korean War and the disastrous Suez expedition, the NHS was the main target for economies in social expenditure, imposed to finance the UK's operations as a world power. Following the 1959 general election, fought by Macmillan on the theme of 'preservation of prosperity', there followed a phase of expansion, with a growth target of 4 per cent. This ushered in a general increase in public expenditure, in which the NHS absorbed its share, facilitating for the first time since the health service had begun such major initiatives as the hospital plan. Notwithstanding this upturn, the annual rate of growth in public resources devoted to health care and indeed welfare in general was considerably in arrears of the UK's Western partners.

After a long period of relative wage stability, the slide towards wage-led inflation was evident during the final years of the Macmillan administration. The Macmillan government resorted to a pay pause, after which some attempt was made to adopt a 'guiding light' set between 2.5 and 3.5 per cent, but wages tended increasingly to move ahead of these limits. As noted below, the situation concerning pay determination for doctors and dentists was stabilized only after a Royal Commission and the establishment of a new review body. To the relief of the government, the review body kept in line with the guiding light during the first years of its operation, but, as indicated in the next chapter, this created such resentment that the Wilson administration was driven into making generous compensatory awards. For others in the NHS sector, the Whitley system operated to keep pay within the government guidelines, but at the cost of a build-up of demoralization that exercised its adverse effects during later administrations. This problem is well illustrated by the experience of the nurses and midwives, the largest group of personnel within the NHS. After accepting economic pay rises in the course of the first decade of the service, the nurses insisted on a revaluation exercise, which in 1959 resulted in a 12 per cent pay increase. However, this left nurses in arrears of comparable groups, even non-graduate teachers, while manual groups in the NHS improved their position relative to nurses. Consequently, the nurses returned to their demand for revaluation, but this was rejected, and in the summer of 1961, the pay pause was used to rule out this objective. Enoch Powell, the new Minister of Health, used the nurses to indicate his own political commitment to strict interpretation of government pay policy, which in the spring of 1962 provoked the nurses into their first concerted public campaigning over their pay grievances. Given the intransigence of Powell, the nurses twice took their case to the Industrial Court, which awarded increases in 1962 and 1963 totalling 14 per cent, compared with the 5 per cent regarded as the upper limit within the government's pay policy as interpreted by Powell.

In 1950/1, the first year of stability of NHS spending, the new service absorbed 4.1 per cent of GDP; thereafter, there was a steady decline in the proportion of national resources absorbed by the NHS to reach a level of about 3.5 per cent in the mid-1950s, after which there was a slow rise, until the level of 4.1 per cent was regained in the year 1963/4, the last year of the Conservative administration. Unlike many other public services, owing to an important policy change introduced by Labour and built upon by the Conservatives, it was possible to offset increases in the cost of the NHS by higher charges and an increased NHS Contribution. In 1950/1 direct charges and the NHS Contribution accounted for only 9.4 per cent of the gross cost of the NHS, whereas in 1963/4 they supplied 19.5 per cent of the cost.

On the basis of various objective comparisons, the NHS was also not particularly successful in the competition for resources. In 1950/1 the NHS absorbed about 25 per cent of total government social spending, whereas in 1963/4 this had fallen to 20 per cent. By comparison, education, which more successfully forced itself ahead to become a main policy priority, increased its share of social expenditure from 18 to 26 per cent over the same period.

By virtually all criteria, over the 1948–64 period the NHS cannot be regarded as a drain on national resources. Indeed, its costs were contained without difficulty, to the extent that resources were denied for obvious and urgent prerequisites, such as those connected with demographic change, medical advance, capital investment, or policy changes needed to keep up with rising expectations and the pace of improvement experienced elsewhere in the Western world. The inferior status of the health service was disguised by the political rhetoric; this effectively induced a sense of complacency concerning the state of the NHS, which vanished from the headlines. Owing to the effectiveness of this propaganda, reinforced by the evident improvement on the previous system, habitual stoicism and misplaced confidence among the public concerning the prospects for improvement, and a general disinclination to criticize a cherished national institution, the new health service drifted into a political limbo and thereby risked becoming a neglected backwater of the welfare state.

This story of decline is confirmed by the sequence of events in Westminster and Whitehall. The NHS was adversely affected by machinery-of-government changes even before Bevan's resignation from the government. The Cabinet reshuffle in January 1951 was taken as an opportunity to break up the Ministry of Health by transferring its housing and local-government functions to the new Ministry of Town and Country Planning. The much-reduced Ministry of Health was almost exclusively concerned with the health service; it was no longer an attractive career opportunity for high-flyers within the Civil Service and its minister no longer merited a seat in the Cabinet. The break-up of the Ministry of Health was therefore distinctly disadvantageous to the NHS. The Minister of Health remained outside the Cabinet from after the departure of Bevan for the rest of the life of the Ministry of Health, except for the brief period from July 1962 until May 1964.[38] A further disadvantage stemmed from the rapid rotation of Ministers of Health; no fewer than eight ministers held office between Bevan's transfer to the Ministry of Labour and the 1964 general election. None of these figures exercised anything like the influence of Bevan, although, on the grounds of their high political profile, both Iain Macleod and Enoch Powell have attracted the attention of analysts.

Although Macleod and Powell were blood brothers in the formation of the new One Nation Conservative grouping, and in this context jointly produced the pamphlet *Social Services: Needs and Means*, published in 1952, their political paths soon diverged, and this was strikingly reflected in their records as Ministers of Health. Macleod effectively purged residual rancour towards Bevan's health service in the Conservative Party. According to Macleod's revisionism, the new health-service was viewed as the logical culmination of a respectable tradition rooted in the social philosophy and sanitarian reforms presided over by Disraeli. As Minister of Health, Macleod was quietly protective of the health service and he continued to use his influence in the interests of continuity of health policy as he subsequently rose through the Cabinet ranks.

Powell started with the same benign attitude towards the health service but his brief spell as Financial Secretary to the Treasury induced a hardening of attitude. His inflexible pursuit of economy in social spending, in which the health service was a main target, contributed to the celebrated confrontation between the Treasury team of ministers and the rest of the Cabinet, ending with the resignation of the Chancellor of the Exchequer, Peter Thorneycroft, as well as his junior ministers Powell, and Birch in January 1958. On the basis of his undoubted ability, Powell soon returned from the wilderness to become Minister of Health, in which capacity he embarked on an exercise of self-vindication by once again applying his retrenchment philosophy to the health service. The confrontation with the nurses mentioned above was merely one manifestation of this effort, and further characteristic interventions concerning health-service charges and the NHS Contribution are noted below. Powell was the last Minister of Health actively to subscribe to the view that the health service was a realistic target for economies in public expenditure.

In the main, after the departure of Bevan, although evident tensions existed between the Conservative right and the Labour left, the two parties converged in their policies. The issue of charges was particularly controversial, but it was Labour which introduced dental and eye service charges in 1951 and only narrowly avoided introducing the prescription charge. As Labour's Chancellor of the Exchequer before the 1951 election defeat, Hugh Gaitskell actively advocated increased charges and cuts in services well beyond anything contemplated by any of his successors, Labour or Conservative.

The Conservatives periodically increased both dental and eye service charges; they also introduced the prescription charge in 1952; this was increased in 1956 and again in 1961. The biggest policy change in the financing of the NHS related to the NHS Contribution. There was some vague idea, usually, but wrongly, attributed to Beveridge, that the contribution from the National Insurance Fund to the NHS should be set at about 20 per cent of the cost of the service. This norm was not, in practice, observed, with the result that the share from the NHS Contribution during the early years of the NHS steadily declined from about 10 per cent to reach a low point of about 6.5 per cent in the mid-1950s. Thereafter, owing to a policy initiative stemming from the Prime Minister, Harold Macmillan, the NHS Contribution was substantially increased on three occasions until its share reached a peak of about 16.5 per cent of the gross cost of the NHS at the date of Macmillan's retirement. This episode is not much remembered, but it represented the only point in the history of the NHS when there was a determined attempt to transfer to an insurance basis of funding. This idea was pursued with vigour by Macmillan and a few Cabinet allies, but it was actively opposed by other Conservative ministers. This policy seemed viable until 1961, when it came to a grinding halt owing to the zeal of Enoch Powell, who simultaneously imposed a substantial increase in the NHS Contribution, a higher prescription charge, and increased dental and eye charges. Although these increases were introduced, they were deeply damaging politically, and no further attempt was made during the 1959–64 administration to pursue this combination of measures, or to reintroduce the idea of basing the funding of the NHS on a hypothecated tax raised through the social-security system. The Treasury was by no means consistent in its attitude to the funding of the NHS, but the nearest thing to an authoritative conclusion emanated from the interdepartmental Working Party on

NHS Finance chaired by F. E. Figgures, which expressed scepticism about all alternatives to the existing system of funding based on general taxation.[39] The arguments contained in the Figgures Report proved apposite and convincing on the many future occasions when alternative methods of funding the NHS were reconsidered.

A National Hospital Service

The hospital service was in all respects the dominant element within the new health service, to the extent that unkind critics called the NHS a 'National Hospital Service'. From the outset of preparations for a new health service rationalization of the chaotic hospital system dominated the attention of policy-makers. The new system of regional hospital administration was the most radical aspect of the Bevan plan. It constituted by far the largest feature of the new service, whether measured by resources invested, or by personnel employed. At the beginning of the health service the hospital sector absorbed about 54 per cent of the available funds; this increased steadily until it reached a peak of about 70 per cent in 1975. As the most innovative feature of the new service, for which high expectations were aroused, the hospital service absorbed almost the entire health-service planning effort. Indeed, it was the only part of the NHS for which a plan developed, although in England and Wales comprehensive regional planning was undermined by the administrative separation of teaching hospitals, and also by ambiguities in relations between the regions and HMCs.

The birth of the NHS coincided with the dawn of a golden age of high-technology medicine. Before the Second World War, despite some notable advances, treatment for many acute conditions was limited in its effectiveness and often hazardous to the patient. By 1948 the situation was changing rapidly. Notable advances included the widespread availability of natural and synthetic antibacterials, anticoagulants, reliable blood transfusion, innovations in anaesthetics, diagnostic X-radiology, and electrocardiography, as well as more refined techniques of pathological investigation, and mechanization in the operating theatre. Such revolutionary changes transformed the capacities of hospital medicine and created conditions for the proliferation of medical and surgical specialities, which were capable of performing on a substantial scale a range of ambitious interventions that were virtually unknown before the Second World War. The continuation and ever-accelerating pace of these developments entailed inescapable increases in funding, as well as a much larger and more skilled workforce. Without these increased material and human resources, the expanding life-saving capacities of modern medicine would remain incompletely realized.

It was anticipated that a coordinated system of hospital services, radiating out from large regional teaching and research centres, would directly or indirectly dominate all aspects of care. Academic centres of excellence were expected to become spheres of enlightenment that would transform the practice of medicine and lead to enormous benefits in treatment and health. Anticipating this extraordinary sense of therapeutic optimism, in 1945 the Oxford regional commissioners had already referred to the 'growing consciousness, both within and without the medical profession, that our Hospitals, of which we are rightly proud, should spread their influence over a still wider sphere'. This was the best means of response to the modern belief in the 'supreme importance of Health', or the aspiration to 'Perfect Health' and of 'an urgent desire to promote the mental and physical fitness of our race for the exacting tasks which lie ahead'.[40]

Arguably the greatest permanent achievement of the early NHS was its rapid establishment of a universal specialist and consultant service. Even by 1950 there existed the nucleus of a comprehensive district general hospital system, with specialist staff sufficient at least for providing basic cover in general medicine, general surgery, and obstetrics and gynaecology. In the course of the first decade of the service there was rapid build-up of specialists in support services such as anaesthetics, pathology, and radiology, and also in such areas as psychiatry and geriatrics. By 1964 the foundations were also in place for regional specialities such as plastic surgery, neurosurgery, thoracic surgery, and radiotherapy.

The growth of advanced specialist treatment exposed to an even greater degree the inadequacies of existing hospital accommodation, much of which dated from the age of Florence Nightingale, with a substantial nucleus of the buildings dating from the original foundation of the voluntary hospitals in the mid-eighteenth century. As Sir George Godber pointed out, the NHS was saddled with hospitals 'largely old and defective in structure, wrongly located, not only had to waste effort maintaining service with inefficient plant, but also had to spend what little capital there was making these bad old units usable for modern treatment'.[41] Every type of hospital was defective, but massive institutions housing some 200,000 mental-illness, mental-handicap, and chronic elderly patients were the worst. As the North West Metropolitan region frankly admitted:

> The Board inherited mental hospitals, some of which are in the neighbourhood of a hundred years old and most of them have been victims of damage and destruction by bombing during the last war. In addition, they were in varying degrees of disrepair, and generally were ill-adapted to the needs of patients under treatment in them. The patient population in the hospitals was predominantly composed of chronic and long-stay patients in various stages of deterioration resulting from prolonged hospitalisation [42]

With the improving economic position, a great national building effort was initiated, spawning huge new housing developments and new towns, replete with such public buildings as schools of all types. Provision of these amenities underlined the failure of the NHS to capture its share of capital resources. Consequently the new community developments possessed neither hospitals nor health centres, and they continued to be served by any old hospital that happened to be located in the vicinity. As Sir George Godber recollected, the slender resources available were dedicated to repairing bomb damage and supplying desperately needed facilities such as outpatient and casualty departments, operating theatres, X-ray departments, and pathology laboratories. Any extra resources were used for replacing antiquated heating systems or attempting to improve the amenities of overcrowded wards. Patching and extending existing hospitals was in many respects a false economy. There was an urgent need for entirely new hospitals, ranging from district general hospitals for new centres of population to teaching hospitals, almost all of which required complete rebuilding.

On the basis of its initial survey of needs, even the small Oxford region estimated that it required £3.5 million for urgent schemes, whereas the allocation for capital needs in the first full year of the service was a miserly £225,000. Oxford was in advance of most other regions in preparing its capital development plans; it also enjoyed good relations with the central department. Even with these advantages the Oxford region was not able to begin work on its highest priority scheme until 1957. This was the first district general hospital to be started in England under the NHS. The modest first phase of this Princess Margaret Hospital at Swindon, comprising mainly out-patient facilities, was completed in 1959; the larger second phase containing ward blocks was completed in 1964, leaving two further stages of this half-completed hospital, still to be constructed. The nearest equivalent in Wales was the West Wales General Hospital at Glangwili near Carmarthen, the first phase of which was opened in 1959. Swindon and Glangwili were two out of a total of only six such schemes in England and Wales at this date. In Scotland the first separate hospital development was the main part of the small hospital at the Vale of Leven, south of Loch Lomond, which was opened in 1955. Most of the capital investment in Scotland before 1960 was directed into modest schemes of improvement.

In England, the problems faced by a large region are illustrated by the North West Metropolitan RHB. This possessed the largest agglomeration of new towns; it listed ten urgently required major building projects, the total cost of which amounted to some £30 million. The total resources available annually for capital outlays of all kinds averaged little more than £500,000 for most of the first decade of the NHS, but it then climbed steadily from 1960 onwards, reaching a peak of about £7 million in the mid-1960s. From a situation in the first decade of the health service where the outlay on new hospitals was negligible, it became possible to plan these developments with realistic chances of their completion. The Queen Elizabeth II Hospital for the new towns of Welwyn/Hatfield was opened by the Queen in July 1963. This was the first district general hospital to be completed since the beginning of the health service. This was quickly followed by the Wexham Park Hospital in Slough and two other largely rebuilt hospitals. These developments in the North West Metropolitan region comprised merely one segment in the new ring of hospitals serving the Home Counties, which progressively reduced reliance on hospital facilities in central London.

The modest rises in staff and limited investment in new facilities yielded substantial returns, as measured by the increase in the hospital workload. For instance, in the North West Metropolitan region, in the period 1949–64, with about a 5 per cent reduction in occupied beds, there occurred a 60 per cent increase in the number of in-patients treated and a reduction of about 35 per cent in the average duration of stay in hospital. The total out-patient attendances increased by 23 per cent, the new out-patient attendances by 46 per cent, and the accident-and-emergency attendances by 40 per cent. These figures were paralleled by spectacular increases in such inputs as quantities of blood supplied by the regional transfusion service, or the units of bacteriological, biochemical, haematological, and histological tests performed by pathology departments. This greater diversity and productivity in the diagnostic field were made possible by such innovations as automation of testing procedures, application of tests involving radio-isotopes, computerized scanning techniques, including the use of ultrasound, and advances in endoscopy.

By 1964 the equivalent of 20 per cent of the population in a hospital region was likely to utilize some in-patient or out-patient service in the course of a year. The character of hospital work was changing not only on account of medical advance but also because of epidemiological and social factors. For instance, in orthopaedics, older conditions relating to the effects of tuberculosis and rickets faded away to be replaced by such problems as poliomyelitis, which was at its height in the 1950s. Orthopaedics greatly advanced during the Second World War; technical improvements and the introduction of new materials brought about further advances in treatment and permitted more rapid rehabilitation. Fresh challenges to orthopaedics arose from the toll of accidents associated with modern transport. Orthopaedics also became more concerned with multiple corrective operations on infants with congenital deformities who would formerly have perished, but now survived owing to advances in paediatrics and neurosurgery. At the other end of the age scale, orthopaedics became involved in the repair of fractured necks of the femur among large numbers of elderly patients who would have remained disabled in earlier times. The work of chest surgeons was no longer dominated by tuberculosis, but was increasingly concerned with the new evil of lung cancer attributable to tobacco-smoking. Cancers became diagnosed earlier and were better understood as a result of advances in the national cancer registration scheme, while treatment and management altered continually in line with innovations in drug treatment and radiotherapy.

As considered further in Chapter 2, owing to medical preference and social fashion, the early years of the new health service witnessed a strong move for hospital maternity departments to be recognized as the normal location for childbirth. Maternity departments thereby became leading features of new hospital schemes. The advantages of hospital confinement were particularly evident for sick or premature babies, where special-care baby units constituted an important new development. Intensive-care facilities were also relevant for many of the new and advanced surgical specialities, such as cardiac surgery, which by 1964 was able to offer as routine many interventions such as valve replacements and correction of septum defects. Such open-heart surgery had required the development of heart–lung machines, and advanced surgery in general was dependent on the availability of advanced equipment in anaesthetics such as the Barnet Ventilator. By 1964 a start had been made with the installation of implantable pace-makers as an alternative means to assist those with cardiac abnormalities.

The process of innovation and improvement extended slowly into the intractable environment of the long-stay hospitals. With the help of small injections of funds, some steps were made towards creating a more humane environment. More important was the emergence of a more constructive approach to therapy. In the early years of the new service, a small band of innovators demonstrated the effectiveness of rehabilitation regimes. By such means, even before the Report of the Royal Commission on Mental Illness and its sequel, the Mental Health Act of 1959, the tide of growth of in-patient numbers had been arrested. This trend was reinforced by important innovations in drug therapy, which stabilized hitherto serious conditions and opened up the possibility for treatment as out-patients of individuals who hitherto would have been destined to join the helpless legions of the institutionalized. The proven success of these new modes of treatment opened up the prospect of a complete break with the old institutional system. Quite quickly, the plans for new district general hospitals were modified to include psychiatric units, the first to be opened being that at the Queen Elizabeth II Hospital in Welwyn. It was anticipated that the centre of gravity of mental health services would gradually switch from the old mental hospitals to these new psychiatric units.

By 1964 the hospital service possessed a firm record of achievement in the relief of suffering. This was rendered possible by virtue of additional resources, but equally important were the gains in efficiency brought about by transfer from the chaotic market of the pre-war period to the planned system of the NHS. However, there remained the unremitting problems experienced in meeting the demand for hospital modernization with slender resources. The failure to invest in hospital modernization was an increasing cause of political embarrassment. The newspapers drew attention to the contrast between modern hospitals springing up throughout Europe and the UK's dilapidated hospital stock. Russell Brock, the distinguished thoracic surgeon, soon to become President of the Royal College of Surgeons, attacked the duplicity of the political parties for unscrupulously deriving political capital from their support for the NHS, but in practice allowing the UK hospital system to degenerate to a state where it was both derelict and dangerous.[43]

The first significant concession by the government was announced on 1 July 1955, when a list of some twenty major capital projects was given official approval, but there was no timetable for these schemes, or guarantees about expenditure to meet these commitments. Many of these schemes had still not been started by 1962. The first tangible targets for spending on hospital development were laid down by the Guillebaud Report in 1956, which calculated that £30 million a year would be required to replace the existing hospital stock over a reasonable period. Thereafter this poorly authenticated figure became adopted as the scientific basis for hospital planning. The first significant political commitment in response to Guillebaud was contained in the 1959 Conservative general-election manifesto, which promised to 'double the present capital programme'. This represented the fruits of the campaign launched by the Minister of Health in July 1958. Following the government's adoption of a five-year plan for school building, Derek Walker-Smith insisted on parity of treatment for hospital building. Only in 1960 was the case for a 'New Deal', 'New Look', or 'Forward Look' for hospitals accepted by the government; in recognition of the large scale of individual hospital building schemes, it was agreed to adopt a ten-year plan. Health authorities were notified about preparations for this plan in January 1961, and a White Paper collating the schemes submitted by regions was published in January 1962.[44] This hospital plan and its subsequent revisions constituted the blueprint for hospital development. It was envisaged that capital investment in hospitals in Great Britain would rise steadily to reach about £50 million a year by 1964. It was anticipated that, through a slow process of replacement of obsolete facilities, the district general hospital containing some 600–800 beds, serving a catchment population of 100,000–150,000, would become established as the basic building block for planning purposes within the hospital service and indeed for the health service as a whole. This hypothesis was built on slender intellectual foundations, and it was outlined in only the vaguest terms in just five pages of the 280-page White Paper. On the basis of the available evidence, it was far from certain that the bed norms adopted for the various specialities were realistic. The plan tended to understate the needs of services where expansion was envisaged, but overestimate the capacity for contraction in services where economies in provision were both sought and needed to prevent escalation in costs. The net effect of this reasoning was consistently to apply minimum values for the component costs of modernization. Consequently, even by 1964 it was evident that the hospital plan would be hugely more expensive than first envisaged. Initial expectations concerning completion by 1970/1 of 90 new and 134 substantially remodelled district general hospitals, together with 356 other major schemes, were soon consigned to the realms of fantasy. Despite this shortfall in the capacities of the hospital building programme, the new policy at least converted hospital renewal into a feasible option. For the first time since before 1914 comprehensive new hospital facilities became a conspicuous feature of the capital investment landscape.

Primary and Community Care

Independent-contractor services administered by Executive Councils, together with the miscellaneous services administered by LHAs, comprised the disciplines soon to be known as primary and community care. These services were immediately important for remedial and emergency purposes; they also served a crucial front-line function, the effectiveness of which was essential for relieving pressure on expensive hospital facilities. From the outset it was also appreciated that for a diversity of client groups optimization of these services represented a more humane and desirable alternative to hospital care.

Although admittedly administrative relics, and not specially favoured by planners, the Executive Council and LHA services represented a point of stability and continuity, which was in some respects helpful, since they were called upon for a much larger burden of work than originally anticipated. The extent of their contribution is illustrated by the explosion of demand for medication after the Appointed Day. In June 1948, the last month of NHI, 6.8 million prescriptions were dispensed by chemists; by September this monthly figure had climbed to 13.6 million. The drug bill was one of the greatest expanding costs of the new health service. It increased from £18 million in the first year of the service to £114 million in 1963/4. Even allowing for price changes, this represented an increase of about 250 per cent. At the beginning of the service the cost of the pharmaceutical service was only about half the cost of the general medical service. The pharmaceutical service overtook the general medical service in its costs in about 1960 and was about 40 per cent greater by 1964. This change was brought about primarily by the growth in costs of individual prescriptions rather than by their number, indicating the remarkable advances brought about by the 'pharmaceutical revolution'. In 1951 the average number of prescriptions per person a year was 5.2, while in 1964 it was only 4.4, which was a very modest figure considering that a progressively higher level of demand might have been expected from an ageing population. In constant price terms, the average net ingredient cost per prescription increased by about 210 per cent between 1949 and 1964. This change reflected the rapid pace of pharmaceutical innovation. Not only had the majority of drugs dispensed been unavailable before the onset of the NHS, but about 45 per cent of the preparations dispensed in 1965 could not have been prescribed in 1960.

Big advances were made with respect to both drug therapy and vaccines. Both contributed to the more effective control of acute infectious diseases, many of which ceased to be regarded with the dread that had been associated with their names before the First World War. A few recent discoveries such as sulphonamides, penicillin, and streptomycin were in use at the beginning of the NHS; by 1964 these were joined by dozens of other natural and synthetic antibacterials. Other important advances during this period were recorded with respect to corticosteroids, anti-hypertensives, anti-inflammatories, oral diuretics, analgesics, anti-epileptics, and psychotropic agents. In 1961 the introduction of oral contraceptives into general use represented a revolution in itself; among many repercussions of this change, as discussed in the next chapter, it forced the government to review its policy regarding family-planning services.

The inexorable rise in the drug bill caused alarm in government circles; many expedients to arrest this trend were tried, but none succeeded. In 1957 the Voluntary Price Regulation Scheme (later the Pharmaceutical Price Regulation Scheme) was introduced to curb the profits of pharmaceutical companies, but in the short term this generated only trivial savings. Each increase in direct charges produced only a temporary reduction in the number of prescriptions dispensed. In 1959 the government-appointed Hinchliffe and Douglas committees reported on prescribing practice in the health service, but neither offered prospects of significant economies. Indeed, from the government's perspective they made matters worse by concluding that prescribing practice, although not always efficient, was not generally irresponsible, that innovation would result in escalating costs, and that prescription charges were undesirable.

Apart from introducing ethical dilemmas, the advances in drug therapy introduced dangers as well as benefits, as indicated by the tide of congenital deformities consequent upon the introduction of thalidomide in 1960, or by a rising problem of addiction, much of which was associated with the misuse of drugs available on prescription. The thalidomide tragedy underlined the need for more effective systems for the regulation of medicines than existed under the early NHS. On a voluntary basis, with the agreement of the pharmaceutical industry and the medical profession, in 1963 the government established the Committee on Safety of Drugs to advise on marketing, clinical testing, and adverse reactions of drugs. This Committee was given a statutory status and renamed the Committee on Safety of Medicines under the Medicines Act of 1968, which introduced more comprehensive arrangements for the control of drugs.

The NHS gave rise to a more concerted effort by LHAs to promote vaccination and immunization. Prior to the Second World War, vaccination for smallpox had been the only one of these procedures to be undertaken systematically. Immunization for diphtheria and BCG vaccination for tuberculosis had been available but not widely utilized. By 1964 protection against diphtheria, tuberculosis, poliomyelitis, whooping cough, and tetanus were available as a matter of routine. The control of tuberculosis was also advanced by systematic campaigns of mass miniature X-radiography among the civilian population. These had their origins during the Second World War, but were continued and extended under the NHS.

The torrent of demand experienced by general medical practitioners and pharmacists also applied to a small and struggling workforce of dentists and opticians, who accommodated a far greater volume of services than had been anticipated or allowed for in the financial estimates of the new health service. During the first eight months of the new service, the rate of demand for the general dental service ran at about eight million cases a year, which was twice the expected level. One-third of the patients treated required dentures, which indicated the terrible state of the nation's teeth and the extent of the backlog of demand. By the tenth anniversary of the new service, the balance had swung towards conservation dentistry, with dentures accounting for only one-tenth of the cases treated. Pressure on the general dental service steadily increased, with the result that the already severe shortage of trained dentists became even more acute. By 1964 the UK was well in arrears of its Western neighbours in its ratio of dentists in relation to the population. This problem looked set to become steadily worse owing to the continuing resistance to fluoridation of water, the unfavourable age-structure among dentists, and the failure to implement in full the recommendations of the McNair Committee, which reported in 1956 on the crisis of recruitment in dentistry.

Although, as its name suggests, the Supplementary Ophthalmic Service was introduced as a stop-gap arrangement pending the development of a comprehensive hospital-based eye service, it proved to be cheap, effective, and popular; it was thereby the least problematical part of the Executive Council services. In the first eight months of the new service, some five million persons had their eyes tested and were able to select from ten different types of spectacle frames available free of charge. In 1950, when the industry was at last able to meet the full demand, about the same number had their eyes tested and the public was supplied with no fewer than 8.3 million pairs of glasses. After this initial peak, both sight tests and the supply of spectacles continued at a steady rate of about five million a year.

Some of the remedial functions of the new health service were met through the hospital service, which by 1968 had supplied some 600,000 hearing aids, but also such old-fashioned items as auricles, ear trumpets, and speaking tubes. The hospital service also provided large numbers of such varied items as surgical shoes and boots, artificial eyes, wigs, wheelchairs, and hand-propelled tricycles. For the most severely disabled, in line with provision for war pensioners, the new service also supplied power-propelled tricycles, which became the object of much experiment, with both electric and petrol-driven varieties. In the first decade of the new service, the old, open motorized invalid vehicles were superseded by all-weather machines which were designed to imitate saloon cars with their steel or glass-fibre bodies, hydraulic controls, and modern suspension units. The more advanced machines even contained folding invalid chairs for use at the end of journeys. Although small in scale, these facilities indicated the real attention of the new service to the needs of the severely disabled.

From the time of the Dawson Report, the ideal of unified

primary and community-care services had been tied up with the concept of the health centre. This idea was carried over into the new health service, providing an opportunity for all classes of independent contractors and LHA staff to work in cooperation. In practice medico-political tensions virtually precluded agreement on the establishment of health centres embracing both groups of staff. In the rare cases where concord was achieved, the health centre tended to be blocked by the health departments on the grounds of resource constraints, since virtually all funds available for health-service capital investment were pre-empted by the hospital sector. Consequently the health-centre plan was abandoned, thereby hindering functional unification of the primary and community services, and preventing attainment of their greater parity with the powerful hospital sector. The handful of health centres existing under the early NHS were a heterogeneous collection of institutions, some inherited from before the NHS, a few experimental centres mainly financed by philanthropic bodies, and a handful of new health centres only roughly conforming to the expectations of the NHS legislation. The latter were modest in their scale and pretensions, and, in the absence of leadership from the central department, they were not conspicuous for any concerted drive towards integration of functions. A review of health centres conducted in 1960 concluded that they failed to promote the kind of cooperative practice intended by the original planners, even to the extent that, in the few cases where independent contractors and LHA staff worked under the same roof, the two groups were partitioned off from one another; indeed even groups of general practitioners working in such centres developed no collective working relationship.

The virtual death of the health-centre concept under the early NHS contributed to the ossification in their pre-NHS form of the services administered by Executive Councils and LHAs, thereby impeding any shift towards a modern system of primary and community care. The general practitioner's surgery or the maternity and child-welfare clinic remained much the same unedifying environment as it had been during the Depression. In most respects the new health service conspicuously failed to reduce the traditional atmosphere of animosity and suspicion that for at least half a century had characterized relations between the MOH and the general medical practitioner. In the past this cold war had not particularly mattered, but in the new health service absence of an effective working relationship was disastrous for the development of the primary and community services and, of course, fatal to the balanced development of the health service as a whole.

There was a real danger that general practice might retreat into its ghetto, deteriorate, and ultimately face extinction. The backward state of general practice at the beginning of the health service was described at length and in alarming detail by J. S. Collings in the *Lancet* in 1950. This review was greeted with fury at the time, but it is now generally accepted as a statement of the true situation. As summarized by Sir Theodore Fox, the editor of the *Lancet* at the time, the practices inspected by Collings were characterized by 'poor premises and equipment, deficient organisation and declining morale. Many practitioners inevitably deteriorated; ceasing to be the family doctors of the past, they did not fully use the methods of the present.'[45]

It was particularly difficult to ensure that medical practitioners were reliably informed about the most efficient therapeutic agents and educated to prescribe economically, reliably, and to the safety of their patients. The big differences in prescribing costs and habits exposed in the Hinchliffe and Douglas surveys, even between neighbouring general practitioners, suggested that many of them were not equipped to optimize the benefits of the therapeutic revolution.

Although the NHS excluded general practitioners from much of the hospital work that they had previously undertaken, they were by degrees granted full access to hospital diagnostic and pathological facilities. However, this important asset was exploited unevenly. A study of general practitioners in a large north-western industrial town reported in 1962 that three-quarters of the requests for hospital pathological facilities emanated from only one-quarter of the doctors, who were usually the younger and more recently qualified practitioners. The full range of available diagnostic facilities was exploited by some 10 per cent of these doctors. This neglect to employ the available diagnostic tools resulted in failure to detect identifiable and treatable asymptomatic conditions such as diabetes. In view of such findings, it is not surprising that Forsyth concluded his review of evidence concerning the state of general practice before 1966 on the gloomy note that 'the family doctor is far from fulfilling the role assigned him within the NHS'.[46]

In the early years of the NHS the prospects for general practice were far from auspicious. Young practitioners were discouraged by the collapse of the health-centre scheme and by a system of remuneration that was indifferent to professional competence and enlightenment. More established practitioners lapsed into a perpetual state of distraction over NHS remuneration levels, which they regarded as a cheat. There was a vacuum of leadership owing to continuing divisions between the bureaucrats and medical politicians, rooted in their endless wrangles over pay and the legacy of hard feeling lingering over from a variety of old disputes going back as far as 1911. The medical schools and medical education were dominated by the hospital specialities. The NHS closed the door on flexible career patterns; it was no longer possible to combine hospital specialization and general practice; the high-flyers took command of the hospital specialities, regarding general practice as the province of the failure. General practice seemed to belong to an ageing remnant left over from the panel system, and to those doctors satisfied to play an ancillary role as 'gatekeepers' determining access to hospital services. Increasing specialization within the medical profession, entailing the elimination of general practice elsewhere in the West, suggested that the UK also was likely to fall into line with this aspect of modernization.

In the event, general practice not only survived, but slowly struggled to its feet and achieved a respectable and independent professional identity. Although the main consolidation took place after 1964, even before that date there were some encouraging signs of improvement. The Danckwerts Award of 1952 removed the worst complaints about levels of remuneration. Residual anxieties were quelled by a full review of the pay problem, conducted in an authoritative manner by the Royal Commission on Doctors' and Dentists' Remuneration chaired by Sir Harry Pilkington, which reported in 1960. This not only produced further economic gains, but set in place the Doctors' and Dentists' Review Body, which was designed to remove the confrontational system for determining pay. Although this objective was not always attained, in general the review body served the profession extremely well. Naturally, this has not given the government much satisfaction, but its failure to evolve a better alternative has allowed this method of pay determination to survive with little alteration until the present.

Changes in pay arrangements following the Danckwerts Award introduced minor incentives to group practice. A special fund was established to assist those doctors wishing to improve their practice premises. At the beginning of the health service about half of the independent general practitioners, known as 'principals', were practising single-handed; by 1964 this had fallen to one-quarter. The larger and more active partnerships proved to be a credible substitute for health centres. They led the way in the building of attractive practice premises, the employment of ancillary staff, and the utilization of hospital diagnostic facilities. Eventually, in a few areas with more innovative MOHs, attachment schemes were devised whereby local-authority staff were located in general practices rather than working separately on a territorial basis. At first this arrangement was largely confined to district nurses, but its success paved the way for the attachment of other local-authority staff. This innovation therefore constituted an important step in the development of the primary-care team. By 1964 group practices were the norm, but the groups were still extremely small; only 3 per cent of groups comprised six or more general practitioners. The predominant small-group practices were therefore not able to avail themselves of the full benefits of attachment schemes or other vehicles of collective activity.

In 1953 a minor change in medical education introduced an intern year following the undergraduate clinical period. This first year of vocational training involved no direct component relating to general practice, but it set a precedent, and experimental schemes were introduced in a few areas enabling trainees to gain experience of both hospital and general-practice work. The further development of education in general practice, as well as improvement in professional standards, became the special province of the College of General Practitioners, which was founded in 1952 and by 1964 had achieved a position of settled authority.

The steady advance of the hospital medical specialities and the introduction of a long-term plan for hospital development underlined the need for more coherent policy guidance on primary and community care. This was especially urgent from the perspective of the government, since optimization of the capacities of these front-line services was indispensable for containing within reasonable limits the cost of the potentially ruinously expensive hospital development programme. Pressure for accelerating the development of local-authority residential and domiciliary services emanated from the Guillebaud Committee in 1956 and from the Report of the Royal Commission on Mental Illness in the following year, with the intention of reducing reliance on long-term hospital care for the elderly and the mentally ill. From the earliest stages of the campaign for a long-term hospital programme, it was also recommended that there should be a 'shift away from hospital and institutional treatment towards community care'.[47] Consistent with this aim, the Deputy-Chief Medical Officer insisted that 'hospitals must be organised primarily for the support of home care', for which purpose he called for much greater cooperation between medical staff from the three parts of the NHS.[48] Thereby both the terminology and the concept of community care assumed importance at this early stage in the history of the NHS, but the realization of this aspiration was much slower to come about.

In practice, local health and welfare services were treated as a low priority in the government's social programme. These services were therefore a favoured target for cuts in each expenditure round. Indeed, the gradual build-up of hospital capital development itself contributed to pressures for cuts in community care. Although ministers promised balanced development of the three parts of the health service, in practice plans for primary and community-care services were framed in order to avoid significant expenditure commitments. Even implementation of small policy advances, such as the establishment of standardized training for non-graduate social workers following the recommendations of the Younghusband Report of 1959, minor steps towards establishing a chiropody service, or permitting local authorities to provide a meals-on-wheels service, were held back for years, with the consequence that in 1964 these elementary and economical reforms were only just being realized.

In order to prevent the impression of complete inactivity and as a defensive measure against likely criticism, the Ministry of Health asked local authorities to provide information concerning their current services and intentions about medium-term expansion plans. In order to give this miscellaneous collection of information greater authority and a semblance of unity with the hospital plan, in April 1963 it was issued as the Community Care White Paper.[49] This was even more provisional and vulnerable to criticism than the hospital plan. It made virtually no attempt to establish objectively defined norms of provision for the many component services, merely assuming that the present pattern of services would be slowly expanded. This approach possessed two unfortunate limitations: first, the plans for expansion were unduly modest, especially considering the need for accelerated development of community care; secondly, no attempt was made to establish uniform standards, or even to reduce some of the more glaring disparities in provision between local authorities. Shortcomings in the estimates for expansion in community-care staff were exposed by the National Institute of Economic and Social Research (NIESR), which compared the local-authority plans for expansion between 1962 and 1973 with its own estimates based on the proposition that it was desirable to raise standards to the level of the 20 per cent best-performing authorities. Projections for expansion regarding three main community-care professional groups are summarized in Table 1.3. This indicates the extent to which notions of expansion held within central and local government were open to question.

TABLE 1.3. *Projected increases in selected community-care staff, England and Wales, 1962–1972* (%)

Staff	1963 White Paper forecast	NIESR estimate
Health visitors	44	88
Home nurses	27	70
Social workers	66	145

Source: D Paige and K Jones, *Health and Welfare Services in Britain in 1975* (Cambridge: Cambridge University Press, 1966), 112–13

Even the relatively lay perspective of the NIESR implied that the bureaucrats needed to double their targets for expansion, while other expert voices believed that even greater increases, as well as major changes in policy direction, were needed to achieve a realistic programme of community care.

Although a limited exercise, the community-care policy document at least possessed a degree of government authority. Some thought was given to a similar policy statement on general practice, but in view of the risk of offending the medical politicians and on account of fear of expenditure consequences, it was decided to remit the question of the future of general practice to a low-status investigation conducted by a subcommittee of the Standing Medical Advisory Committee of the Central Health Services Council. Paradoxically, the resultant report, produced by a committee of experts chaired by Annis Gillie, a prominent woman general practitioner and leading figure in the College of General Practitioners, was superior to both the hospital and community-care plans. It was based on sustained investigation and contained a reasoned defence of its proposals, neither of which was a feature of the two White Papers.[50] The Gillie Committee was handicapped because of its remit, which excluded expenditure issues, and on account of background interference by the Ministry of Health, which prevented trespass into sensitive policy areas. Departmental intervention steered the Gillie Committee away from support for many reforms, including reorganizing the health service, reducing the maximum list size, accepting deputizing arrangements, or introducing stricter regulation of obstetric practice, all proposals which either possessed expenditure implications or were likely to be politically contentious. The scope of the Gillie Committee was therefore severely limited. In the main its report encouraged widely supported trends that were already underway, such as inducements to group practice, or loans for practice improvement, and greater assistance with provision ancillary help. A series of recommendations related to the improvement of general-practice vocational training in line with the thinking of the College of General Practitioners. By contrast with the 1961 Platt Report on hospital medical staffing, the Gillie Report rejected the idea that general practitioners should enhance their status through service in hospital as 'medical assistants'. The Gillie recommendations envisaged some participation in the hospital service in such fields as psychiatry or obstetrics, but located the main field of work in the autonomous sphere of group practice.

Persisting Inequalities

The various parts of the new health service were successful in meeting immediate objectives relating to the extension in the scope and scale of services according to the most pressing priorities of the time. On the other hand, none of the sectors addressed itself effectively to problems connected with geographical and social inequality. The NHS therefore tended to mirror and perpetuate the accumulated idiosyncrasies and inequalities in health-care provision contained in the inherited system, which in the main reflected deep-seated patterns in the distribution of wealth, which had determined that those sections of community experiencing the greatest problems of ill health were provided with the worst health services. At the outset of the new health service, the better hospitals and more generous services tended to be concentrated in the areas around London, whereas the least well-provided hospital regions coincided with the former depressed areas, which in the main were the centres of heavy industry.

Although some measures were taken to iron out the worst anomalies concerning the distribution of general practitioners or the provision of consultant services, the impact of these efforts was limited. The resource distribution system therefore tended to preserve the disadvantages of the deprived regions. It was also evident that disadvantage with respect to one part of the health service was not likely to be compensated for by more generous provision in another. The metropolitan regions and their neighbours possessed the more generously resourced hospital service, also the greater concentration of general practitioners, group practices, and dentists, as well as the lion's share of younger and more innovative practitioners. Conversely, the northern regions and Wales were likely to have the less-well-resourced hospital service, the least concentration of general practitioners, group practices, and dentists, and a preponderance of older practitioners. Since there was no retirement age for independent contractors, there were large numbers of older practitioners, including many in their eighties, who were likely to be out of touch with modern and safe practice. In 1958 about 16 per cent of dentists were aged over 65, while 7 per cent of general practitioners were aged over 66.

Inferior quality of service and lower patient expectations also followed the gradient of resource provision. Thus in the more prosperous south-east of England better-qualified dentists predominated and conservation dentistry gained ground more rapidly, whereas in the industrial areas there were greater numbers of the untrained '1921 dentists' and a predominance of extractions and dentures. In London and the south-east in 1958, for every tooth extracted, more than three were filled, but in Wales and the north of England less than one tooth was filled for every one extracted.

In 1952, comparing the West Midlands and the south-west of England, the latter held a 26 per cent advantage with respect to the number of general practitioners per 100,000 population; by 1963 this gap had been reduced to 20 per cent. The original intention of Bevan to correct imbalances in the distribution of general practitioners was almost completely thwarted by the obstructionism of the BMA. Consequently, in 1964 the distribution still reflected the historic pattern, with average list sizes ranging from 3,116 in the Burton-on-Trent Executive Council at one end of the league table to 1,434 in Radnorshire at the other extreme.

At the start of the health service the Manchester and Sheffield regions were at the bottom of the league table of consultant numbers, while the North West Metropolitan region was at the top. At this stage, estimated in whole-time equivalents, there were 17.5 consultants per 100,000 population in the North West Metropolitan region, with 8.2 per 100,000 in the Sheffield region. The corresponding levels for 1965 were 22.8 per 100,000 population in the North West Metropolitan region and 11.8 per 100,000 in the Sheffield region, which represents increases of 30.3 per cent and 43.9 per cent respectively. The gap between the two regions therefore narrowed, but the metropolitan region retained a comfortable advantage over its northern partner. The higher concentration of teaching hospitals provided the main explanation for the huge lead of the metropolitan regions at the beginning of the health service, and this was sufficient to guarantee a continuing advantage. The league table of regions was not entirely unchanging. At the start of the NHS, Newcastle was firmly among the impoverished regions with respect to consultant numbers, but by 1964 it had joined the leaders. However, with respect to the independent-contractor and community services, with the exception of Newcastle itself, the area covered by the Newcastle hospital region remained conspicuously backward.

Although the occasional voice was raised concerning the questionable character of the mechanism for resource distribution within the hospital service, this issue never attained the prominence it deserved during the early years of the NHS. The first tabulation designed to draw attention to disparities in resource distribution dates from 1950, when the Welsh Hospital Board pointed to its own disadvantageous position. The first more elaborate presentation seems to date from 1964. Although this adopted a different methodology from the Resource Allocation Working Party (RAWP) a decade later, it is useful to draw together, as shown in Table 2.2, the 1964 calculation, the findings of RAWP relating to the mid-1970s, and the situation arrived at in the 1980s indicating the full impact of the RAWP system.

Despite their limitations, the calculations made in 1964 are valuable for indicating the large scale of the disadvantage of the less-favoured regions. Also, since the situation had changed little since 1948, the tabulation from 1964 arguably gives some indication of the scale of the inherited disadvantage of these regions that the NHS had singularly failed to address. Therefore, although the NHS had laudable consequences from the perspective of the poor, the historic north–south divide in social welfare and health care remained very much in evidence. This inertia with respect to questions of spatial resource distribution was obviously a substantial obstruction to progress with the declared egalitarian objectives of the new health service.

Awkward Questions

Unquestionably the health service gave ample proof of its capacity to deliver great humanitarian benefits at a surprisingly low cost.

Many of the limitations of the NHS were attributable to shortage of resources. Consumers tolerated this situation with their habitual stoicism; but unlike their attitude to earlier disappointments, they were optimistic that the new system was basically sound and able to move forward as circumstances permitted.

Resource constraint was indeed a main handicap, but, as indicated above, the problems of the new service were more deep-seated than was realized by the public. Despite a superficial impression of well-being, the health service was riddled with anomalies and basic flaws. The interests of social justice were hardly served by the distribution of resources according to past precedent rather than proven need. It was also not clear that resources were used to the best effect, or with regard to the stated policy priorities of the government. By contrast with the above-mentioned Guillebaud Committee and the Abel-Smith and Titmuss investigations, the Public Accounts Committee and the Select Committee on Estimates were less concerned with inadequate resources than with evidence concerning profound inefficiencies in their utilization. The main targets for criticism were the new hospital administrative bodies, which were regarded as extravagant and badly managed. Persistence of this reputation provided a ready excuse for denying the health service additional resources, even for purposes for which there was a proven need and where the investment represented a contribution to longer-term economies. Within Whitehall and among experts on the machinery of government, the new and unfamiliar system of administration adopted for the NHS was, therefore, not regarded as a success. Rather, it was the object of distrust on account of its complexity, lack of accountability, confused management arrangements, and alleged inefficiencies.

Of course, the complexity of the system was not a matter of design, but a reluctant necessity, aiming to accommodate a variety of powerful interest groups. The resultant arrangements were suspect; such fundamental goals as the balanced development of the system, functional unity and continuity of care, or the promotion of such important objectives as teamwork within primary care, or community care within the local-government sector, were dependent on effective leadership from ministers and their bureaucrats, which proved well beyond their capacities, especially before 1960.

The performance of the Ministry of Health noticeably improved after 1960. This advance was assisted by the appointment of Sir Bruce Fraser as Permanent Secretary and Sir George Godber as Chief Medical Officer. The former was the first Permanent Secretary in modern times to be recruited from the Treasury. Sudden retraction of the Treasury's objections to a long-term plan for hospital building was the first fruit of this change at the top of the Ministry of Health and it ushered in a new phase of constructive partnership. The experienced Sir George Godber adopted a robust approach to his duties, reasserting the role of the medical administrators within the department and providing much-needed leadership in the many areas where changes in policy required delicate negotiation with the various arms of the medical profession. Under Fraser and Godber various working parties were instituted which laid the foundations for the Family Doctors' Charter and new medical management structures adopted in the hospital system.

It was inevitable that at some stage the longer-term viability of the tripartite system of administration should come into question. In line with the prevalent ethos in social administration at the time, the Ministry of Health and other advocates of the status quo placed their faith in the capacity of cooperation to overcome problems associated with the over-complicated administrative structures of the NHS. Despite exhortation from ministers and reports on cooperation from committees of the central consultative structure, there remained persistent and serious problems of duplication, fragmentation, and lack of cohesiveness, all characteristics horribly reminiscent of the defects of services before the NHS. The passage of time produced no evidence of meaningful cooperation between the three main arms of the health service. Although introducing some elements of simplification, the system adopted in Great Britain in 1948 divided responsibility for the new health service between no fewer than 850 main administrative bodies. In any one natural geographical area it was likely that services would be distributed between a variety of autonomous health authorities, each with its separate tradition and fiercely protective of its autonomy. The situation was in some respects more complicated than before the NHS, when, with respect to such services as maternity and child welfare, tuberculosis, or the mental sector, some individual local authorities had provided reasonably comprehensive services. In such fields, the new health service effectively disrupted some hard-won gains in continuity of care.

The dysfunctional characteristics of the NHS administrative system were particularly evident in areas such as Tyneside where numerous authorities were crowded into a small geographical area, or when it was necessary to develop services for new towns, such as Milton Keynes, which compared in scale with major cities. When Humberside was created as a new health service administrative unit in 1974, it was constituted from no fewer than six LHAs, six Executive Councils, and eight HMCs belonging to two different regions.

With the above disadvantages in mind it was inevitable that the case for reorganizing the health service should eventually force itself onto the political agenda. No encouragement for this move emanated from the Ministry of Health, which used its influence to determine that a series of independent reports, beginning with the Guillebaud Report of 1956, were unsympathetic towards reorganization. This view prevailed, for instance, in the Salmon Report on nursing administration and the Farquharson-Lang report on hospital administration in Scotland, both dating from 1966. However, the line against reorganization was difficult to hold. Already in 1956, Sir John Maude's long note of reservation to the Guillebaud Report had called for the administrative unification of the health service under local government.[51] The same conclusion had been reached by Aneurin Bevan, who since 1945 had accepted that 'If at some future date local government can be reorganised on a wider regional basis—as we all want to see it—a situation may well arise in which we could adapt this system of hospital regional boards to the reorganised local government system, and perhaps get the hospital services back into a more modern form of local government.'[52] Both Maude and Bevan had no doubt been influenced by the revival of plans for local-government reorganization, which inevitably revived consideration of the merits of reversion to local-authority control over the health services.

Apathy on the part of the Ministry of Health and assertiveness from the local authorities created conditions for a recapitulation of earlier competitions for dominance. Not to be left out of the race, as after the First World War or at the outbreak of the Second World War, the medical profession buried its internal differences in order to mount a spirited pre-emptive strike. With the advantage of their superior forces, specialized knowledge, and a powerful investment of political energy, the doctors were well equipped to outpace all their rivals. The vehicle for their initiative was a committee formed in 1958 by nine leading medical organizations to review the state of the medical services in Great Britain. This committee, under the chairmanship of Sir Arthur Porritt, the former Olympic athlete and leading surgeon, completed its report in November 1962.[53] This report contained a competent and critical survey of the health services, but it is primarily remembered for its conclusion that requisite improvements in health care were unlikely to be attained without reorganization of the health service. The Porritt Report called for assimilation under a single authority of all health services located in each natural area of administration. In most respects this represented a revival of the model favoured by the Dawson Report of 1920 and the BMA in 1938. Accordingly, the Porritt Report rejected local-government administration of a unified health service. It was therefore firmly outside the tradition represented by the Royal Sanitary Commission, the Minority Report of the Poor Laws Commission, Sir Robert Morant in his capacity as architect of the Ministry of Health, and this department during the first decades of its existence.

Although not widely publicized, or particularly well received even within the medical profession, the Porritt Report became the effective catalyst to furthering the case for reorganization. Only with difficulty was the Gillie Committee dissuaded from giving explicit backing for the Porritt Report. Nevertheless, the Gillie Report, like most other expert reports after this date, concluded that effective integration of functions was unlikely to be attained without reorganization. This conclusion clearly echoed the mood at the grass roots, indicating that mutual suspicions between the various professional groups were at last beginning to fade. John Revans, the Senior Administrative Medical Officer of the Wessex region, and a member of the Gillie Committee, in November 1962 issued a questionnaire to all general practitioners asking them to state what further hospital facilities they would like provided, on the assumption that 'sooner or later greater integration would appear to be inevitable'.[54] Wessex was also the area with the fullest development of schemes whereby LHA staff were attached to general-practice groups. In both Scotland and Wales the BMA quickly drew up schemes for the application of Porritt principles to their health services and there was sympathy for this development in Northern Ireland. Thus by 1964 the principle of reorganization was widely conceded throughout the UK. Apart from higher levels of funding, this was seen as the single most effective measure likely to bring about improvement in the efficiency and effectiveness of health care. The groundswell of support for reorganization was impressive and it suggested a new mood of constructiveness and commitment to the NHS on the part of the medical profession, but this opportunity for fundamental reappraisal required, as a necessary condition for its success, leadership or at least a degree of compliance from the Ministry of Health. Given the sovereign position of the Ministry, little progress could be made without its acquiescence. In the event, the bureaucrats displayed their customary reticence, with the result that the opportunity for decisive action soon melted away; reorganization was thereby converted into an intractable problem, delayed for a decade, and then accomplished without conviction or success.

2

PLANNING AND REORGANIZATION

> If England seems to be content with the general framework of the Health Service, that does not mean that country is completely satisfied with the actual workings of the program, either qualitatively or quantitatively. In many areas, performance has not measured up to expectations. It is recognized that, however sound are the basic concepts, their translation into a highly efficient system will require years of effort and careful planning. It is generally accepted that only through experimentation and the application of improved techniques can the Health Service remain a dynamic force.[1]

The period from 1964 to 1979 conveniently circumscribes the second phase of the NHS. The health service entered this stage of its existence with a heavy legacy of unsettled problems, without realistic prospects of attracting a substantial influx of additional resources, and lacking clear guidelines for the future direction of policy. Despite these impediments and the gathering economic storm, the second phase of the NHS witnessed a higher rate of growth in its resources than in the preceding or following period. The generally more relaxed atmosphere generated conditions favourable to a series of major planning exercises, the most ambitious of which were connected with the reorganization of 1974. This huge investment of energy by expert working groups in seeking consensual solutions to the problems of the health service provided one of the defining cultural characteristics of the NHS during the second stage of its history. Not all of these initiatives were successful, and inevitably the expectations aroused by these planning exercises far outstripped the capacities of available funding. Especially after the oil crisis of 1973, as elsewhere in the Western system, this period became characterized by the dilemma of 'doing better and feeling worse'.

Government and Politics of Health Care

Labour resumed authority over the NHS in 1964 after an intermission of thirteen years. The general election of October 1964 ushered in a Labour government headed by Harold Wilson. Except for the interruption of the Heath administration between 1970 and 1974, Labour remained in office until May 1979. In addition to overturning the Conservative majority in 1964, Wilson successfully survived three further elections, one in 1966, and two in 1974, but retired in April 1976, when he was replaced as Prime Minister by James Callaghan. With the exception of the period from 1966 to 1970, when Labour enjoyed a comfortable majority, the other administrations during this period were handicapped by slender or even negligible parliamentary majorities.

The NHS was affected by changes in the machinery of government, especially the assimilation of the Ministries of Health and Social Security in November 1968 to form the Department of Health and Social Security (DHSS), which, like the pre-1951 Ministry of Health, was one of the largest spending departments in Whitehall. The head of this department, the Secretary of State for Social Services, was naturally a senior member of the Cabinet. By contrast with the mostly inexperienced or uninfluential figures who had served as Minister of Health between 1951 and 1968, heavyweight politicians assumed this important office. Between 1968 and 1979 Richard Crossman, Sir Keith Joseph, Barbara Castle, and David Ennals served as Secretary of State. All but the last were figures of major political stature. Crossman, Joseph, and Castle each represented the interest of the health service efficiently, and this was perhaps reflected in the better record of the NHS in the competition for resources during their period of office. All three notably contributed to increasing the profile of Cinderella groups such as those requiring long-term care, which involved awkward decisions, bringing little beneficial publicity or personal gain for them as politicians. Each found the health-service assignment more daunting than they had anticipated. Consequently, despite their undoubted achievements, they left office in a state of frustration and dissatisfaction. In the cases of Crossman, Castle, and Ennals, the health assignment marked the end of their ministerial careers, and their reputations were not unscathed by this experience. Both Crossman and Joseph believed that they had adopted a completely wrong approach to health-service reorganization. Barbara Castle's reputation was damaged by a series of bruising encounters with the medical profession. She was removed from office by Callaghan in an evident atmosphere of bad feeling, and with some sense of humiliation owing to the unsatisfactory outcome of the dispute over pay beds in the health service. Ennals hardly put a foot right during his term of office and appropriately left the health service in a state of seemingly terminal crisis. The health portfolio therefore largely preserved its reputation as a political graveyard.

The health service obviously gained through direct ministerial representation in the Cabinet. However, the Secretary of State was inevitably distracted by the wide range of other responsibilities. The complexities and controversy surrounding social security and the inexorable rise in its budget was a particular source of their anxiety. Although the two sides of the department operated largely in isolation, it is arguable that the health service was adversely affected by its administrative association with a larger and dominant partner. The Secretary of State's disadvantage was to some extent compensated for by the appointment of a Minister of State specifically concerned with health. However, in the period under consideration, only between 1974 and 1976 was this particularly advantageous, owing to the tenure of David Owen, who was both energetic and innovative. Owen was only the third medically qualified politician to hold a senior ministerial office in the health department since the formation of the Ministry of Health in 1919.[2]

When the NHS confounded its critics and proved to be a resounding success, opposition rapidly melted away; most of the service's erstwhile foes became supportive and indeed proprietorial. Consequently by 1964 the essential propositions of the health service commanded a broad consensus of support. The new health service was therefore effectively immune from destructive assault, but consensus was also the enemy of constructive self-criticism and progress. Identification as a national institution was a mixed blessing, inviting indifference and neglect as much as veneration. Despite rhetoric to the contrary, health lapsed into a low-priority issue for both main political parties, an outcome welcomed by the technocrats, who cultivated the idea that the health service belonged to the province of the expert. Busy politicians advanced their careers by taking up other issues of more immediate topical interest and media appeal, leaving the accumulating and inaccessible complexities of the health service to the concerns of a handful of uninfluential parliamentarians. Consensus among the politicians was accordingly at least in part attributable to their failure to engage with health-care issues. During the early 1960s a rash of newly formed or reconstituted pressure groups sprang up to fill this vacuum. Bodies such as the Aid for the Elderly in Government Institutions, the Association for Improvements in the Maternity Services, the Consumers' Association, Help the Aged, the National Association for the Welfare of Children in Hospital, and the Patients' Association struggled to prevent the plight of patients and vulnerable groups from being ignored by the powerful NHS establishment.

Besides lack of political salience, there were plenty of other reasons conspiring to perpetuate the entrenched regime of inertia within the health service. Small parliamentary majorities were themselves a disincentive to controversial policy initiatives. Opportunity for expansive developments in social policy was also impeded by the strain of economic crisis which persisted for virtually the whole of the second phase of the NHS. Finally, in the competition for scarce resources, although health made some gains, in many respects it continued to lose out to its competitors.

Out of indolence rather than active conviction, Labour became accustomed to the compromises adopted at the outset of the NHS, while the Conservatives were insufficiently sure of their ground to advocate significant departures from the existing system. The politicians limited themselves to vague promises of improvement and pursuit of established policy objectives. The parties were therefore pushed along by the tide of external events and periodic crises which largely determined the political agenda. Consequently, the general-election manifestos of the major parties systematically failed to anticipate the health service problems that were making their appearance on the horizon.

Voluble demonstrations of political disagreement over the NHS continued to be conducted in parliament, but many of these took on a ritual character; they were often artificial constructs lacking in substance and conviction. For the most part, the parties were either in positive agreement or were unable to work out their ideas sufficiently to enter into effective controversy. This situation was of course frustrating to the radical wings of both parties, where there was constant agitation for fiercer ideological definition of policy, but in practice these extremes exercised little influence at the level of policy.

Between 1970 and 1974 the new right continued to advocate measures to encourage the extension of private health care and the adoption of compulsory insurance as the basis for funding the health service. Despite some support from Conservative ministers, neither of these objectives came near to adoption as policy.

Given the longer tenure of Labour government and the buoyancy of the left during this period, there was greater opportunity for exercise of influence from this quarter. The left undoubtedly exercised influence in the health unions, but its impact in the policy field was negligible. Paradoxically, the left and the right came together in their scepticism about the medical establishment. Their main effect therefore arguably lay in their radical critique and generalized assault on the value system inherent in the medical system, which was not immediately translatable into policy action, but had a beneficial effect in inducing a greater spirit of self-criticism within the health and social-service professions, as well as wider assertiveness and activism among the public. The charismatic voices of Illich, Foucault, the Neo-Marxists, and the anti-psychiatry movement, together with the new-found confidence within complementary medicine, contributed a new dynamic and plurality of thinking about medicine that proved capable of sustaining itself long into the future as a constructive force.

The drift towards consensus was therefore not altogether able to eliminate party political differences or indeed other traditional sources of tension. As noted below, the two parties remained at odds in their attitude to such important questions as health-service charges, pay beds in NHS hospitals, the consultants' contract, democracy in the health service, and in their approach to NHS reorganization. Despite some positive developments, Labour continued to enjoy troubled relations with most arms of the medical profession, not only in the celebrated confrontation over pay beds, but also on various occasions over remuneration, contracts, and other professional issues. The displays of friction in parliament were after all not merely confined to inessentials, but indicative of real ideological difference, perhaps suggesting that, in the sphere of health care, consensus among the politicians was never more than a fragile construct.

Paying for Health Care

From the previous chapter it is evident that funding of the new health service was determined less by objective merit than by the state of the UK economy. Trends in the UK reflected the pattern elsewhere in the Western economy, although the UK was noticeably low in the league table of health-service spending, as indeed in most social expenditures.

During the second phase of the health service, funding came to reflect the contortions of an economy in a state of acute crisis. The period between 1960 and 1975 is generally depicted as the golden age of social expenditure in the Western economies. In the OECD group an average rate of expansion in social expenditure of no less than 8 per cent was maintained during this period. The UK was one of only two OECD states with an average rate of increase below 4 per cent.

In its projections for the period from 1960 to 1975, the NIESR suggested that current expenditure needed to rise at a rate of 3 per cent, and that capital investment should be maintained at no less than fourfold the level appertaining in 1960. These estimates were made in the light of expectations of rising industrial productivity and prosperity, with the result that a high rate of expansion could be managed without increasing the share of national resources absorbed by health care.[3] The NIESR predictions were consistent with the mood among economists at the beginning of the Wilson administration, when it was confidently anticipated that there would be a 25 per cent increase in output over the period from 1964 to 1970, permitting an increase in public expenditure of 4.5 per cent a year.

The Wilson administration was launched on this note of optimism and commitment to even higher rates of growth than had been attained in the last years of the previous Conservative administration. Extravagant commitments concerning public expenditure adopted on the assumption of this rapid growth became the cause of major embarrassment when this growth failed to materialize and when other adverse factors plunged the economy into a spiral of catastrophes.

The gentle seesaw of the stop–go economy of the Macmillan years was replaced by the violent motion of the switchback, in which occasional upturns failed to compensate for the dramatic falls. Some ominous signals of declining confidence were evident in the course of 1964. The big package of public-welfare concessions, of which abolition of the prescription charge was a minor element, announced in the first Labour budget in November 1964, was therefore sufficient to precipitate the first of a succession of rounds of speculation against sterling.

Inadequate responses on the part of the Wilson government led to the humiliation of devaluation in November 1967, which in turn necessitated a major review of public expenditure and a substantial package of cuts announced in January 1968, of which the re-introduction of the prescription charge was a small part. This constituted the first big reversal in the slow incremental rise in public expenditure that had been taking place since the end of the Second World War. Devaluation in fact produced few immediate benefits and it was not until the last months of Wilson's second administration that a balance of trade surplus was recorded. Even then the situation was unstable owing to a low rate of growth, rising unemployment, and rapid rises in earnings.

Labour failed to import order and stability into public-sector pay. At first Wilson relied on a vague agreement with the TUC, which produced a norm for pay rises, but this was only indifferently observed. In the face of the threat of devaluation, a much stricter pay and price regime was introduced in July 1966. This was effective until the summer of 1969, when the *In Place of Strife* initiative collapsed, which was the signal for a dramatic escalation in pay. Once again, the case of nurses and midwives illustrates the general trend of pay settlements in the health service, which for the most part are themselves indicative of the general pattern in the public sector. Nurses were left in a state of dissatisfaction concerning their treatment under Powell. Their pay increased at an average of about 3 per cent a year after 1964, but with Wilson's establishment of the National Board for Prices and Incomes (NBPI), nurses recognized an opportunity to achieve the complete revaluation in their pay that had been resisted under the Whitley system for nearly a decade. The NBPI Report was issued in March 1968. Although the review was sympathetic to the nurses' case, and was generous to nurse managers, for most nurses the award itself amounted to an annual rate of only just above 3 per cent. The settlement was especially detrimental to the worst paid on account of the greater impact on them of higher charges for meals. The latter indignity once again shot nurses into the headlines and led to a prompt retreat by the government. This episode created unease among nurses and sensitivity among ministers, finally reflected in a large one-year pay settlement of 20 per cent taking effect in April 1970.

As noted in the previous chapter, doctors and dentists negotiated their remuneration outside the Whitley system, with the consequence that from 1962 onwards their pay was determined by their Doctors' and Dentists' Review Body. Since this mechanism proved advantageous compared with the Whitley system in maintaining pay comparabilities with other top professions, it was broadly acceptable to the doctors and dentists, and thereby seemed likely to eliminate the much-publicized confrontations that had plagued the health service during its first decade. This goal was realized only imperfectly. As noted below, the general medical practitioners rebelled over the first settlements proposed by the review body and thereby succeeded in gaining both improved remuneration and more favourable contractual terms through their Family Doctors' Charter. When the new general medical practitioner contract was introduced in 1966, the government succeeded in reducing the extent of this gain in line with the provisions of its new pay policy, but the advantage was clearly on the side of the general practitioners. This episode was important because it renewed suspicion about Labour on the part of the BMA. The prospects for industrial harmony with the doctors was further undermined when Labour dragged its heels over implementation of the review body's recommendation for a massive 30 per cent increase shortly before the 1970 general election. Although the incoming Heath government granted the doctors less than they would have obtained under Labour, it was the latter that carried the blame for this alleged betrayal of the review-body procedure.

The Heath administration embarked on a succession of reflation measures and succeeded in increasing the rate of output, but at the cost of a further effective devaluation of sterling and mounting problems of industrial unrest. The government's position was finally undermined by the Middle East war and the associated fourfold increase in the price of oil imposed in stages, starting in October 1973. The government's troubles led to the State of Emergency declared in November 1973, the three-day week imposed in January 1974, and the first miners' strike since 1926, which began in February 1974. The latter prompted Heath to declare a general election, which brought a premature end to his administration.

The miners' strike was merely the most dramatic manifestation of the degeneration of industrial relations under the Heath administration. Following the huge pay awards at the beginning, Heath opted for a new approach in the form of restrictions on trade unions, attempted through the Industrial Relations Act of 1971. When this blunt instrument failed, in November 1972 Heath turned to an incomes policy, which successfully brought down wage rises in the public sector, but at the cost of much bitterness. The Whitley Councils and a revived pay-review body for doctors and dentists fell into line with pay policy, but with much complaint about its arbitrary features and anomalous results. This tension sparked off industrial unrest on many fronts, among which was the first ever outbreak of serious strike action in the NHS, which occurred among ancillary workers between February and April 1973. Although the strikers made almost no gains, this episode signalled the escalation of industrial militancy in the NHS.

In February 1974 Harold Wilson returned to office under singularly inauspicious circumstances. Under Labour, pay ran out of control, the unemployment situation further deteriorated, output again slumped, and the external deficit remained high. The UK was experiencing problems common to the advanced Western economies, but, on account of a greater endemic weakness, it was affected to a noticeably greater extent.

The oil crisis precipitated an economic collapse throughout the Western world. The economic growth rate, which had been maintained since 1960 at an average of about 5 per cent in the OECD area, slumped to nothing. From 1975 onwards the entire OECD area shared the UK's experience of low growth, high inflation, high unemployment, and an adverse balance of trade. All Western nations experienced a sudden crisis of confidence in their welfare regimes, which necessitated a general reappraisal of the viability of their social spending commitments. Gloomy voices declared that 1975 represented the death knell of the welfare state.

Among its many problems, the Labour government risked public expenditure running out of control. In 1974/5 the government overspent its original supply estimates by almost one-third and this crisis further deepened in the following year. The continuing struggle to protect sterling necessitated recourse to massive foreign-currency borrowing, the condition for which was a series of cuts in public expenditure and the introduction of entirely new financial tools and information systems, which soon turned into permanent controls on public expenditure.

This sudden downward plunge in fortunes generated shock and disbelief within the NHS. From the moment of return of his administration, Harold Wilson was met with urgent calls from the health professions for reinstatement of commitments to growth. In order to pacify the professions, in 1976 the government reluctantly agreed to establish a Royal Commission to examine the 'best use and management of the financial and manpower resources of the National Health Service'. This was the first and only comprehensive review of the health services of the UK ever to be initiated by the government. The Commission, chaired by Sir Alec Merrison, reported shortly after the end of the Labour administration.[4] Its findings were therefore too late to assist with the mounting problems overtaking the NHS during the period of its deliberations.

Some of the economic indicators improved towards the end of the Callaghan administration, but the sense of crisis persisted, partly owing to escalating problems of industrial unrest, culminating in the 1978/9 Winter of Discontent, which determined the atmosphere in which Callaghan's administration sank towards its demise.

Precipitated by the general state of crisis in the economy, the period between 1974 and 1979 represented the worst phase of industrial unrest in the history of the NHS. By scrapping the Heath incomes policy, Labour unleashed huge wage demands, which resulted in wage and price rises running at well above 20 per cent in its first year of office. Nurses and midwives again provide a useful indication of the general course of events. Nurses regarded the NBPI Report in 1968 as an inadequate response to their long-running campaign for comprehensive revaluation of their incomes; in the light of further prevarication under Heath, their patience was exhausted. In response to threatened industrial action, Barbara Castle set up an inquiry under Lord Halsbury which examined the pay, not only of nurses and midwives, but also of other groups claiming comparability with them. The Halsbury Report, issued in September 1974, resulted in a pay award of 30 per cent for nurses and midwives, which was of course substantial, but only on a level with pay increases in the industrial sector.

From July 1975 onwards pay increases were determined by the three stages of Labour's prices-and-wages policy, which worked tolerably well, but in the summer of 1978 the attempt to impose further restrictions in phase 4 was rejected by the unions, precipitating the winter pay crisis of 1978/9. In common with other groups, nurses refused to accept a 5 per cent limit on their pay rises, and demanded compensation on account of their ineligibility for increments on productivity criteria. With considerable public support, the nurses pressed for a 15 per cent interim increase pending a full review of their case for 'exceptional treatment'.

The nurses' campaign took place against a background of widespread industrial action, which inevitably spread into the health service, particularly among ancillary workers and ambulance staff. More than half the staff of the NHS were involved in strike action; 1.4 million days were lost, which makes this Winter of Discontent by far the greatest episode of industrial unrest in the history of the health service. The interim increase eventually granted to the nurses was about half the level originally demanded and followed the lines of agreements reached with other groups of NHS personnel. The Labour government came to an end before the promised comparability study was completed.

Doctors and dentists stood outside the structural negotiation framework applying to other NHS staff, but their review system was similarly affected by the strains of the situation, as indicated at an early stage, when in the autumn of 1974 Lord Halsbury was forced to resign as chairman of the review body owing to inadvertently suggesting that his clients should abide by the twelve-month pay rule. Owing to a variety of complicating factors, confrontation with the medical profession became arguably worse than ever before or since. In summary, the main additional causes of friction comprised: negotiations over a new contract for consultants, which dragged on intermittently between 1974 and 1979 without final agreement being reached; the short but damaging dispute over junior hospital doctors' hours and pay in the autumn of 1975, which occasioned the first disruption in hospitals caused by medical staff since the beginning of the NHS; and, finally, a further short but even more acrimonious dispute occasioned by Labour's attempt to phase out pay beds in NHS hospitals, an aim that was effectively thwarted owing to intransigent opposition from the medical profession and an absence of conviction within the Labour Cabinet. Each one of these disputes with the medical profession possessed significant and unwelcome expenditure implications for the NHS.

The review mechanism proved efficiently protective of the interests of doctors and dentists. The review body went along with pay policy, but complained throughout that this was unreasonably restricting the incomes of its clients. The end of phase 3 was taken as an opportunity to signify refusal to comply with further controls on public-sector pay. The review body demanded and obtained an agreement for an immediate increase of 10 per cent from April 1978, together with further adjustments amounting to 18 per cent by April 1980, which in the summer of 1979 secured for doctors and dentists an increase of 26 per cent, placing them well in advance of Whitley groups in securing their economic interest in the final stages of the Callaghan government.

The above combination of adverse economic conditions and industrial strife determined that there was almost continuous pressure from internal and external paymasters for containment of public expenditure. Consequently, no sooner was the health service released from its probation and set on course for a mild regime of expansion than it was once again subjected to tough controls.

Successive economic failures inevitably exercised their impact on spending on the public services. With respect to the health service, the slow process of incremental advance described in the previous chapter was replaced by an unstable pattern in which there were sharp changes from one year to the next. The first Wilson administration began on a euphoric note, with the elimination of the prescription charge and the promise to review other direct charges. Health-service expenditure increased at a higher rate than under the Conservatives, but then, following the devaluation crisis, the engine went into reverse. Constituting something of a humiliation, dental charges were increased and the prescription charge was re-introduced, albeit with exemptions for the over-65s and other priority groups. Notwithstanding these setbacks, when deflated using the NHS price index, health-service current spending increased at a rate of about 4.5 per cent during Wilson's first period in office, and about 5.5 per cent under Heath. Spending between 1974 and 1979 repeated the Wilson pattern of high spending at first but ended in two years with virtually no growth. The first year was artificially inflated owing to high wage settlements, especially the Halsbury award to nurses. The increase in current spending between 1974 and 1979 averaged at about 5 per cent a year. Every effort was made to protect capital investment on hospitals, where spending continued at a high level, doubling in real terms between 1965 and 1975, before falling back to the 1969 level during the Callaghan period.

In a situation of low growth, the share of GDP absorbed by the health service increased from 4.1 to 5.3 per cent between 1964 and 1979. As a proportion of total social spending, the health service remained constant, but the personal social services increased from 4 to 5 per cent largely as a result of the expansion consequent upon the Seebohm reforms. The position in the social-spending league table of the combined health and personal social services therefore marginally improved, but the biggest gainer during this period was social security, reflecting the increase in unemployment. After a long period of buoyancy, both education and housing fell back sharply in the late 1970s.

Between 1964 and 1979 the sources of health-service funding fell into a settled pattern. The Macmillan–Powell experiment with high direct charges and insurance contributions was abandoned and it was not resurrected. Direct charges settled down to providing only about 2 per cent of gross costs, while about 10 per cent was derived from the NHS Contribution. This stability disguises uncertainty in both parties concerning the funding of the health service. As already noted, Labour was committed to abolishing direct charges, but went no further than a temporary abolition of the prescription charge, and in 1974 removal of the charge for family-planning services. Labour had previously vigorously contested increases in the NHS Contribution, but Crossman made no secret of his preference for insurance rather than direct charges. The Heath administration favoured increasing health-service charges, and was particularly committed to introducing a proportional charge for NHS prescriptions, but in practice it found these measures impracticable on account of its prices and incomes policy. In response to rising support for insurance funding of the health service among senior Conservatives, including Sir Geoffrey Howe, and also in the BMA at this date, an interdepartmental working party was established in 1970 to look into the question of NHS finance. This recapitulated the work of the Figgures Committee and reached precisely the same negative conclusion about alternatives to the current system. Notwithstanding vociferous campaigning in favour of compulsory insurance funding of the health service, there was even less support under Heath for pursuing the insurance option than there had been under Harold Macmillan.[5]

Planning, Priorities, and Equality

The progressive sophistication of public-expenditure controls, and later the opportunity for improvement in management and planning structures presented by reorganization, conspired to produce substantial changes in resource-management and strategic-planning methods within the NHS, the total effect of which left few parts of the system unaltered. The roots of these changes were located in the early 1960s. The Plowden Report and the introduction of the Public Expenditure Survey Committee (PESC) system in 1961 imposed a new level of discipline, but also fresh prospects for growth and rational planning in the public sector. Although evoking much complaint, the PESC operated to smooth the course of expansion in social expenditure, even serving to reduce the impact of the post-devaluation economies, although health was not one of the main beneficiaries.

In an attempt to improve the performance of spending departments, the Heath administration imported business advisers, and shared their enthusiasm for planning, programming, budgeting systems, and techniques such as cost-benefit analysis. Among the immediate practical outcomes were the establishment of the Central Policy Review Staff (CPRS), a programme-analysis and review system, and general encouragement of programme budgeting.

The absence of strategic planning containing an indication of broad developments over the medium term or a firm statement of priorities was a constant source of complaint about the NHS from the Treasury in the course of the 1960s. This lack of a rational framework was used as an excuse to block bids for additional resources emanating from the health departments. The hospital plan introduced a model for strategic planning, but it was highly provisional and uncertain in most of its major aspects. For instance, it was by no means certain what impact new hospitals would exercise on current spending. The Treasury therefore engineered a joint investigation into the revenue consequences of capital schemes, which evolved a formula for suitably compensating the owners of new facilities, but this had the unfortunate consequence of giving generous compensation to prosperous authorities in the south-east, thereby increasing the disadvantage of the generally less-favoured authorities which tended also to benefit less from the hospital plan. As noted below, this scheme therefore came into conflict with the rival attempt at rationalization represented by RAWP and its antecedents.

The DHSS stumbled towards a comprehensive planning system in its habitual erratic and indeterminate manner, the course of progression being to some extent dictated by unforeseen events. Arguably the first block in the planning puzzle was the long-gestated and impressive White Paper, *Better Services for the Mentally*

Handicapped, which appeared in 1971. This planning initiative was hardly a spontaneous gesture. Rather it represented a defensive move rendered necessary by the Ely Hospital scandal, discussed further below, which suddenly precipitated long-stay hospitals to the head of the policy agenda. By a fortunate coincidence of timing, *Better Services for the Mentally Handicapped* was completed at a rare point of relative relaxation over medium-term expenditure commitments, with the result that it was allowed to adopt specific targets and norms. Indeed, this was the first occasion in the community-care field that such precise objectives were stated.

Once mental handicap had obtained its planning statement, it was necessary to proceed with its logical sequel, a White Paper on improving services for the mentally ill, the publication of which occurred after a long delay in 1975. This exercise was completed in a renewed climate of retrenchment, dictating avoidance of commitment to targets and norms of the kind contained in the earlier document on the mentally handicapped. The next logical product of this sequence was a White Paper on services for the elderly, but this exercise was all but abandoned.

The ongoing hospital plan, the complex of initiatives relating to the groups needing long-term care, and other items such as the plan for maternity services emanating from the Peel Committee in 1970, and the proposals for an integrated child health service produced by the Court Committee in 1976, represented strategic initiatives of different types and contrasting character. They showed up the need for integration into a comprehensive planning framework. In the early 1970s the Treasury sought to impose order on this patchwork by channelling the health departments' priorities reviews into one of its programme-analysis and review exercises, but this was deftly avoided by the DHSS in favour of a planning study controlled by the health department itself. Given the new emphasis on output budgeting, the DHSS calculated that its leverage in PESC negotiations would be enhanced by the use of this form of analysis. Methodological limitations prevented direct reference to health outputs; the best that was possible was drawing information into natural programmes, the progress of which could be measured against stated policy priorities. Although beset with technical difficulties, programme-budgeting was much more than a dry academic exercise. Great expectations were aroused concerning the capacity of this instrument to enhance the credibility of the health departments' planning capacities and bring about a major shift in resources in the direction of more economical and desirable services.

This DHSS planning system was devised in the course of preparations for reorganization. The general objectives of this system were sketched out in the Management Grey Book which appeared in September 1972, and the full scheme was outlined in the *NHS Planning System* Blue Book published in 1976, by which time the programmes had been running on an experimental basis for some time. Completion was repeatedly held up by the recurrent expenditure crises of the time. The system aimed to provide broad strategic plans covering all parts of the health and personal social services for a ten-year period, together with detailed operational planning statements relating to two or three years. For practical purposes the new planning system classified health services into eight care groups, most small in scale and relating to specific dependency groups, but with two (general, acute, and maternity hospital services; and primary-care services) being massive and heterogeneous in character.

The first attempt to state the objectives of health expenditure according to the new planning system was contained in the consultative document *Priorities for the Health and Personal Social Services*, which appeared in March 1976.[6] This document bore all the signs of the uncertainties of the times. Reflecting its early origins, it contained the first comprehensive statement of norms and targets for service provision produced since the beginning of the health service. Indicating its publication at a time of mounting crisis, it embodied only the most limited assumptions concerning growth. It was anticipated that spending on the health service would rise by 2.6 per cent in the first year and at a rate of 1.8 per cent thereafter. For the personal social services an increase of 4 per cent was assumed in the first year and 2 per cent thereafter. Given the inescapable priority assumed by community care on the basis of previous policy statements, 6 per cent was taken as the annual prospective increase for this provision. On account of the demand-led system and demographic change, a 3.7 per cent annual increase for the independent-contractor services (after the 1974 reorganization known as Family Practitioner Services (FPS)) was envisaged. Given these priorities, it was necessary to adopt very limited rates of growth for the elderly (3.2 per cent), for the mentally ill (1.8 per cent), for the mentally handicapped (2.8 per cent), and for children (2.2 per cent). These modest targets were not attainable without even more severe restriction on the acute and general hospital services, where an increase of 1.2 per cent was allowed, or the maternity service, where an actual fall of 1.8 per cent was projected. Although not admitted, the low rates of growth outlined for the hospital services effectively undermined the effort to redistribute hospital resources spatially according to a more egalitarian formula, which was one of the other stated objectives of the *Priorities* document. This planning exercise therefore sacrificed spatial equality in order to benefit its client-oriented priorities, but even here certain high-priority client groups were set to fare much better than others. However, since this was a provisional exercise, the outcome was far from certain, especially since it was evident at the time that shifting resources from the acute hospital sector to the Cinderella specialities was unlikely to succeed.

Lack of conviction concerning the possibility of moving with any speed towards the objectives of the *Priorities* document was confirmed by a second consultative document, *The Way Forward*, issued in September 1977.[7] This slight publication pathetically reiterated the general objectives of the earlier document, but acknowledged that forward progress was likely to take place at a snail's pace. Paradoxically *The Way Forward* attached even greater emphasis than its predecessor to correcting spatial inequalities, although the task was virtually impossible to achieve in the light of the government's recurrent public expenditure cuts and priorities dictated by the new planning system.

Although not exercising much direct practical effect, at least the planning system enabled the new Regional Health Authorities (RHAs) and Area Health Authorities (AHAs) to compile their strategic plans, albeit with the usual variation of practice and differing degrees of competence. As a consequence of the general atmosphere of crisis surrounding the production of these voluminous regional Doomsday Books, they were in the main left to gather dust until the date arrived in 1982 for their revision. On account of the absence of 'growth moneys' it was again not possible to make more than token progress with operational planning; planning teams representing the various sectors were set in place, only to face frustration and embarrassment owing to their inability to achieve any meaningful redistribution of resources according to the guidelines laid down in the *Priorities* consultative documents.

The ultimate failure of the programme-budgeting initiative to act as an instrument for redistribution is illustrated in Table 2.1, which compares the situations at the outset of the priorities exercise and at the date of the first formal revision.

When it came to the point of decision, even by the modest aspirations of the *Priorities* documents, the programme-budgeting exercise adopted targets that entailed only a slight departure from the existing pattern of expenditure. Given the absence of growth, it was in practice not feasible to shift resources away from the hospital acute sector in the interests of community care on anything like the scale originally anticipated. The balance between programmes therefore stayed much as before the redistribution exercise.

Importation of cash limits into the NHS represented a

TABLE 2.1. *National Health Service revenue programme budget, England, 1976–1982* (%)

Programme	1976/7 (outturn)	1981/2 (projected)
Primary Care	19.7	19.9
General, Acute, hosp.maternity	38.7	37.5
Elderly, Phys.handicap	13.1	13.9
Mental handicap	4.3	4.5
Mentally ill	7.7	7.7
Children	5.7	5.9
Others (mainly PSS)	10.9	10.6
TOTAL	100	100

Source: Based on data from G T Banks, 'Programme Budgeting in the DHSS', in T A Booth (ed), *Planning for Welfare: Social Policy and the Expenditure Process* (Oxford: Blackwell, 1979), 150–72, 159–61

fundamental development in control, the ramifications of which continue to the present day. From the onset of the new service, budgets were determined by historic costs plus a small allowance for growth. Compensation for price increases and pay awards was made by means of retrospective additions to allocations to enable the existing volume of services to be maintained. This convention was terminated from the financial year 1976/7 onwards. Cash limits, already applied in other sectors of public expenditure, were extended to the Hospital and Community Health Services (HCHS) administered by the new RHAs and AHAs. The cash-limits system introduced a ceiling embracing growth, prices, and pay increases. Furthermore, the inflation factor was set at a minimum, with the result that, if prices or pay awards breached the inflation limit, the excess would be deducted from the growth allocation, and, if this was not sufficient, cuts in services would be incurred. At first, the practice was not quite as draconian as the theory. Compensation was in fact applied for price and wage increases above the predicted levels. However, the increasingly severe interpretation of cash limits introduced an important cultural change into the NHS, creating severe pressure on resources available for modernization and innovation. Cash limits also exposed a yawning disparity between the HCHS and the FPS sectors, since in the latter expenditure continued to be demand led.

Regional Resource Allocation

The onset of preparations for reorganization, involving the application of a more scientific approach to resource management in the health service, highlighted the embarrassing problem of irrationalities and disparities in the prevailing system of spatial resource distribution. This issue had been taken up in 1969 by Richard Crossman, whose advisers were sensitive to this issue, and who was understandably receptive since he represented a constituency in Coventry, located in the Birmingham RHB, known to be one of the main deficit regions.

The government's new-found alertness to the problem of spatial distribution had been signalled in the unlikely context of Crossman's 1970 Green Paper on health-service reorganization, where it was declared:

> In the long run, it is intended that the basic determinant of area health authority budgets will be the population served by the area, modified to take account of relevant demographic variables, underlying differences in morbidity, the characteristics of the capital plant inherited by each authority and any special responsibilities undertaken for wider care and particularly for special needs of teaching and research.[8]

In fulfilment of this intention, beginning in 1971/2 a hospital revenue allocation formula was applied, which was designed gradually to diminish inequalities in distribution by reducing the role of bed and case data in the calculation, and placing a new level of emphasis on demographic and epidemiological criteria. It was accordingly proposed to phase out the system of distribution based on the established pattern of service provision and replace it by a method reflecting objective needs.

As evident from Table 2.2, the Crossman formula was successful to only the most limited extent. The bed- and service-based formula used in 1963 indicated two regions with double-figure deficits, compared with two metropolitan regions with a surplus above 8 per cent. The calculation applying to 1975, which reflected a population bias, indicated a slightly different pattern of advantage and disadvantage, with the excess in the metropolitan regions being even more pronounced. For the first time this impression was confirmed by a substantial body of independent research, which drew attention not only to regional variation, but also to the even greater extent of disparities within regions.[9]

The Resource Allocation Working Party, established in May 1975, was commissioned to improve on the Crossman formula. An interim RAWP formula became the basis for distribution in 1976/7, while the revised formula contained in the final report was applied thereafter.[10] Similar distribution formula exercises were undertaken for all other parts of the UK. The RAWP system was designed to give 'equal opportunity of access to health care for people at equal risk' and thereby achieve a much greater degree of equality than attained under the Crossman formula. The RAWP approach extended the demographic and epidemiological basis of the distribution calculation. The main innovation was to use Standardized Mortality Ratios as a proxy for morbidity, on account of the paucity and unreliability of information relating to levels of

TABLE 2.2. *RHB/RHA distance from revenue target allocations, 1963–1988* (%)

Region[a]	1963[b]	1975	1981	1988
Newcastle/Northern	−5.34[c]	−7.81	−5.21	−2.14
Leeds/Yorkshire	−11.65	−4.92	−3.71	−2.21
Sheffield/Trent	−5.66	−14.29	−6.71	−3.22
East Anglia	−9.48	−6.66	−5.56	−3.79
NW Metropolitan/Thames	+8.19	+21.88	+12.33	+5.68
NE Metropolitan/Thames	+5.14	+18.75	+8.85	+9.01
SE Metropolitan/Thames	−1.20	+15.63	+8.87	+2.72
SW Metropolitan/Thames	+6.80	+10.94	+5.67	+0.26
Wessex	+1.20	−6.66	−4.78	−0.68
Oxford	+5.88	+10.94	−1.18	−1.84
South Western	−3.29	−4.92	−4.74	−1.01
Birmingham/W. Midlands	−6.26	−6.66	−3.89	−2.21
Liverpool/Mersey	−19.23	−1.59	−0.30	+0.15
Manchester/N. Western	−7.45	−14.29	−6.14	−2.06

[a] In cases where two names are given for a region, the second relates to any alteration made in the 1974 reorganization, which converted RHBs into Regional Health Authorities (RHAs)

[b] The estimates for 1963 exclude teaching hospitals The latter are included for the three other dates If teaching hospitals had been taken into account, the 1963 estimates would have added a further 5% advantage to each of the metropolitan regions

[c] Minus indicates below target, plus above target

Sources: *Hospital Service Finance* (1964), 7–11; calculated from DHSS, *The Way Forward* (Sept 1977); DHSS, Circular RRA 16/2 (Feb 1981); DHSS, *Health Services Cash Limits Exposition Booklet, 1987/88* (London: DHSS, 1987)

sickness. As indicated by the 1975 column in Table 2.2, the RAWP formula amply confirmed fears that there existed endemic shortcomings in the NHS distribution system. It was not clear what part this had played in contributing to existing disparities in health between the regions, but continuation of this degree of irrationality within the system was obviously intolerable. RAWP defined a needs-based expenditure target for each region, which it was anticipated might be reached within about ten years. In fact, resource constraints placed limitations on the rate of movement towards the RAWP targets. Consequently, as indicated in the third column of Table 2.2, only limited progress had been made by 1981, although the gulf between the extremes had been noticeably reduced. The RAWP exercise and its counterparts undoubtedly brought some benefit; at least they represented an attempt to seek a solution to a problem that had for long been ignored. Although RAWP was vulnerable to criticism, it formed the basis for further conceptual and practical progress on questions of resource allocation. An expert Advisory Group on Resource Allocation was established to undertake an ongoing review of problems raised by the RAWP formula, but this had produced only one report by the time it was disbanded as part of the Thatcher government's early onslaught on public-interest quangos.

Initially, the two main redistributional exercises achieved only limited results. Neither spatial nor client-group redistribution proved possible to anything like the extent merited by the evidence, or anticipated by planners. The economic crisis provided a ready excuse, but it is by no means evident that a more relaxed public expenditure regime would have yielded markedly different results. The more affluent regions and acute specialities were efficient at obstructing any rapid shift of resources according to the criteria of spatial equality or in the interests of the groups dependent on community care.

Reorganization

Reorganization represented the dominant and most intractable policy challenge relating to the NHS. As indicated in the previous chapter, by 1964 the case for reorganization had been widely accepted, but this cause evoked little sympathy on the part of the Ministry of Health and this view was shared by Kenneth Robinson, the new Minister of Health. The health department kept resolutely to its official line, recognizing that 'securing maximum cooperation between the different branches of the Service' represented the largest administrative challenge within the health service, but this was not regarded as insuperable. Accordingly there was no inclination to consider deviating from the existing organization. The Ministry sheltered behind the Guillebaud Committee's conclusion that the 'Service works much better in practice than it looks on paper'.[11]

Coordination undoubtedly continued to improve and was actively assisted by the leadership of Sir George Godber and Sir John Brotherston, the new Chief Medical Officers in London and Edinburgh respectively, and by the efforts of such organizations as the King's Fund and the Nuffield Provincial Hospitals Trust.

As already indicated, especially after the Porritt Report, the tide of opinion turned decisively in favour of abandoning the tripartite structure and undertaking complete reorganization of the health service. Especially significant were some major policy reviews instituted early in the lifetime of the Wilson administration, which collectively made it impossible for the Minister of Health to avoid the question of reorganization. By favouring unification of social work under social-service departments of local government, the Seebohm Committee threatened to reduce the functions of LHAs to the extent that their continuing existence was thrown into doubt. The Royal Commission on Medical Education chaired by Lord Todd suggested improvements in education and training that could not be achieved without ending the administrative separation of teaching hospitals, the reorganization of hospital services in London, and greater administrative integration of health administration. Especially significant was the Royal Commission on Local Government in England chaired by Lord Redcliffe-Maud, which opened up the possibility of placing the entire health service under new multi-purpose or 'unitary' local-government agencies. Although this was not appreciated at the time, once Richard Crossman in September 1965 had committed himself to a comprehensive review of local government, a similar review of the health service was rendered unavoidable, if only as a defensive gesture against local-government takeover.

The above major reviews were merely the most potent forces affecting thinking on reorganization. The opening years of the Wilson administration witnessed the emergence of an irresistible tide of demand for reorganization emanating from many bodies and even unexpected directions. For instance, in reviewing the pay of both manual workers and nurses in the NHS, the NBPI concluded that the current 'diffusion of authority in the Health Service is a grave source of weakness'; it called for a much simpler system of administration, preferably entailing establishment of a relatively small number of single-tier authorities.[12] The NBPI was undoubtedly influenced by the respected National Institute of Economic and Social Research, which in 1966 published a comprehensive review of prospective trends in spending on the health and welfare services, in the course of which it was emphasized that there was an inescapable argument for 'basic reorganization and administrative improvement' within the NHS.[13] In the absence of convincing guidance from the Ministry of Health, lay bodies such as the NBPI and NIESR were at risk of reaching poorly thought-out conclusions about reorganization, based on inadequate understanding of the argument; therefore they were liable to complicate further an already confused situation.

Owing to the failure of the Ministry of Health to take command of events, the opportunity for consensus was lost and the scene was set for the re-enactment of the fractious debates that had occurred at the end of the First and Second World Wars, with precisely the same alternatives and a similar line-up of forces. Once the long-delayed reorganization of local government was in sight, local-government associations could see no convincing reason why the health services should not be returned to local-government administration. Their case was strengthened by the evident shortcomings of the specially invented tripartite health-service organization, by the desirability of harmonizing social-service and health-service administrations, by the advantages of strengthened local accountability, and by the superior management possibilities promised under strengthened unitary local government.

The medical profession was convinced by none of these arguments. It had lost none of its antipathy to local government, and it remained vigilant against its membership sliding under the heel of the MOH. The Porritt Report represented in essence a revival of the Dawson Report's proposals for the unification of the health service under a separate administration. This alternative was always favoured by the medical profession because it ensured a substantial degree of professional influence in the health-service administration. Separation from local government was also defended on the grounds that local taxation was inadequate to support the health service, and on account of the notorious lack of uniformity in the standards of local-authority services.

Reorganization in Scotland

The reorganization problem proved easier to resolve in Scotland and Wales than in England. Both the Scottish and the Welsh BMA were attracted by the Porritt scheme; in neither case was local government in a position to mount a rival bid for the control of the health service. In Scotland difficulties experienced in the ambitious plan for integrated health care in Livingstone new town, and the likelihood of even greater problems in other new housing developments, persuaded the Scottish health department that reorganization would represent a simpler and more effective alternative to isolated local exercises in integration. In the course of 1965 agreement was reached that reorganization in Scotland at the local level should involve unification of health services under some eighteen 'area health boards'. Scottish ministers agreed enthusiastically to this scheme. Despite this flying start, the momentum in favour of reorganization in Scotland was soon lost, partly owing to changes of junior ministers in Scotland after the March 1966 general election, and also through the exercise of a veto by the English Minister of Health, who insisted on a slower timetable involving in the first instance the issue of Green Papers. The latter were a new invention of the Wilson administration designed to give an airing to tentative government policies. The Green Paper was also an ideal vehicle for impeding unwanted change, and it was used for this purpose by Kenneth Robinson.

The Scottish Green Paper appeared in December 1968, after which there was further delay occasioned by a series of sharp changes of direction in England.[14] For this reason the Scottish White Paper was not issued until after the change of government, and indeed after further delays mainly connected with the need for harmonization with the English scheme. The Scottish White Paper was finally issued in July 1971.[15] The Scottish Reorganization Bill was introduced in the House of Lords in January 1972, and the National Health Service (Scotland) Act received the Royal Assent on 9 August 1972.

Notwithstanding repeated delays, Scotland at least enjoyed the benefit of seeing its reorganization legislation reach the statute book almost a year in advance of the legislation relating to England

and Wales, with the helpful consequence that preparations for the new system scheduled for introduction on 1 April 1974 were conducted at a more relaxed pace.

The final plan was consistent with the 1968 Green Paper and was therefore the filial descendant of the Porritt scheme. In Scotland, the Porritt approach was more readily applicable owing to the more fragmented structure and lesser power of local government. Also Scotland was in advance of England and Wales in deciding its policy on social work, with the result that the Green Paper contained assurances to local authorities concerning their control of unified social-service departments. Finally, the Royal Commission on Local Government in Scotland was known to be much less favourable than its counterpart in England to local-government administration of the health service. The way was, therefore, tolerably clear for introducing a scheme for unification of the health services outside local government.

A more difficult and controversial question related to the future of the regional tier. Again, as favoured by Porritt, the Scottish Green Paper's stated preference for the abolition of the five regional authorities was confirmed. This raised some objection, but was overwhelmingly favoured on the grounds that Scotland was small enough for the central health department to exercise a span of control over a single tier of local administrative units, at first called by the Porritt name 'area health boards', but later retitled Health Boards in the legislation. Indeed, the 1948 system had already embodied a greater degree of central control than was exercised by the health department in London. Accordingly the Scottish Home and Health Department (SHHD) seemed well suited to take on an additional degree of responsibility. However, out of sensitivity to legitimate fears of over-centralization, the planners allowed Health Boards to be strongly represented on two important and newly devised central bodies: the Scottish Health Service Planning Council, and the Common Services Agency. The former was concerned with strategic planning and the latter with the supply of common services to both the health department and the Health Boards. Of these two bodies only the Common Services Agency was anticipated in the 1968 Green Paper. The Planning Council was added to give greater assurance concerning the health department's commitment to partnership. In determining the characteristics of the Planning Council, the SHHD found it difficult to meet the mutually incompatible expectations of the Treasury and the incipient Health Boards. The Treasury feared that the Planning Council would erode the Secretary of State's responsibility for management efficiency, whereas the Health Boards suspected that the Planning Council would degenerate into a complicated and time-wasting talking shop.

The number and boundaries of Health Boards were adjusted slightly in the course of the planning exercise, the final pattern being adapted to achieve compatibility with the units of reorganized local government scheduled for introduction in April 1975. There were nine regions of the new local-government structure. Of these, two regions were subdivided, each into four Health Boards: on account of geographical diversity, the Highland Region was divided into four Health Boards (including three representing the island groups), while four Health Boards were constituted from the populous Strathclyde Region. The other boards coincided with the seven other regions of local government, making a total of fifteen Health Boards. Also on grounds of geographical diversity or population density, most of the Health Boards were subdivided into Health Districts for administrative purposes.

Reflecting the close ties of the BMA with the Scottish scheme, unlike the situation in England, independent contractors agreed to place their contracts directly with Health Boards, thus obviating the need for separate Family Practitioner Committees (FPCs). The changes in Scotland accordingly introduced both unification and a radical simplification in administration, reducing the number of administrative units from about 160 to 45.

As in England, the most contentious aspect of the new scheme related to the composition of the Health Boards. Both local government and the medical profession anticipated substantial representation on the Boards as a condition of their compliance with reorganization. The SHHD was sympathetic to representation, but consistently resisted eroding the Secretary of State's freedom of action in appointing chairpersons and in determining the membership. In practice, the boards included significant local-government and professional representation, and universities in the case of the five boards containing medical schools. The *Democracy in the NHS* exercise mounted by Labour in 1974 marginally increased the local-government share and added to the range of health-service personnel on the boards.

Indicative of the concern that the influence of the patient and the local community was weakened under the reorganized health service, in common with arrangements being made south of the border, the Scottish legislation provided for a Health Service Commissioner and Local Health Councils, the latter being the approximate equivalent of Community Health Councils (CHCs) in England and Wales. Separate from the legislation, but connected with reorganization, this opportunity was taken in Scotland to introduce a standardized code for complaints procedures in hospitals, which placed Scotland more than a decade ahead of England and Wales in this respect.

Reorganization in England and Wales under Labour

Scottish preparations for health-service reorganization were subject to many delays, but the entire operation was characterized by a high degree of consensus and genuine enthusiasm for the agreed objectives. Thus, Scotland required only one Green Paper at the beginning and one White Paper at the end of the planning process. The reorganization operation in England and Wales displayed little of this continuity or confidence. Disregarding the three policy documents relating specifically to Wales, in England between 1968 and 1970 Labour produced two Green Papers containing entirely different plans, followed by a White Paper which was suppressed on account of the general election. After the change of government, there followed a Conservative consultative document containing yet another variant scheme. In a slightly modified form, these proposals were embodied in the 1972 White Paper, which formed the basis for the 1973 legislation. The entire planning process was marked by discord; although resistance to the final scheme died away, this was as much indicative of inanition as positive confidence in a scheme that was to suffer the fate of being disowned almost at its birth.

As already noted, following the Porritt Report, there was strong and consistent support within the Welsh BMA for reorganization, but further progress was blocked owing to the lukewarm response from the BMA in London, and a refusal to discuss this issue on the part of the Welsh Board of Health, encouraged by the Ministry of Health.

Until 1967, at the insistence of Kenneth Robinson, the Ministry of Health clung to the philosophy of coordination. The only concession to administrative change was provisional agreement to legislation that would allow ministers to introduce local variant forms of administration to suit special circumstances such as new towns. However, within the department there was increasing support for the more radical approach adopted in Scotland, as, for instance, indicated by the two (Cogwheel) reports on the organization of medical work in hospitals. The joint working parties in Edinburgh and London, each under the supervision of the respective Chief Medical Officer, tactfully but firmly concluded that the objectives of coordination and continuity of care were unlikely to be achieved without administrative integration. The English report aptly summed up the case for reform:

> Unfortunately, there has to date been a lack of coordination and communication between the three component parts of the National Health Service. Recognition of the need for continuity of care and integration of the constituent services, including the preventive services of the local authority, is widespread and seems at variance with the continuance of administrative divisions within the National Health Service.[16]

Despite such sentiments, it was not until the summer of 1967 that the Ministry of Health began serious consideration of the case for reorganization. The first public admission that health ministers were examining this issue dates from November 1967.

The Redcliffe-Maud Commission's evident support for local-government administration of the health service added urgency to the reorganization review within the Ministry of Health. In April 1968, the publication of the Todd Report on medical education and the completion of the Seebohm Report on personal social services effectively forced Kenneth Robinson to declare his hand on reorganization.

Within the Ministry of Health there was no consensus concerning the way forward. Local-government administration of health care was ruled out on grounds of the known opposition of the medical profession. The department was divided over the merits of the models for unification of health administration deriving from the Porritt Report and the hospital plan. The former approach envisaged a single tier of 'area' health authorities compatible in their boundaries with the units of reorganized local government, which were expected to number fewer than 100. The rival scheme anticipated that the fourteen existing RHBs would assume wider health responsibilities, and that about 200 lower-tier 'district' authorities would be created around the nuclei of district general hospitals. Given the shortage of time and Robinson's unwillingness to conduct outside consultations, there was little investigation of the degree of support for the two rival plans. Robinson opted for the single-tier plan, which was the model entailing maximum simplification and unification. Under this scheme some 700 administrative units in England and Wales would be reduced to fewer than 100. Politically, Robinson's option at least had the merit of being derived from a prestigious medical source, and was therefore likely to be better received by the profession. Robinson also calculated that the Porritt formula would be palatable to local government, since it preserved compatibility of boundaries, and allowed for substantial local-authority representation on the area authorities. Finally, the Porritt scheme was known to be widely accepted in Scotland, where extensive discussions had preceded the publication of the Green Paper. With these hopeful thoughts in mind, the Green Paper embodying Robinson's preferred plan was published on 23 July 1968.

The prospects for Robinson's scheme were never good. Although Whitehall departments and Cabinet members insisted on only one major alteration, preventing Robinson from conclusively eliminating the local-government option, there was little enthusiasm for his scheme, which was widely regarded as an abstract exercise unlikely to command support within the health service.

The first Green Paper attracted some support on account of its aspiration to establish a single authority in each natural planning area responsible for the administration of all health services. In this regard it lay in the honourable tradition extending back to the Royal Sanitary Commission. Robinson's Green Paper was in fact the last government policy document to propose this degree of unification and simplification in health administration. Despite its rational appeal, Robinson's scheme was badly received. There were two main criticisms. First, the regional concept was regarded as basic to the success of the health service; its abandonment was therefore regarded as retrogressive. Secondly, the area was regarded as an inappropriate entity for health-service administration, being too small for planning purposes, but too large for efficient administration or for local accountability. These doubts were also associated with fears among medical groups that a scheme harmonizing with the structure of reorganized local government might eventually fall into local-authority hands.

The first Green Paper was consigned to the wastepaper basket in the autumn of 1968, when union of the health and social-security departments was taken as an opportunity to transfer Robinson to other duties. Although Robinson had been a dedicated and worthy departmental minister, his horizons were limited, and this weakness showed up badly in his handling of the reorganization problem. On this issue there was need for leadership from a politician with a capacity to appreciate the broader problems of the social services, and more capable of dealing with academic and medical experts from a position of strength. Richard Crossman was well equipped for this task, and he was appointed by Harold Wilson as the first Secretary of State to head the combined department of health and social security on the expectation that he would bring to this office something of the dynamism of Aneurin Bevan. Wilson himself enjoyed an important link with Bevan through having been his main Cabinet ally in resisting health-service charges, and he had joined Bevan in resigning from the government over this issue.

Although Crossman was, like Wilson, a former Oxford academic, he was more firmly from the Bevanite stable, and as a politician he was prone to acts of audacity of a kind characteristic of Bevan himself. Crossman possessed the advantage of ready familiarity with the arguments relating to reorganization, partly on account of his earlier responsibility for local government, but also because of his role as the minister charged with coordinating policy in the social services. He believed that Robinson was mistaken in not undertaking consultations in advance of publication of the Green Paper, and from the outset he was sceptical about its chances of success. Armed with inestimable confidence in his own capacity to succeed, Crossman undertook a radical policy rethink, or more accurately a series of rethinks, in the course of which his expert advisers played a leading part, and all relevant interest groups were fully consulted. Crossman's initial instinct was to pacify the powerful hospital administrative lobby by giving a firm hint that the government's revised thinking would entail reversion to the region–district structure. However, this obvious solution was quickly ruled out on account of its offensiveness to local government. Crossman and his Cabinet colleagues appreciated that, if local authorities were to be stripped of their health powers, this would be politically embarrassing, contrary to the recommendations of the Redcliffe-Maud Commission, and subversive to Labour's commitment to strengthen local government. It was, therefore, necessary to offer substantial countervailing concessions, the main one of which was local-authority control over the new comprehensive social work departments, as recommended by the Seebohm Report. However, this was insufficient, and not even attractive throughout local government, where a strong body of opinion opposed the Seebohm proposals and was favourable to a lesser degree of integration, in which one of the entities would be combined health and welfare departments, ensuring that health-related social services would remain under medical supervision. Even those local authorities favouring the Seebohm formula insisted on compatibility of health-service and local-government boundaries in order to facilitate the development of community care. Even if the government was not entirely convinced by the above arguments, political factors dictated that it was imprudent to further assault the dignity of local government. Political considerations therefore determined that coterminosity of health-authority and local-government boundaries was adopted as a non-negotiable principle, indeed one of the few fixed points of policy regarding reorganization. Accordingly, for political reasons rather than for merit with respect to health planning, the area tier became the fixed anchor point of the reorganization process.

As a second major shift in perspective, Crossman's enthusiasm for retaining the region soon evaporated. He was irritated by the stubborn refusal of the existing regions to comply with his policy initiatives, particularly their failure to deflect small amounts of resources to address the scandalous conditions in long-stay hospitals. As already noted, he was also indignant that the resource distribution system had been allowed to run on unchecked for decades without any significant attempt to bring about a greater degree of equalization between regions. Crossman's impatience soon grew into distrust of what he was apt to call the 'regional satrapies'.[17] This change of attitude regarding regions was reflected in the second Green Paper on reorganization issued in February 1970.[18] Only with reluctance was Crossman persuaded to reprieve the region; even then his 'regional health councils' were to be granted only the most limited functions.

Given Crossman's earlier dismissive attitude about Robinson's 'area health boards', it is interesting to note that these now emerged as the main feature of the second Green Paper, but rechristened as 'area health authorities', of which it was intended to establish ninety in keeping with the system of local government proposed in Labour's recent White Paper on local-government reorganization. The novelty of Crossman's scheme was a proposal for an additional district tier of administration, to be controlled by 'district committees', but these were specified in only the most general terms.

Although the area remained paramount in Crossman's Green Paper, his scheme contained the germ of a three-tier system of administration, thereby sacrificing much of the simplification that had been the main attraction of the first Green Paper. This was taken by the Treasury as a sign that the form of organization outlined in the second Green Paper would embody a crippling degree of inefficiency. This conclusion was further confirmed in the eyes of the Treasury by Crossman's emphasis on 'local participation', which he aimed to achieve by granting local authorities substantial representation at all levels in administration. The Treasury was also unsympathetic with the proposal to allow independent contractors to retain separate statutory committees for the administration of their services, and it was antagonistic to a variety of other measures designed to protect the interest of consumers.

Within the limits imposed by political realities, Crossman was satisfied that his Green Paper struck a reasonable balance between the demands of unification, efficiency, central control, and local accountability. From the rival perspective of the Treasury, the Crossman scheme was a bizarre folly, and worse in most respects than the existing system. Crossman's plan was little better received than its predecessor, but this was a matter of academic interest, since the Labour government came to an end before Crossman had been able to issue a White Paper outlining his legislative intentions.

Robinson's Green Paper related to England and Wales, Crossman's only to England. As already observed, the early Welsh lead on reorganization was lost on account of a veto exercised from London, symptomatic of the low status occupied by Wales in health policy-making. Although, in fulfilment of a Labour policy pledge, a Secretary of State for Wales was appointed by Wilson in 1964, this minister was granted much more limited powers than his counterpart in Scotland. Health was among the powers promised but not granted. Only in April 1969, after an arduous campaign, was responsibility for health transferred to the Secretary of State for Wales. To the annoyance of its politicians, Wales was given virtually no special consideration in the first Green Paper of 1968. During preparations for a second Green Paper, the Scretary of State for Wales insisted on a separate Green Paper, which was issued in March 1970.[19] The plan for Wales departed little from the Porritt-inspired scheme proposed by the Welsh BMA in 1964. Although adopting much of the English terminology, the administrative plan was more akin to the Scottish scheme. The Green Paper proposed a single tier of seven area health authorities, with no intervening regional tier; it also suggested, as in Scotland, an increased degree of control by the central department and a separate common services agency. No central planning council of the Scottish type was proposed, but the Green Paper included a vague promise to consult the Welsh Council on matters relating to the health service.

Reorganization in England and Wales under the Conservatives

Indicative of the lack of progress over reorganization, the incoming Heath administration was not committed to this objective and it was not mentioned in the 1970 Queen's Speech. In Whitehall departments there was more than a residual feeling that reorganization was a mistake. However, the Green Papers had aroused the expectation that the health service would be reorganized, and these had already created uncertainty and adversely affected morale within the NHS. It was, therefore, essential to bring policy discussions to a speedy and decisive end. Given the imminence of unified social-work departments in local government and advanced preparations for reorganization of local government, some kind of simultaneous reorganization of the health service seemed inescapable. For the purposes of the comprehensive reorganization exercise, April 1974 emerged on the political timetable as an analogue to July 1948, but the Conservatives were considerably less confident than Bevan had been about the solution to be adopted.

It was not until November 1970 that Sir Keith Joseph issued a brief written statement indicating that the government would continue with its predecessor's plan to unify the administration of the health service outside local government and that the changes would come into effect at the date of local-government reorganization. The Secretary of State became more enthusiastic for reorganization when he appreciated that it provided an opportunity to apply his own and the government's commitment to management efficiency. This criterion had been relevant to the Labour Green Papers, but it had never achieved the prominence desired by the Treasury, while Crossman had intentionally relegated management to a place of secondary importance.

Sir Keith Joseph was not only an enthusiast for management reform, he also had the advantage of access to the advice of the newly appointed Business Team, headed by Sir Richard Meyjes. The latter was persuaded to take a personal interest in health-service reorganization. In view of the urgency for a rapid decision on the main lines of policy, a brief and self-evidently provisional consultative document, of amateurish appearance, was issued in May 1971.[20]

On one of the central issues of contention, the number of tiers of administration, the Joseph plan represented continuity with Crossman's suppressed White Paper. Sir Keith Joseph rejected both the Porritt area scheme and the rival region–district alternative. Like Crossman, Joseph attempted to satisfy all parties by fusing the two rival plans together to produce a three-tier structure. However, Joseph adopted an entirely different approach to the management role and interrelations of the three tiers. He reverted to a strong regional tier not dissimilar to the existing RHBs, while the district was converted into a management rather than a statutory entity. Joseph further increased the management emphasis by reducing the representative character of the regional and area authorities. The precise manner of operation of this highly complex structure was remitted to a separate expert investigation. The second topic set aside for expert review was the awkward question of collaboration between health authorities and local government, which was likely to be especially difficult and important owing to the increasing role of community care. In order to give some compensation to the public for the reduction in local accountability of the management structure, Community Health Councils (CHCs) were introduced as a new feature and a fresh complication in the scheme. Independent contractors were reassured that the promised separate administration of their services would not be prejudiced.

Sir Keith Joseph's consultative document proclaimed that 'throughout the new administrative structure there should be a clear definition and allocation of responsibilities; that there should be maximum delegation downwards, matched by accountability upwards; and that a sound management structure should be created at all levels'.[21] This theme may have been redolent with meaning for the expert, but it was opaque to the public. The media therefore paid little attention to Joseph's scheme, which tended to be regarded as a technical management exercise. Discussions among the experts made little impact on the media. The consultative document contained sufficient concessions to the main NHS interests to merit a positive reception. However, there was general suspicion about excessive management orientation, increase in central government control, and decline in protection for the consumer. Unease about these features was expressed by Crossman, who now urged that Joseph was fundamentally mistaken in failing to grasp the opportunity to return the health service to local-government control:

> there is, in reason, no case for saying that the new great local authorities, with very extensive powers, should not take over the health services. That would be infinitely more logical. It would have resolved at one stroke the appalling division between the local authorities and the health service. There would have been proper democratic representation . . . if there had been any sense in the world, the health service would come under the new local authorities and their extensive new powers and responsibilities.[22]

Other senior Labour figures echoed Crossman's criticisms, but they conspicuously avoided suggesting any root-and-branch alteration of Joseph's scheme. The path to Sir Keith Joseph's White Paper issued in August 1972 and the legislation that followed in 1973 was superficially uneventful. However, this impression of harmony in government circles during this planning process was to some extent misleading.

The main problem related to the precise form of the intended management intervention. It soon became apparent that divergent ideas were held about the means to bring about a managerial revolution in the NHS. For instance, there was a long-established proposal for a fundamental change in NHS central-management arrangements, involving hiving off the NHS to an autonomous national corporation headed by a director-general, together with management by chief executives at lower tiers of NHS administration. Under this scheme it was suggested that the regional function should be exercised from regional offices of the DHSS. In 1971 this model was advocated by the Civil Service Department and by the government's Chief Business Adviser; it gained the sympathy of Joseph himself, but it was regarded as impracticable within his department. Joseph reluctantly sided with his department, causing Meyjes to resign from the reorganization project on the grounds that the alternative preferred by the health department perpetuated the fundamental weaknesses of Crossman's scheme.[23] With the abdication of one school of management, another was left to work out some means of imposing management order on the three-tier system bequeathed by Crossman. This task was rendered even more complex through structural additions introduced by Joseph, or limitations imposed by the need to avoid offence to the many vested interests in NHS management. This riddle was referred to a team of experts which included the American management consultants, McKinsey & Co. Inc. The results of the management study were summarized in Joseph's White Paper, and published in full shortly afterwards as the management 'Grey Book'.[24] For the most part the Grey Book comprised a more structured and detailed expression of policies contained in other policy documents. Its main original features related to spelling out relations between officers at the three levels of administration and describing the lines of accountability. Central to this operation was the concept of consensus management, exercised by multi-disciplinary teams of officers, constituted at each level in the administrative hierarchy. Although it was diagrammatically ingenious, and impressive as a paper exercise, it was evident from the outset that in operation the Grey Book was liable to expand the NHS bureaucracy, complicate decision-making, and erode initiative, without bringing about proportionate benefits in increased efficiency. The government's business advisers regarded the Grey Book as confirmation that the management system of Joseph's devising was no more capable of solving the problems of management and efficiency in the NHS than the Crossman system that had been discarded.

Sir Keith Joseph's second main problem related to preserving his conception of the health authorities as management bodies. He was successful with respect to the non-statutory district level of organization, where it was accepted that control would be exercised by a consensus management team. Regardless of proposals for CHCs and a complicated professional advisory system, Joseph's colleagues were unhappy about expunging the representational element in the statutory regional and area authorities. This issue almost monopolized debates among ministers on the consultative document and the White Paper. Finally a compromise was reached whereby it was agreed to allow a greater element of representation than had originally been intended for both local government and the professions on regional and area authorities. This dispute indicated that within the Cabinet various ministers were in sympathy with Crossman's view that health authorities should retain local accountability as one of their main characteristics.

The period between Joseph's consultative document and his

White Paper represented the last opportunity to clear up a series of awkward problems that had been debated since the onset of discussions about reorganization. It was, for instance, easier in theory than in practice to determine the distribution of health and personal social-service functions between health authorities and local government. On the grounds that nursing and medical functions should reside with health authorities and social care with local government, such groups as *psychiatric social workers* were transferred, largely against their wishes and to the detriment of unified care teams, to the new social-work departments. There was much vacillation about *environmental health*, but this was allowed to remain with local government. On account of the transfer of public-health doctors to the new health authorities, their century-old association with environmental health officers was severed. The most difficult transfer to arrange was that of the *School Health Service*, which possessed an honourable tradition as a separate service extending back to 1907. This service was reformed and extended in 1944 in advance of the establishment of the NHS, and was an important part of the Local Education Authority (LEA) empire. It was agreed to transfer this service to the NHS, but the Department of Education and Science was sceptical about the chances of success of this arrangement; it fought unsuccessfully to leave LEAs with residual powers to appoint staff for health purposes. This change had the effect of breaking up local-authority child-guidance and child-psychology services; it also indirectly weakened the position of supplementary nutritional services such as school meals.

Also unresolved until the eleventh hour was the organization of the health service in London. Failure to arrive at a solution agreeable to the politically influential metropolitan local-authority interests, or to the numerous and prestigious teaching-hospital Boards of Governors, risked making enemies capable of embarrassing the government at the legislative stage. Since these groups occupied mutually incompatible positions, reconciliation was in fact impossible. It was, therefore, necessary to introduce sufficient concessions to induce capitulation on one side without leaving a sense of humiliation. This issue bristled with difficulties. The two main controversies concerned definition of Area Health Authorities (AHAs) and the relationship of these bodies with the ubiquitous undergraduate and postgraduate teaching hospitals. Each of the London boroughs aspired to separate AHA status, with the absorption of teaching hospitals according to their location. Even if the provincial undergraduate teaching hospitals agreed to assimilation into the unified system, the London teaching hospitals were determined to retain their cherished independence. As a fallback position they were willing to consider a federal structure in the form of a health authority dominated by teaching hospitals for the Inner London area. Something like this arrangement had been anticipated in the first Green Paper, which proposed two area health boards for Inner London, but the second Green Paper proposed five area health authorities for Inner London, and a working party set up by Crossman expanded this to seven. Under Joseph, local-government bodies and DHSS officials settled on six Inner London health authorities constituted mainly from pairs of London boroughs. The rival scheme evolved by the teaching hospitals entailed eight areas for the whole of London, involving amalgamation of larger groups of boroughs.

Conservative ministers were only reluctantly persuaded to abandon continuation of the existing Boards of Governors. A compromise was reached whereby the postgraduate hospitals were granted at least temporary continuation of their independent status, leaving only the undergraduate teaching hospitals to face assimilation. This drove a wedge between the two groups of teaching hospitals. Since the provincial undergraduate teaching hospitals agreed to assimilation into the health-authority structure, it seemed reasonable to expect the London undergraduate teaching hospitals to follow suit. The undergraduate teaching hospitals were offered a further concession whereby the teaching groups would be granted area rather than district status, which duly increased their strength within the management hierarchy. Even with these and other concessions, lengthy negotiations were required before the undergraduate teaching hospitals accepted that they would be distributed mainly in pairs between six AHAs in Inner London, leaving a further ten peripheral London area authorities as non-teaching groups.

The above arrangement had important implications for the organization of hospital services in London. Granting continuing independence to the postgraduate teaching hospitals effectively thwarted implementation of the Todd Commission's recommendations for linking postgraduate institutions with the nearest undergraduate partners. On the other hand, the pairing of undergraduate teaching hospitals within teaching areas facilitated the implementation of the Todd proposals for their amalgamation, although the implied unions were different from those proposed by Todd.

The main residual disagreements in Wales related to all-Wales arrangements. The earlier disagreements both inside and outside the Welsh Office concerning the abolition of the Welsh Hospital Board continued during preparation of the Welsh Consultative Document and the White Paper, issued in June 1970 and August 1972 respectively.[25] Advocates of the region were defeated, allowing for the elimination of the Welsh Hospital Board, thereby offering some saving in staff and a simpler structure of management. However, this was counterbalanced by the need for more civil servants and the establishment of the Welsh Health Technical Services Organisation to provide common services. The DHSS argued that the better way to efficiency was to preserve the region and cut out Welsh Office involvement in health administration. The increased role of the Welsh Office provoked demand for some kind of central consultative machinery. Welsh ministers rejected the advice of their officials and insisted on retaining the arrangement suggested by their predecessors, involving consultation with the Health and Social Services Panel of the Welsh Council. This outcome was feared by officials, who believed that the panel would constitute a 'Frankenstein's monster', which would become even more threatening if developed into an elected Welsh Health Council as a consequence of devolution. Owing to the collapse of the Welsh devolution initiative, this threat to officialdom failed to materialize, only to revive again in the context of the 1997 decisions concerning a Welsh Assembly.

Many issues of contention were cleared up only shortly before the publication in November 1972 of the National Health Service Reorganization Bill relating to England and Wales. After all the preparatory activity by the working parties on management and relations with local government, and the negotiations with health-service interests reported above, the Bill itself was a relatively modest and straightforward exercise. The reorganization legislation communicated little of the idealism associated with Bevan's Bill establishing the NHS.

The Scottish Bill provided a convenient rehearsal for the England and Wales Bill. Given the smooth passage of the Scottish legislation, it was decided to introduce the England and Wales Bill in the House of Lords, a procedure reserved for Bills of a technical nature. This expedient proved successful. The only clauses occasioning real difficulty related to the CHCs and family planning. The latter is discussed more fully below. As a completely new element in the health service, CHCs were likely to give problems at the design stage. The peers were rightly suspicious that the government was attempting to emasculate these bodies in order to prevent the new managerial structures from being discomforted by the prying eyes of potential trouble-makers. The government's unwillingness to offer concessions proved to be counterproductive, since it only served to fuel the suspicions of the sceptics and intensify their determination to strengthen the independence and the powers of CHCs. This was the only major point in the reorganization legislation upon which the government was forced to offer significant concessions.

Implementation of Reorganization

The unanticipated complications relating to family planning and CHCs delayed the legislation, but the National Health Service Reorganisation Act received the Royal Assent on 5 July 1973, the exact twenty-fifth anniversary of the NHS. The main features of the 1974 reorganization are indicated in Fig. 2.1. On account of the late date of the legislation, it was necessary to commence preparations for reorganization well in advance of the Royal Assent, establishing where necessary shadow authorities that were converted to statutory equivalents immediately it became procedurally possible. Especially important were the Joint Liaison Committees, which were effectively shadow area officer teams acting without reference to any health authority. These committees drew up plans for area services and establishments, and also for district arrangements.

Compared with the tangles regarding London, the construction

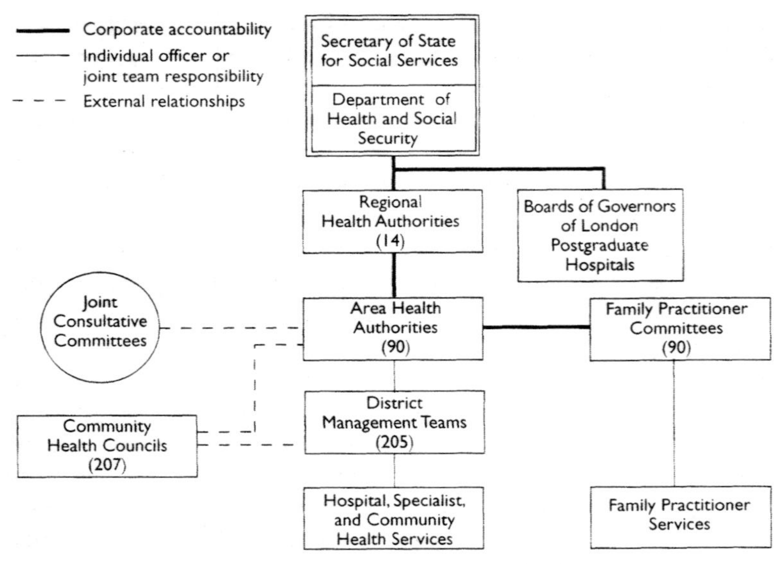

Figure 2.1. The National Health Service in England, 1974

of the rest of the system was a relatively straightforward technical exercise. After brief consideration of splitting some of the regions, it was decided to retain the existing regional pattern, but with alteration of boundaries in order to avoid breaking across local-government boundaries. Reflecting their increased powers, the fourteen Regional Hospital Boards in England were renamed Regional Health Authorities. As indicated in Table 2.2, the names of the regions were slightly modified to reflect geographical location, correcting the impression given by the previous nomenclature that provincial regions were colonial possessions of regional teaching centres.

The number and boundaries of AHAs were consistent with the local-government structure determined by the Local Government Act, which became law in October 1972. This implied seventy-four AHAs outside London, and sixteen in Greater London. The former were constituted from thirty-nine non-metropolitan counties and thirty-six metropolitan districts, the one complication being the joining of two of the latter (St Helens and Knowsley) to form a single area. Of the ninety AHAs, nineteen were designated as Area Health Authorities (Teaching); as noted above, six of these were located in London. The AHAs determined the pattern for the statutory committees promised for the administration of family practitioner services. These successors of the Executive Councils were renamed Family Practitioner Committees (FPCs).

As already noted, Wales dispensed with the region, leaving the area structure to be determined by the Local Government Act of 1972, on which basis eight AHAs were established, of which Cardiff was the sole teaching area. Three of the AHAs were undivided, leaving the others to be divided into fourteen districts, most of which were concentrated in South Wales.

In England designation of health districts led to much disagreement. Joint Liaison Committees operating at the area level produced schemes for districts, but these were frequently radically altered by the DHSS on the basis of political representations. The final scheme established 205 districts, but these were whittled down to 199 by 1979. Thirty-eight areas, usually called single-district areas, were not subdivided into districts. Completing the geography of the new scheme, CHCs were established at the district level.

Once the design had been completed, the Secretary of State appointed the members of RHAs and AHAs, beginning with their chairpersons. Notwithstanding the greater emphasis on management qualifications, the new authorities were similar in character to their predecessors. Following earlier practice, men from professions such as law and accountancy predominated; women were a small minority. On the eve of their abolition, none of the chairs of the RHBs was occupied by a woman; in the RHAs that supplanted them, only two of the chairs were allocated to women, then only on account of a last-minute intervention by Joseph. Within the ninety AHAs only six chairs went to women. This gender imbalance was little different in consensus management teams. The only locations where women achieved substantial numerical strength were the CHCs, where little influence resided. The flow of women into the CHCs reflected their high degree of participation in charities, voluntary organizations, and campaigning groups.

The degree of unification and simplification in health-service administration attained in England and Wales was less than in Scotland. The first Green Paper had aimed to reduce the number of administrative bodies in the NHS in England and Wales from 700 to fewer than 100. Each further planning document involved the addition of substantial complications. If the districts are taken into account, the final scheme comprised a core of about 325 administrative bodies. Only if consumer, advisory, and consultative bodies are left out of account is it possible to claim that any significant degree of simplification was achieved in 1974. The extent of unification was also diminished by the fragmentation arising from the continuing presence of health-related functions in environmental health and social-work departments of local government.

Despite its reservations about the Joseph reorganization scheme, the 1974 Labour administration had no choice but to oversee its implementation, and attempt to make the new system work as smoothly as possible. In the short term Labour was limited to introducing marginal alterations, the primary vehicle for which was the *Democracy in the NHS* exercise launched in 1974, which had the effect of increasing the local-authority membership of health authorities and slightly increasing the powers of the CHCs. Proposals to improve industrial democracy in the NHS remained unimplemented owing to lack of agreement between the bodies representing staff groups.

Although the Joseph reorganization achieved nothing like the desired management revolution, it proved to have some advantages. However, as the economic climate worsened, the volume of criticism increased. The government demanded action to arrest the increased cost of health-service bureaucracy. Between 1968 and 1979 the numbers of administrative and clerical staff increased almost threefold. Hospital administrators retorted that these increases were entirely determined by management complexities imposed by the government. It was universally agreed that some radical simplification in the system of administration was required, and it was generally conceded that consensus management and the complexity of operational relationships were a recipe for paralysis. Even analysts sympathetic with management reforms concluded that the 1974 reorganization had made the service neither more efficient (the managerialist objective) nor more effective.[26] Unkinder critics urged that 'the platitudes of American management theory, plastered over the informal and rather lethargic amateurism of UK hospital administration, have produced the worst of both, a still inefficient but now faceless bureaucracy'.[27] Indicative of its difficulty in locating a solution that would avoid making a bad situation worse, the Labour government failed to address the issue, and excused its equivocation on grounds of awaiting the findings of the Royal Commission on the NHS, thereby handing determination of policy on vital issues of health-service organization and management to the incoming Thatcher administration.

Hospital Services

As evident from the previous chapter, the NHS hospital service was always hard-pressed to meet its obligations, but in the circumstances the acute sector at least succeeded in keeping up with the demands of modernization. The 1962 hospital plan signified a move towards a comprehensive system of district general hospitals, while the 1974 reorganization created a matching district administration. The economic climate was never sufficiently positive to allow lavish expansion, but at least before 1974 the hospital service had been protected from cuts, allowing slow incremental growth to be maintained. This state of affairs ended suddenly in the wake of the 1973 oil crisis. The hospital service not only faced a relentless increase in its obligations owing to such factors as demographic change or the rising capacities of high-technology medicine, but, as noted above, it was forced to submit to stricter financial disciplines associated with cash limits and RAWP, and also alter its priorities in response to programme-budgeting. The labyrinthine management structure introduced in connection with the 1974 reorganization introduced some advantages, but it is also saddled the hospital service with many dysfunctional characteristics.

In earlier decades, the hospital services had reaped the benefit of a substantial dividend associated with the decline of tuberculosis or other infectious diseases, but the later dividend associated with the anticipated run-down of long-stay hospitals in the mental sector proved more difficult to collect. Some saving was derived from the sharp reduction in length of stay of in-patients in almost all specialities, and by increasing use of day surgery. Such social measures as the introduction of compulsory seat belts in 1967, or crash helmets in 1974, undoubtedly saved lives, and altered the pattern of injuries associated with motor accidents, but it is doubtful whether the cost of treating these patients was much reduced. Indicative of these costly new obligations, more than half of the children admitted to Accident and Emergency departments were victims of road accidents.

Modern hospitals and high-technology medicine inevitably required higher levels of skill and were generally more demanding in their use of human and material resources. Consequently big increases were recorded among most groups of NHS staff. Consultant and nursing numbers each increased by two-thirds between 1964 and 1979; hospital medical staff numbers doubled; professional and technical staff increased nearly threefold. In Great Britain as a whole, the staff having employment or contracted status with the NHS increased from half a million in 1948 to just over one million in 1979, of whom only about 60,000 worked outside the HCHS sector. Hospital medical staff were approximately equal in number to general practitioners in 1964 but they were almost twice as numerous by 1979.

Reflecting advances in medicine, changing therapeutic regimes, and increases in staff, the productivity of the hospital service continued to increase. Steady rises were recorded in units of diagnostic service, blood products supplied, the in-patient workload, the numbers of new out-patients, or accident-and-emergency cases. This was achieved without increasing the numbers of available beds in most specialities, and in the mental-illness sector there was a steady reduction. The length of stay of patients steadily declined in most specialities. A summary indicating some of the more important changes in hospital in-patient activity is given in Table 2.3. The throughput in the acute sector was understandably greater than the average for all beds, by 1979 reaching about thirty cases per available bed, compared with a level of about nineteen in 1960. These productivity indicators were broadly in line with experience elsewhere in Northern Europe.

TABLE 2.3. *Hospital in-patient beds and activity, England and Wales, 1949–1977* (000s)

Bed and activity levels	1949	1959	1969	1977
Average available beds	422	449	429	376
Available beds per 1,000 pop.	10.3	10.5	9.4	8.1
Discharges and deaths	2,788	3,783	4,968	5,345
Discharges and deaths per available bed	6.6	8.4	11.6	14.2

Source: DHSS, *Review of Health Capital* (DHSS, 1979), appendix II

It is not surprising that, despite daunting staff numbers and impressive levels of productivity, staff shortages were endemic to the system and affected all groups of skilled staff. Even among consultants, although the prestigious medical and surgical specialities were not short of recruits, difficulty was experienced in many areas, including pathology, radiology, mental health, geriatrics, anaesthetics, and public health. Medical staff shortages were more pronounced in the regions at the bottom of the RAWP league table, which placed a heavy reliance on overseas doctors. In 1979 about 35 per cent of the NHS medical workforce was from overseas.

The pattern of work of hospital departments was subject to a process of relentless change. In part, this was a response to epidemiological factors, the major feature being the rising population of the elderly, who were no longer primarily consigned to long-stay beds, but became the main user of acute services. Their particular requirements determined the higher demand for such services as replacement surgery or ophthalmic surgery. The second major cause of change was technical factors, especially relating to information technology and medical advance. In response to the accelerating pace of technical innovation, the NHS was forced to establish entirely new and highly expensive facilities, which usually moved rapidly from the experimental stage to being demanded and provided throughout the system.

Across the board, the diagnostic techniques at the command of pathology and radiology departments continued to expand and become further automated. Radiology facilities gradually evolved into diagnostic imaging departments, owing to the exploitation of non-X-ray techniques such as ultrasound, the utilization of contrast media, image intensifiers, television systems, and computerization which facilitated the use of digital images. The 1970s saw the rapid development and increasing availability of X-ray computed tomography, and the 1980s magnetic resonance imaging; these techniques were applied both to the brain and to whole-body scanning. The high cost of this equipment was beyond the capacities of many district general hospitals; funds to support such projects were often raised by charitable appeals, often to the embarrassment of health authorities, which were forced into adopting this expensive diagnostic service as a high priority.

With the development of flexible endoscopes employing glass-fibre technology in the 1960s, the endoscope became an infinitely more powerful tool for observation, testing, and finally minimum invasive surgery, employed in most systems of the body. Catheters were similarly developed for a wide range of diagnostic and therapeutic purposes. The capacity of non-invasive techniques greatly to simplify treatment was indicated by the introduction in the 1980s of lithotipsy for extracorporeal treatment of kidney stones.

During the 1960s, developments in medical engineering and materials science permitted the development of hip replacement. These methods became refined during the 1970s and alternatives to total replacement became more readily available, although application of these techniques to other joints proved much less successful. In 1979 some 24,000 hip-replacement operations were performed. In 1995 this figure had risen to 58,000.

For those suffering from end-stage renal failure, renal transplantation and intermittent dialysis gradually became available. These techniques were at the experimental stage during the 1950s, but with substantial risks of failure, owing, for instance, to rejection in transplantation and infection in dialysis. These problems were gradually overcome during the 1960s. Transplantation was sufficiently well established for a national organ match and distribution service to be established in 1972. The demand for transplantation outstripped supply, but the UK kept up with its European partners in its level of this service. In 1979 about 800 kidney transplant operations were performed; in 1995 this figure was more than doubled. Those without transplants were thrown back on the less satisfactory and more expensive option of intermittent dialysis. Dialysis facilities were only at the experimental stage in 1964, but, following conferences of experts held shortly after that date, regional centres for this purpose were planned and fully established during the 1970s. However, the rate of intake of new patients for renal dialysis of 22 per million population in 1979 was only half the level adopted as the target during the 1980s, and the target was again doubled in the 1990s. Despite these higher targets and the introduction of continuous ambulatory peritoneal dialysis, which was cheap convenient, even in 1998, UK acceptance rates were among the lowest in Europe.

The period after 1964 witnessed spectacular advances in cardiac surgery. It became possible as a matter of routine to replace heart valves with mechanical or transplanted substitutes. It became possible to correct major abnormalities of the heart, in children as well as in adults. During the 1970s coronary bypass graft surgery became established on a routine basis and became the biggest growth area in cardiac units. After early experiments elsewhere, in the late 1960s heart transplantation was attempted in the UK, but discontinued in 1969 owing the adverse results. Thereafter caution was observed and heart transplantation was reintroduced with greater safety in 1979.

In common with cardiovascular disease, cancer presented a series of changing and persisting problems. Despite huge efforts in research, few cancers were amenable to a fully effective treatment. However, the prospects for recovery were improved with earlier diagnosis, and in some cases screening was introduced for this purpose. Screening for cervical cancer and breast cancer became a possibility in the mid-1950s. After much vacillation, in response to consumer pressure, a cervical cancer-screening service was introduced in the mid-1960s. This screening system remained somewhat haphazard, with the result that serious doubts about its effectiveness began to be voiced during the 1970s. Screening for breast cancer was periodically considered from the mid-1960s onwards, but on each occasion it was resisted by the government on expert advice on the grounds that the benefits were unlikely to merit the costs. Despite the availability of convincing evidence concerning the value of breast screening in the early 1970s and the existence of widespread demand, this was not given full imprimatur by the health service until the late 1980s.

Treatment of cancers by radiotherapy and chemotherapy was well established before 1964, but only partly effective, and it occasioned much suffering among cancer victims. With the advent of supervoltage radiotherapy and more refined methods of surgery, the evolution of transplantation techniques, and development of combination chemotherapy, the suffering decreased and the success rate improved. Inevitably centres capable of providing comprehensive care according to the best standards of practice were limited in number. Also, on account of the high cost, such equipment as linear accelerators was limited to a few hospitals. By these means, such conditions as Hodgkin's disease, as well as various forms of leukaemia, were treated with success.

The Smithers Report published in 1971 presented a depressing picture of the limitations in data-gathering, lack of coordination, and absence of standardization in procedures in the cancer services, which was undoubtedly detrimental both to early detection and to safe and effective treatment. The Smithers proposal for oncological centres at regional level was watered down into a plan for regional cancer organizations. Professional and parochial jealousies obstructed even this modest development. By the date of the NHS reorganization only four regions had produced provisional regional cancer schemes. Reflecting continuing slow progress with the organization of cancer services, in 1995 it was admitted that the quality of cancer care was patchy and variable in the 'skills and technology available in different hospitals, but also in clinical outcomes'.[28] This pessimistic conclusion was borne out by all too frequent evidence of errors in treatment by radiotherapy. In order to address this serious lack of uniformity, renewed efforts were announced to rationalize cancer care on the basis of district general hospital cancer units and regional cancer centres, very much as advocated in the Smithers Report of 1971.

Modernization was not equally successful on all fronts in the hospital service. There were, for instance, weaknesses in organization at points both of entry and of exit from hospital. Accident and Emergency departments were not points of prestige, and there were no settled arrangements for their clinical oversight and management. Disagreements about their organization have proved a continuing phenomenon and have impeded their development. There was a long delay before establishing a standardized major accident service. Responding to pressure from the Casualty Surgeons' Association, and confirming the recommendations of the Bruce Committee, the Joint Consultants Committee in 1978 recommended that these departments should be headed by full-time Accident and Emergency consultants rather than orthopaedic surgeons, as was the dominant practice previously.

Rehabilitation was a further Cinderella of the hospital services. This was a further specialist area falling between the stools of the established specialities. It also experienced difficulties in the recruitment of its mainly female staff owing to poor pay and status. Even after the exhaustive Tunbridge Report of 1972, progress towards the development of comprehensive rehabilitation departments remained lamentably slow, and there was resistance by other specialists to the Tunbridge proposals for placing authority for this service in the hands of specialists dedicated to rehabilitation.

The pattern of changing expectations and increasing burden on the hospital service is well illustrated by the dramatic change in the location of childbirth. At the beginning of the NHS confinement predominantly took place in the home. Traditionally, institutional confinement was reserved for the pauper and the aristocrat. The Royal College of Obstetricians and Gynaecologists (RCOG) consistently advocated hospital confinement. The RCOG adopted 70 per cent as the desirable norm for hospital confinement in 1944; in 1954 this figure was revised to 100 per cent. The Ministry of Health was loathe to plan on the basis of more than 50 per cent. An independent inquiry under the Earl of Cranbrook was established to break this impasse as well as resolve other divisive problems relating to maternity care. In 1959 the Cranbrook Report opted for a compromise of 70 per cent, but in 1970 the Peel Committee, reflecting intransigent RCOG orthodoxy, once again insisted on 100 per cent.

The health departments were reluctantly dragged along with RCOG dogma, which, notwithstanding the absence of convincing supportive evidence, successfully persuaded the public that childbirth outside hospital was unsafe. The hospital plan adopted 70 per cent as its assumption for the provision of maternity beds, which was only slightly above the levels prevailing at the time. The 70 per cent target was reached in the mid-1960s and by 1979 hospital confinement stood above 90 per cent. This trend gave an incentive for a new level of priority for maternity departments in the hospital plan. In the event, this turned out to be less demanding on resources than anticipated, owing to the steady reduction in the length of hospital stay. The Cranbrook Committee assumed ten days after confinement, but the mean length of stay was rapidly reduced; in 1979 it stood at only five days, with some regions such as Oxford discharging one-third of mothers before the third day. The less economical side of the equation was the rapid development in this period of Special Care Baby Units, which by 1979 were used by no fewer than 20 per cent of live births in the two most northerly English regions. This trend was to some extent associated with the sharp rise after 1960 of episiotomies and induced labour. Desperate to discover some area of economy within the hospital service, the DHSS fastened upon the hospital maternity service. The ongoing trend towards reduction of length of stay and a decline in the birth rate enabled the *Priorities* document to impose a 1.8 per cent annual reduction in this area of expenditure.

The colder economic climate stimulated reconsideration of policy in the field of obstetrics, driven partly by the growing campaign against the medicalization of childbirth, which aimed to reassert the authority of the mother and the midwife. The reformers were particularly concerned to counteract the unnecessary use of induction in childbirth. On the basis of a wide constituency of support, the 'new obstetrics' gradually took hold and many of its elementary humane and care objectives became widely adopted, including officially in the policy document *Changing Childbirth* in 1993. However, this movement has had little effect in reducing the dominance of childbirth in hospital.

As noted in the previous chapter, higher expectations about rehabilitation, the new community-care philosophy, and numerous innovations in drug therapy stimulated optimism that the gloomy asylums housing some 150,000 mental patients might soon become completely superseded. On the basis of their successes with rehabilitative regimes and experiments with day hospitals, geriatricians were equally confident about releasing their long-stay patients from the old workhouse infirmaries. Furthermore, in the late 1960s opinion finally turned firmly against institutional confinement of the mentally handicapped. In their respective spheres, organizations such as Aegis, Mind, and Mencap proved effective critics of institutional regimes. Their vigilance determined that, for the first time since the workhouse and asylum system began, the shameful negligence, brutality, and humiliating excesses of the practices prevalent in long-stay hospitals were exposed to public scrutiny. Following the Ely Hospital Report published in March 1969, action on behalf of long-stay patients was no longer avoidable.[29]

Some ameliorative action would have been undertaken in any case, but the record of Kenneth Robinson demonstrated that the health department was more concerned to discredit complainants than to address the problem in a realistic manner. Complaints about the treatment of mentally handicapped patients at the Ely Hospital, Cardiff, came on the heels of a series of similar complaints relating to long-stay hospitals throughout England. The Ely Report, which contained exhaustive and alarming detail, contributed to the indictment of the whole system of care existing in long-stay institutions, and especially the treatment of the mentally handicapped. The impact of the Ely Hospital Report was increased owing to its production under the chairmanship of the lawyer, Geoffrey Howe, who was at this time a relatively little-known, but rising Conservative politician with a special interest in health care.

Crossman was new to his office when the Ely Report was completed. He not only intervened personally to ensure that Howe's Report exercised its full impact, but took up the redress of conditions in long-stay hospitals as the main mission of his office. Crossman's personal intervention, during which he liaised with many experts, including Howe, unleashed a new wave of important initiatives, the main elements of which were: establishment in 1969 of the Hospital Advisory Service, which was specifically concerned with monitoring and improving conditions in long-stay hospitals; the appointment in 1973 of the Health Service Commissioner, which extended the Ombudsman principle to the hospital service; establishment of CHCs in the context of the 1974 reorganization; and finally the formation of the National Development Group and Development Team for the Mentally Handicapped in 1975. As noted above, in 1971 and 1975 respectively, mental handicap and mental illness were the first beneficiaries of the new crop of priorities programme planning documents. Also relevant to long-stay patients were the Davies review of hospital complaints procedures published in 1973, and the review of the Mental Health Act announced in 1975; although neither of these controversial issues yielded agreement in England and Wales by 1979, a uniform complaints procedure was instituted in Scotland in 1970.

These investigative, developmental, and strategic planning initiatives helped to induce a fresh spirit of determination with respect to the care and treatment of long-stay patients, but they were successful only to a limited degree in generating increased resources and producing real improvements for their respective client groups. Progress was also hindered by disagreements among professionals concerning the merits of more than partial retreat from the old institutional system. A large lobby favoured a gradualist approach, based on improvement of existing institutional facilities, and moves towards community care only when it was clear that superior services were available in that sphere. In the atmosphere of retrenchment after the oil crisis it was virtually impossible to achieve such an objective. Already strained long-stay services were therefore faced with further uncertainties. Early predictions that the days of the long-stay hospital were numbered proved to be over-optimistic. Large numbers of the mentally ill, the mentally handicapped, and the elderly remained unnecessarily incarcerated in cavernous Victorian asylums and workhouses, which remained starved of resources. This neglect was now additionally justified by health authorities on account of the uncertain future of these institutions. As a consequence of the slow momentum of change, in 1979 some 10,000 elderly patients were still housed in former workhouses inherited from the poor-law authorities in 1948.

The slowdown of the district general hospital programme impeded the development of psychiatric units in these hospitals. By 1979 only one-third of districts provided comprehensive psychiatric services based on their general hospitals, and these were more poorly endowed than originally intended. At this date it was accepted that major capital investment was required in no fewer than 130 districts to provide a basic infrastructure for district psychiatric services. These district services were also hampered by the slow pace of development of community-care services by local authorities. It is, therefore, clear that the best-intentioned and enlightened initiatives of the 1970s merely succeeded in undermining the existing system without decisively introducing a superior alternative. The chaotic situation into which the services for long-stay patients were degenerating was underlined by a succession of embarrassing and much-publicized inquiries into abuses at hospitals such as Warlington Park (1976), Darlington Memorial (1976), St Augustine's (1976), Mary Dendy (1977), Normansfield (1978), Winterton (1979), and Church Hill House (1979).

Hospital Planning

The hospital plan introduced in 1962 represented an opportunity to bring hospital facilities up to the standard required by the advanced services just described. This was by no means a straightforward task in view of the rapidly changing nature of hospital care. Even allowing for the difficulties of the challenge, the hospital plan fell well short of the objectives of its originators. Even upon the most lenient interpretation, both with respect to the execution of individual projects and as a comprehensive planning exercise, the hospital plan was little short of a disaster, the full ramifications of which are still largely unchronicled. The fifteen-year opportunity for expansion was not effectively exploited; incompetent hands determined that precious public resources for capital development yielded only a limited part of the benefits potentially achievable. Our understandable thanksgiving for the many new hospitals constructed under the hospital plan should not be allowed to disguise the limitations of the project as a whole.

The shaky intellectual foundations for the hospital plan have already been mentioned in the previous chapter. Labour's review of the plan left the district-general-hospital concept unquestioned, but conceded that imprecise costing and slow rates of completion would reduce the rate of hospital replacement and therefore prolong the life of existing old and smaller hospitals. Instead of subjecting the hospital plan to high-level critical scrutiny, correctives to policy were introduced only in response to the more drastic mistakes or public embarrassments. The only official review of the district-general-hospital concept took place by chance through the haphazard mechanics of the Central Health Services Council (CHSC). The result was the partisan Bonham-Carter Report of 1969, which provided fresh justification for the district-general-hospital concept, and also sanctioned the centralization of hospital services to a degree not previously anticipated, thereby giving licence for moves towards centralization involving a threefold increase upon the bed maximum envisaged in 1962. On account of the superficial appeal of its bold rationalizations, the concept of highly centralized hospital facilities gained widespread currency among hospital planners before it was belatedly corrected by the Conservatives in revised policies issued in 1974 and 1980. The former allowed for the continuation of small, local, non-specialized community hospitals staffed by general practitioners, for patients who were deemed not to require the expensive and advanced facilities of the district general hospital. The 1980 revision scaled down expectations about district general hospitals and abandoned the idea of single-site centralization. These changes reflected a new spirit of realism appropriate to a colder economic climate.

Of the 250 district general hospitals projected as either new constructions or modernized older buildings, by 1979 only one-third were completed. That left one-third partly finished, and a further one-third hardly started. One-third of the hospital buildings in use in 1979 dated from before 1900. The balance was intended to shift in favour of community hospitals, but by 1979 this programme had hardly started.

This account omits reference to the many innovations intended to bring about improvements in the efficiency and management of building projects. The hospital scene is littered with memorials to the largely unsuccessful 'Best Buy' and 'Harness' experiments dating from the high water mark of the hospital plan, and rather more of the 'Nucleus' projects dating from 1976 onwards. Even the latter were heavily criticized, illustrating the failure of the health service to establish a consensus on the design and management of major hospital projects. McKeown's complaint that 'there are still no satisfactory answers to fundamental questions concerning hospital size, location and function' remained as true in 1979 as it had been in 1974 when these comments were made.[30]

The biggest problems surrounded the largest hospital projects, particularly the teaching hospitals, where the plans of 1962 to proceed on a multi-site basis were often scrapped in favour of single-site plans, often projected to contain 1,500 beds or more. These gigantic schemes were inevitably slow to execute, and their excessive costs attracted attention from the Public Accounts Committee. The first new teaching hospitals completed in the mid-1970s were inevitably out of date, since they represented ossification of the thinking of the early 1960s. The tower blocks at Guy's and Charing Cross or the concrete barbarity of Liverpool represented the excesses of the system. Even the more discreet examples like the John Radcliffe Hospital in Oxford attracted the headlines owing to absence of funds either to complete its final stages or even to open the acute facilities already built. In Oxford the luxurious maternity block incongruously stood for some time in isolation as the only functioning part of the new teaching hospital. Swindon typifies the fate of district-general-hospital projects. The successful early start with the first and second phases was noted in Chapter 1. The second phase, comprising the maternity unit and Accident and Emergency facilities, was completed by 1968; the final phase comprising facilities for gynaecology, paediatrics, acute geriatrics, and rehabilitation was due for completion in the early 1970s, but this project was repeatedly delayed, and, despite confident predictions of completion by 1978, site preparations were delayed until 1990. Swindon then became a victim of the collapse of the government's capital programme. However, Swindon was volunteered for the new Private Finance Initiative (PFI), but this occasioned a full reassessment of the project, resulting in proposals for total rebuilding on a different site of a hospital with rather fewer beds. This plan received approval in principle, but the final decision was deferred on account of legal difficulties in the way of the PFI initiative, and then by the 1997 general election. As noted in chapter four, when New Labour adopted the PFI scheme, in July 1997 Swindon was among the small group of projects selected for immediate implementation. Swindon is an extreme example, but it exemplifies the great difficulty experienced under the NHS of bringing to a successful conclusion the provision of comprehensive district-hospital services.

Community Health Services

The term community health services was increasingly used for the miscellaneous health functions over which local government retained control after 1948. These were important since they embodied the core of the services relating to community care. Many of the curative functions traditionally taking place in local-authority clinics were taken over by the hospital and independent-contractor services. The role of the MOH with respect to such client groups as mothers, infants, and children gradually diminished. However, there were some countervailing points of expansion. Routine immunization and vaccination programmes remained important and were extended to include rubella and measles. The legislation of 1967 gave LHAs broader powers with respect to family planning. As noted below, the greatest point of expansion was health centres, which had hardly existed before 1965, but thereafter became an important feature on the health-service landscape. Even though the MOHs lost a degree of control by locating some of their staff with general practitioners, these attachment schemes and other cooperative developments served to bring the public-health professionals more into the mainstream of health-service planning. Although opportunities for growth were limited, the empire of local health and welfare departments expanded during the 1960s. Although capital investment was small compared with the hospital sector, health centres, residential homes, ambulance stations, and occupational centres for the mentally handicapped added up to a significant commitment. One of the main growth points of health and welfare departments lay in the field of social work. By 1968 health and welfare authorities were employing, in whole-time equivalents, about 4,000 general social workers, 2,000 mental-health social workers, and 30,000 home helps. On account of the expanding need for health visitors, home nurses, social workers, and home helps in various local-authority services, there was increasing tendency to rationalize their administration.

During the 1960s it became increasingly common to establish combined health and welfare departments under the MOH, which further enhanced the authority of public-health doctors, among other things giving them a major interest in the expanding social-work profession. This development was complementary to a second point of consolidation of social work, which took place around the nucleus of local-authority Children's Departments. Any chance of social work stabilizing according to this dichotomy was undermined by a powerful group favouring the creation of a unified social-work profession operating from an independent department of local government and headed by a professional director of social work. This latter force proved politically the most agile. Its views were adopted by the Seebohm Committee, which reported in July 1968, after which the government became committed to establishing unified personal social-services departments in advance of local-government and health-service reorganization. MOHs thereby stood to lose a major part of their staff, even mental health social workers, and many of their important functions in April 1971—sufficient to undermine the continuing viability of local authority health departments. The latter were further adversely affected in the course of preparations for health-service reorganization through the decision to establish environmental health as a further independent function of local government.

The above changes raised doubts about the survival of public health as an independent medical speciality. This issue was addressed by the Seebohm Committee, the Royal Commission on Medical Education, and finally the Hunter Committee, which reported specifically on this problem in 1972. Between them, these committees evolved a rescue package entailing proposals for resuscitating public health as the new speciality of 'community medicine'. As a consequence of the 1974 reorganization, senior public-health doctors were appointed community physicians and attached to the relevant tiers of the new health authorities. The most senior community physicians were members of the consensus management teams at each of the three levels of administration, where they enjoyed consultant status. Their role lacked clear definition; they fulfilled a mixture of management, planning, epidemiological, legal, and public-health functions. Subordinate members of the new speciality continued to undertake clinic work. The rescue effort was not entirely successful; community medicine failed to achieve the status intended by its architects and recruitment fell off. The limited success of community medicine was reflected in the failure to reshape the health service according to the government's stated priorities—for instance, by redirecting resources into community care, preventive, and promotive medicine. Also responsibility for public health and other functions formerly important to the MOH became fragmented, with unfortunate consequences, as demonstrated by the long and disquieting run of public-health alarms during the 1980s and 1990s.

To some extent the shortcomings of the health service with respect to community care were compensated for by the rapid growth of spending on the new personal social-services departments. However, this expansion came to an abrupt end in the mid-1970s, when the personal social services became a prime candidate for economies. Between 1975 and 1978, capital expenditure on the personal social services was reduced by 50 per cent. The cumbersome apparatus of Joint Consultative Committees, Joint Care Planning Teams, and their satellites, created to facilitate cooperation between local authorities and health authorities, made a minuscule contribution and proved incapable of generating any meaningful momentum. Community health services and community care failed to develop on anything like the scale required to provide viable substitutes for obsolete institutional services. In 1979, for mental patients, only 20 per cent of the estimated places needed in day centres had been provided, and only one-third of the places needed in residential homes. For the mentally handicapped, only one-third of the places needed in residential homes and half of the places needed in training centres had been provided. The endemic disparities between local authorities in levels of service provision showed no sign of reduction. For instance, in the field of mental health, some authorities, especially in urban areas, made reasonable provision and were prepared for expansion when resources were available, whereas many rural authorities made little provision and possessed no plans for development.

Primary Health Care

Services administered by Executive Councils represented the part of the health service least amenable to planning initiatives. Executive Councils themselves were scarcely equipped for this progressive purpose, being almost totally absorbed with the elaborate machinery devised for remuneration of independent contractors under their supervision. The changeover to FPCs in 1974 made little difference to these arrangements. By contrast, the situation in the care sector was far from static. From the mid-1960s onwards, general medical practitioners in particular became swept up in changes, which transformed their practices and brought them into the mainstream of the health service. Symptomatic of these altered circumstances was the adoption of new terminology. Before 1970, despite the invention of the primary/secondary terminology and the importance attached to this concept in the Dawson Report, neither the idea nor the term primary care featured significantly in normal discourse, even among the general-practitioner intellectual leadership. By contrast, during the 1970s, primary care began to be used to indicate the distinctive front-line function of the speciality of general medical practice. Gradually the term was expanded to indicate the unified character of the FPS, and also to underline the part in the primary-care team of other health professionals such as nurses and health visitors. For the first time family practitioners gave more than token support for the concept of teamwork and accepted that all professionals involved in primary health care were engaged in an interdependent partnership. In some respects this was an echo of consensus partnership arrangements taking shape in the secondary-care context of the hospital. The idea of primary health care was further refined as a consequence of the Alma Ata Declaration of 1978, which evolved a formula applicable to the Developing World as well as to the Western context. It took a long time before the message of Alma Ata percolated to the backwoods of the independent contractors, but, on account of the moral authority of the World Health Organisation, the new primary-care philosophy constituted a goal which governments and the leadership of the profession were impelled to adopt as their formal objective.

Opticians and pharmacists remained untouched by the primary-care ethos, and dentists were affected only to a limited degree, and then only the minorities working in health centres and community dentistry. Opticians, dentists, and pharmacists continued to exercise their traditional function, without attracting particular attention. Perturbations affecting these groups in the main related to adjustments of fees and contractual conditions. The dominant players in the eye service were ophthalmic opticians, whose solid work was recognized in 1968 when the Supplementary Ophthalmic Service was reconstituted as the General Ophthalmic Service. Recruitment was at this time sluggish, but this problem was resolved in the 1970s. The modest General Ophthalmic Service generally satisfied its customers and, with the increase in fashion-consciousness about spectacle frames, the service became highly profitable for opticians. Sight-testing remained free, but consumers became accustomed to periodic increases in fees for lenses. On account of four increases in these charges between 1969 and 1977, charges accounted for one-third of the cost of the service, which was the highest yield from charges for any part of the NHS.

According to data concerning the supply of dentists, courses of treatment, and dental fitness of all age groups, the general dental service seemed as successful as the eye service. However, the Royal Commission on the NHS complained that levels of expectation remained low and that 'the prevalence of dental disease remains at an unacceptably high level'.[31] The Court Committee heavily criticized dental services from the perspective of young people. Substantial reforms, including a large increase in all categories of dental workers, were recommended in order to raise the standard of service in the less-favoured regions, and for the elderly and the poor.[32] Unequal distribution of dentists remained an intractable problem and it followed the predictable pattern. In 1977 there were only 0.19 dentists per 1,000 population in the Trent region, whereas the level in North West Thames was 0.40. Although in 1979 charges accounted for only 19 per cent of the cost of the general dental service, they were a deterrent to early treatment for those groups experiencing the worst state of dental health.

The Court Report and the Royal Commission complained about the continuing neglect of community dental services, the failure to make more active use of auxiliaries such as dental hygienists, and they were scornful about the failure of successive governments to take effective action to fluoridate water. The latter represented one of the simplest, most effective, and most economical measures capable of being applied in the field of preventive medicine, but a vocal anti-fluoridation lobby effectively undermined the government's resolve, with the result that by 1979 less than 10 per cent of the population had access to fluoridated water supplies.

The crisis of dentistry was arguably worse than the Royal Commission indicated, since it ignored problems of inferior quality of treatment, unnecessary intervention, or the incidence of fraudulent claims, while there also emerged suggestive evidence that improvements in dental health were arising from changes in diet and such factors as use of fluoride toothpaste rather than dental treatment or the preventive measures traditionally advocated by dentists.

The pharmaceutical service was the most expensive part of the FPS. As previously noted, this service overtook the general medical service in its cost in the mid-1960s; by 1979 it was almost double the cost of the general medical service and increasing at the rate of about 4 per cent a year. On account of political objections to increasing the prescription charge and the large extent of exemptions, this charge made only a small impact on the cost of the service. Escalating cost was ascribable to the unremitting process of pharmaceutical innovation. Continuing irrational diversity in prescribing habits among general practitioners indicated that part of this activity was wasteful and indeed positively deleterious to patients. Repeating the experience of governments before 1964, neither the Sainsbury Committee, which reported in 1967, nor later ministerial initiatives succeeded in reducing the extent of wasteful prescribing. The Royal Commission on the NHS concluded that the open-ended commitment of the NHS to meeting the cost of whatever general practitioners prescribed had encouraged their 'bad and expensive habits, such as leaving repeat prescriptions to be handed out by receptionists and prescribing drugs by brand name when cheaper therapeutic equivalents are available'.[33]

As with other independent contractors, recruitment into general medical practice improved between 1964 and 1979. The list size in England remained constant at about 2,300, about 300 higher than in Scotland and Wales. The profession generally favoured reducing the average list size to 2,000, which would have required an increase of 10 per cent in the number of general practitioners. In fact, recruitment into general practice continued to improve, taking the list size down to 1,900 in England by the mid-1990s. By this stage 30 per cent of general practitioners were women. General practice was not reliant on immigrant doctors to the same extent as hospital medicine; nevertheless in 1979 about 20 per cent of general practitioners were from overseas; this figure increased to 25 per cent in the 1990s, with most of the overseas general practitioners coming from the Indian subcontinent.

The distribution of general practitioners mirrored the unequal pattern existing in the hospital services. In 1976 the Trent region possessed 41 general practitioners per 100,000 population, whereas the figure for North West Thames was 49. In 1974 expenditure on the FPS was generally between 6 and 10 per cent above the per capita national average in three metropolitan regions and the South Western region, but between 7 and 10 per cent below the average in the Sheffield, Birmingham, and North East Metropolitan regions.[34] These differentials have narrowed to a small extent since 1979, but even in the 1990s, they remain significant.

The work of general practitioners changed out of all recognition owing to the decline of infectious disease, the growing population of the elderly, and increasing preoccupation with the diseases of civilization. In 1964 Professor Butterfield had already noted that 'the old emergencies, lobar pneumonia, empyema, mastoids, have disappeared: doctors are being cast, whether they like it or not, in a new role as interested in and responsible for all the human frailties'.[35] Not all general practitioners were equipped to meet new challenges associated with the rising importance of treating asymptomatic and psychosomatic conditions. Perhaps an even greater gulf opened up between the avant-garde among general practitioners and their antediluvian neighbours. These contrasting elements coexisted in the same district or even in the same practice, but in general the quality of practice reflected the social gradient. At one end of the spectrum, innovative practitioners drew together in substantial groups, where they exploited the most advanced and enlightened ideas on therapy, practice management, and research; at the other extreme a dismal residuum worked from lock-up surgeries and preserved a practice mentality belonging to the era of the panel.

Emergence of general practice from the dark ages owed much to the leadership of the College of General Practitioners, which in 1967 received its royal charter. On College of General Practitioner inspiration, the Royal Commission on Medical Education made recommendations designed to achieve parity between general practitioners and other specialities with respect to their undergraduate education, postgraduate training, continuing education, and academic role in university medical schools. These reforms were implemented only gradually, but they successfully raised general practice to a status akin to the hospital specialities.

Also important for promoting innovation was the new contract introduced in 1966 and based on the Family Doctors' Charter issued by the BMA in March 1965. Either directly or indirectly, the new contract gave encouragement to group practice, improvement of practice premises, continuing education, and employment of ancillary help. For those general practitioners not wishing to develop their own practice premises, the new contract made it advantageous to participate in health centres, which in turn encouraged their cooperation with LHAs. In 1965 there were only thirty health centres in England and Wales, and three in Scotland. By 1974 there were 566 health centres in England, twenty-nine in Wales, and fifty-nine in Scotland. During the 1970s health centres and group practices became a focus for teamwork and primary care. Public-expenditure economies slowed down capital investment, but the new planning system was designed to sustain the development of primary care and this was assisted by the demand-led nature of FPS spending. There was, however, no protection for the part of the primary-care team located in the HCHS sector, which was subject to cuts associated with cash limits. The Harding and Acheson reports of 1981 confirmed fears that primary-care teams were falling apart under the strains of the public-expenditure economies and the tensions deriving from the NHS management system. The Acheson Report also confirmed that Inner London had largely proved immune to striking advances in primary health care that had taken root elsewhere. The development of primary health care was not, therefore, a smooth and unimpeded process bringing about benefits in equal manner to all social groups. Even in 1979 the Royal Commission on the NHS conceded that 'team-work in primary care is at an early stage'.[36] There were continuing complaints about the inadequacy of primary care in both rural and inner-city areas, as well as the 'continuing reluctance of some doctors to perceive their role as other than responding to episodes of illness'.[37] It was evident, then, that, even in 1979, the revolution engineered by the Royal College of General Practitioners was by no means universal in its effects.

Family Planning

Despite relaxation in social attitudes, family limitation continued to be the subject of emotive debate. This issue faced governments with some uncomfortable dilemmas. Owing to the contentiousness of birth control, at its inception the new health service judiciously avoided any commitment to provision of comprehensive family-planning services. It merely continued the arrangements devised in 1930 whereby local authorities were permitted to apply public funds for birth-control purposes, but this was formally restricted to married women and cases where medical risk was involved. Most of the birth-control clinics were provided by voluntary agencies, subsidized in some districts by local authorities.

On account of the sensitivity of the subject, reliance on voluntary effort, and the usual vagaries of local-government action, family planning was subject to even greater disparities in provision than most other LHA services. For the same reasons, this fundamental facet of preventive health care was consigned to the fringes of the health service, which was a reminder of the disadvantages traditionally suffered by women in the field of health care. Although there was copious reference to services for mothers and infants, family planning was not even mentioned in the 1963 White

Paper on the development of local-authority health and welfare services.

High-profile campaigns for both family-planning services and abortion law reform emerged during the 1960s, reflecting changing social attitudes and also the impact of oral contraception. Family limitation was forced back onto the political agenda. However, once again the government displayed its habitual timorousness, with the result that change in the law was dependent on the vicissitudes of Private Members' Bills. This had the unintended and unfortunate effect of giving precedence to draft legislation on abortion. After a succession of failed Bills, the final success of the abortionists came with a Bill introduced in July 1966 by David Steel, a Liberal MP; after intense controversy the Abortion Act finally reached the statute book in October 1967. The Abortion Act allowed termination of pregnancy upon the recommendation of two registered medical practitioners, limited to cases when the continuation of the pregnancy would involve risk to the woman's life, or injury to the physical or mental health of the woman or existing children within her family. Although the government accepted that facilities for abortion should become available under the NHS, implementation of this provision was left to the discretion of health authorities. On account of the abhorrence of the Abortion Act among certain specialists, in some regions development of abortion facilities was obstructed. In such cases, those women requiring this service were at the mercy of charitable agencies or the commercial sector.

The likely successful passage of the Abortion Bill created the embarrassing anomaly that abortion was likely to become more readily attainable than the more desirable expedient of contraception. This problem was addressed as a matter of urgency by a further Private Member's Bill emanating from the Labour MP Edwin Brooks. The preparation of this Bill forced the government into reassessing its attitude to family planning. With the assistance of the Ministry of Health, the Brooks Bill proved to be relatively uncontentious, with the result that it comfortably overtook the Abortion Bill and became law in June 1967. In order to satisfy the government's health-service economy drive, the provisions of the Family

Planning Act were extremely modest. The services supported by local authorities were now available to all women, without regard to medical criteria, or limitation regarding marriage. The Act was permissive and there was no automatic provision for free facilities, except for family-planning advice. In England and Wales, where the Family Planning Act came into force in 1968, some authorities persisted in making no allowance for these services, whereas others, such as Camden and Islington, established comprehensive and free services. The Scottish family-planning legislation dated from 1968, but this was not implemented until September 1970. As in England, there were wide disparities in practice between local authorities, with Aberdeen being the most active in providing services.

Changes in the law failed to remove abortion and family planning from the political limelight. The critics of abortion immediately campaigned to tighten up the law. In order to buy time, in February 1971 the Heath administration established an independent committee under Mrs Justice Lane to review the workings of the Abortion Act. To the surprise and consternation of the anti-abortionists, the long, authoritative, and unanimous report of the Lane Committee expressed confidence in the Act, although it suggested a variety of measures to improve its effectiveness. The by-now well-organized and articulate 'pro-life' lobby continued on its course, regularly introducing amending Bills, and forcing parliamentary votes. This was resisted by the equally well-motivated abortion-rights lobby, which effectively neutralized the moves for further legislative restrictions on abortion.

Given the government's objections to a free and comprehensive family-planning service on the grounds of costs, and Sir Keith Joseph's special concern with targeting social assistance on deprived groups, he favoured limiting further extension of free family-planning services to cases of special need, an intention that was declared in December 1972 in his statement concerning arrangements for the transfer of family-planning services to the new health authorities under the NHS reorganization. Joseph's proposals were in fact subversive to his declared aims, since they involved eliminating existing free family-planning services, which were concentrated in inner cities, and which therefore reached precisely the groups for whom the highest priority existed. The government's rejection of a free family-planning service was also at variance with the recommendations of its own Population Panel and with the known views of the Lane Committee.

Owing to the hostile reception to Joseph's family-planning policy, the relevant clause 4 of the NHS Reorganization Bill was vigorously contested; indeed it became the Bill's most contentious provision. Joseph's clause was fiercely attacked in both Houses and from across the political spectrum; indeed, the Lords' amendments providing for a free service were reversed only at the eleventh hour, and with the important concession that charges would be limited to the standard prescription charge, which at the time stood at 20p. Labour committed itself to remove the prescription charge for family-planning services—a commitment which was promptly honoured at the beginning of the new administration in 1974. This was by no means the dawn of satisfaction concerning the family-planning service. The voluntary agencies complained about the neglect of the family-planning clinics by the new health authorities, which allowed the clinics to be overshadowed by the considerably more expensive services provided by general practitioners, after the latter fully entered the arena in July 1975, following their securement of a generous scale of fees for this work. Despite the extension of family-planning services, the NHS service was reaching fewer than 30 per cent of women of childbearing age in 1975, and this had increased only marginally by 1979. As with other aspects of the NHS, family-planning services as a whole were least accessible where the need was greatest.

Crisis of Health Care

Despite setbacks associated with such events as the 1967 devaluation, the period from 1964 to 1974 represented the phase of greatest optimism in the history of the NHS. It became possible for the first time to place the emphasis on planned expansion and confront many major tasks that had hitherto been either ignored or shelved. The many initiatives recorded in this chapter amount to an impressive planning effort. However, the success in evolving ideal models was not matched by anything like the same ability to convert these schemes into efficient reality. The reasons for this inertia within the system were different in each case, but the NHS continued to be handicapped by indifferent leadership, lack of a unified management structure, the complexity of its decision-making processes, the limitations of the consensual framework for determination of policy, the power of vested interests to veto change, and a shortage of human and material resources. The resources problem was ultimately decisive. The reverses occasioned by the economic crisis beginning in 1974 were more erosive because they were unexpected. At first there was a brave attempt to keep up the momentum of change, but confidence collapsed on one front after another.

Naturally, although severe in their impact, the adverse circumstances were insufficient to undermine the continuing record of humanitarian achievement in all parts of the health service. Estimates relating to the first thirty years of the health service listed some 135 million hospital in-patient episodes, 1,300 million out-patient attendances, 35 million donations of blood, 7,300 million prescriptions, nearly 500 million courses of dental treatment, and 180 million sight tests. Apart from NHS sight tests, such activity statistics continued on their upward climb in the next two decades. Also impressive was the evidence concerning health outputs, although these improvements were not entirely attributable to the health service. In such indices as perinatal mortality, the health-service contribution was important. In England and Wales the perinatal mortality rate stood at 38.5 in 1948; it declined to 28.2 by 1964, to 14.7 in 1979, and to 8.6 in 1996. In Scotland, the perinatal death rate stood at 46.8 in 1964; it fell to 14.1 in 1979, and to 9.2 in 1996. Such trends were indicative of the continuing success of the health service across a broad range of its operations. The previous sections of this chapter, together with the report of the Royal Commission on the NHS or the annual editions of government publications such as *Social Trends*, furnish ample further evidence concerning the scale of this achievement.

The economic crisis, cuts in public expenditure, and the imposition of new financial disciplines impeded progress with the belated initiatives to meet more realistically the egalitarian objectives of the health service. The process of redistributing resources for the benefit of the deprived regions or for the assistance of groups requiring the facilities of community care proceeded at a snail's pace. As noted above, the human and material resources of the health service remained unequally distributed and this was reflected in the unequal distribution of health benefits, as reflected in indices as diverse as toothlessness or perinatal mortality. During the early years of the health service it was no doubt anticipated that the extent of social and spatial inequalities in health would disappear as natural consequences of rising prosperity. The 1970s were marked by rediscovery of the problem of inequality. Reflective of this awakening, the Black Committee outlined the full scale of this problem in the field of health, and drew attention to the wide range of measures in the field of social support that were required for addressing these problems on a realistic basis.[38] Even before publication of the Black Report, Brian Abel-Smith had pointed out that 'despite 30 years of the National Health Service, mortality rates are in general a third higher in Wales than in East Anglia. Most worrying of all, despite 30 years of the "welfare state", the differences in mortality rates between social classes, are if anything getting wider rather than narrower. These are the problems which need intensive investigation and remedial action in whatever field such action can be effective.'[39]

The issues raised by the Black Report were not universally appreciated as a high priority. For instance, the Report of the Royal Commission on the NHS made little reference to the problem of inequality and made no mention of the existence of the Black Committee. There was also lack of consensus about the solution. While the Black Report saw no alternative to policy initiatives and public-expenditure commitments, this approach was decisively rejected by the incoming Thatcher administration.

The seeds of changing attitudes towards the poor were evident even before 1979, as indicated by the title of the consultative document issued at the outset of the Labour government's preventive health initiative, *Prevention and Health: Everybody's Business*, issued in 1976. In essence, the sick were accused of bringing ill health upon themselves and thereby wasting the resources of the NHS. Even Professor Abel-Smith gave prominence to the idea that the health service would be able to meet its obligations more effectively if the public adopted a healthier life style. This was, of course, a truism, but it invited placing the burden of responsibility for improvements in health on the individual, while giving licence for the state to withdraw from its obligations in the field of prevention and promotion. Inaction by the government was inexcusable and it contributed to the mounting toll of death, disease, and social problems associated with such phenomena as avoidable occupational stress or unemployment, environmental pollution, urban degradation, lax public-health controls, tobacco-smoking, alcohol abuse, drug addiction, or unsound diet. It was unrealistic to pretend that these problems could be addressed without leadership and active intervention on the part of the state, or that they lay outside the remit of a national health service pledged to the principle of comprehensiveness. Also the idea that the individual was able to effect economies in NHS spending by changes in life style raised more problems than it solved. It invited retrenchment-minded governments to cut resources further on account of exaggerated estimates of prospective efficiency savings relating to this factor. It also overlooked the fact that individuals adopting a healthier life style were likely to become substantial charges on the health service owing to a variety of unavoidable degenerative conditions. Finally, it was entirely inconsistent to place a new level of emphasis on healthy life style while ignoring the much larger problem of under-reporting of ill health or obstacles in the way of access to urgently needed services. Lamentations from the government about unhealthy life styles could not obscure the conclusion that substantial sections of the community continued to be deprived of the range and quality of health services appropriate to the later twentieth century.

The years from 1974 to 1979 were of pivotal importance for the health service. Until that time, it was confidently anticipated that the economic system was capable of achieving a rate of growth sufficient to meet rising social expectations. This optimism was swept away in 1974, when the impact of the oil crisis exposed the full extent of the weaknesses of the UK economy. The already tenuous advances enjoyed by the health service came to a sudden end and the system relapsed into a state of siege. In the last phase of the old Labour government, the combined effects of cuts in public expenditure, bitter industrial relations, the incubus of the

Joseph reorganization, the tide of resentment from vulnerable groups about failure to improve their services, and the evident bankruptcy of leadership on the part of health ministers precipitated the NHS into a state of crisis and demoralization worse than ever before or since.

3

CONTINUOUS REVOLUTION

> Yet the basic, though somewhat battered, framework created by the Attlee Government remained—the National Health Service, social security, the education system, support for industry and employment, etc. Ironically, that may have been one of the government's main problems. If the core responsibilities are still to be borne and if the aim is also to hold down total expenditure, it may be impossible to maintain current standards of expected service.[1]

During the two decades ending in 1979 consensus had ruled among the political and policy élite, but this period also witnessed the emergence of high-profile, radical critiques of the system, directed from both left and right. By 1979 these adversaries of the establishment had built up a significant following. Their credit was increased on account of loss of confidence within the agencies of welfare, whose morale was adversely affected under the new regime of retrenchment. All sides appreciated that it was necessary to subject all facets of social spending to critical review, and that it would be difficult to sustain the existing system without radical alterations of policy.

In 1979 the wheel of political fortune placed the onerous responsibility for policy reappraisal in the hands of the political right, while the left began its drift into the political wilderness. It took seventeen years for the political pendulum to swing away from the Conservatives, by which date Labour had become rehabilitated and transmuted into New Labour. In view of the essential continuity between Conservative and New Labour in the field of health-care policy, New Labour's interventions are most appropriately considered in the light of the present chapter's consideration of the impact of the Thatcher revolution on health-care policy.

At the time of its election defeat in 1979, Labour was committed in principle to increasing public expenditure at some future date to the point whereby the welfare system established by the Attlee administration could be fully restored. With respect to both the health service and wider welfare provision, it seemed as if the Thatcher administration would institute a root-and-branch reappraisal, and background noises to this effect were much in evidence. As the quotation at the head of this chapter indicates, this mission proved more difficult to accomplish than seemed likely at the outset. The quotation was addressed to the situation in 1983, but its ready applicability to later dates, indicates that every administration since 1979 has experienced the greatest difficulty in providing the resources required to support the welfare-state commitments to which each party remains irrevocably pledged.

In its unsuccessful contests with this problem, Labour followed a conventional course, in which its policy options were constrained by mechanical deference to traditional policies. The new brand of conservatism represented by Mrs Thatcher was not bound by such constraints. Under the new Prime Minister's direction, in the ever more desperate search to prevent the crisis inherited from Labour turning into a catastrophe, the health service was subjected to a process of recurrent policy reappraisal, the effect of which amounted to a continuous revolution, which brought about a profound transformation in the culture of the NHS. The following analysis suggests that the changes introduced after 1979 were brought about by an act of determined political will, rather than merely representing necessary responses dictated by technical exigencies. This renewed political polarization marked a return to circumstances akin to 1945, but, whereas Bevan achieved his revolution by means of a single ambitious piece of legislation, the Thatcher reforms were evolved incrementally, each step preparing the way for further change. The architects of the new wave of changes soon appreciated that public tolerance would not extend to sudden radical alterations of Bevan's system; accordingly it was necessary to advance by means of progressively discrediting, destabilizing, and supplanting existing institutions until the process of radical transformation was complete. This approach soon developed an attractiveness of its own. It is, therefore, not surprising to find reports that insiders identified this model as their equivalent to the Maoist ideology of perpetual revolution.[2]

Ideological Reorientation

The general-election victory in May 1979, which provided Mrs Thatcher with a modest majority, presented a fresh opportunity for decisive initiative on the part of the right. During the next decade Mrs Thatcher impressed the stamp of her personality on the administration and its policies to a greater degree than is normal for Prime Ministers. Nevertheless, the Thatcher administration experienced a shaky start and only slowly consolidated its position. The adverse impact on the government's political fortunes of high unemployment and economic crisis was compensated for by military glory in the Falklands War and by the visible disintegration of the Labour opposition. Mrs Thatcher was returned with a landslide majority in the June 1983 general election. This huge mandate was reduced in the 1987 general election, but the parliamentary majority remained comfortable. In an unexpected turn of events, and in what was, in retrospect, a landmark in the slide into fratricide of the Conservative Party, Mrs Thatcher was turned out and replaced by John Major in November 1990. Despite this trauma, the Conservatives retained a small majority in the 1992 general election, but this was steadily eroded by subsequent by-election defeats until for the latter part of its term of office the Major administration was without a majority. Between the 1979 and 1997 general elections, seven Conservative Secretaries of State held the health portfolio, of whom Norman Fowler, who held office between 1981 and 1987, was by far the longest serving. In July 1988 the DHSS was split, reversing the changes made in 1968 and re-establishing separate departments of Health and Social Security. By contrast with the situation before 1968, both health and social security retained their Cabinet status and both ministers were Secretaries of State. The first Secretary of State for Health was Kenneth Clarke, who had earlier served under Norman Fowler as the Minister for Health. The Clarke tenure was important, since he was responsible for framing and launching the radical *Working for Patients* policy initiative.

Labour was widely written off after its two humiliating election defeats in 1983 and 1987. Also Labour was weakened by secession of the Social Democratic Party and the emergence of a stronger centre political grouping. In practice Labour proved remarkably resilient and slowly regained its electoral strength. Labour extended its appeal, burying its traditional policy objectives, assimilating policies associated with Mrs Thatcher, and improving its public-relations techniques. The metamorphosis was complete by the May 1997 general election, when New Labour, led by Tony Blair, conveyed the impression of being a less sleaze-infected, fresh-faced version of conservatism. Under Mrs Thatcher's successor, the Conservatives proved unable fully to rebuild confidence, or to end their internal wrangling over Europe. Labour's evident unity and sophisticated media image produced the reward of a landslide majority at the general election on 1 May 1997, even greater than that enjoyed by Mrs Thatcher after the Falklands War.

Thatcherism possessed profound implications for the health service. As claimed by the Conservatives themselves, the cumulative effect of the changes introduced after 1979 were quite as profound as the reforms instituted by Aneurin Bevan after the Second World War. Of the elaborate edifice of health-service administration constructed by Sir Keith Joseph in 1974, only the CHC survived into 1997 in its recognizably original form, and even this narrowly escaped dissolution in 1982. Both the HCHS and FPS administrations were changed out of all recognition. In addition, beginning with the Central Health Services Council (CHSC) and the Personal Social Services Council in 1979 and ending with the Health Advisory Service in April 1997, a whole range of advisory and inspectoral bodies came under the axe. In place of these innocuous public-interest agencies, a much larger legion of quangos was summoned into existence to feed the requirements of the new management culture.

Although the scale of the Thatcher and Bevan reforms is comparable, their strategies were entirely different. In the case of Bevan, the entire system was reformed under a single piece of legislation, according to a comprehensive plan, which remained in place for more than twenty-five years. The Thatcher reforms represented a long-drawn-out sequence of changes, amounting to a process of continuous revolution, in which the end result was not predictable at the beginning, and indeed the whole process of policy-making was akin to a journey through a minefield, advances being made in an erratic manner, as dictated by the exigencies of political opportunism.

This incremental process—its relatively uncontentious inception, the emolliative content of ministerial and prime-ministerial utterances or election manifestos, and the relative late date of emergence of the most controversial policies—has given rise to the suggestion that trends in policy were dictated by technocratic rather than ideological criteria, at least for most of the 1980s, and even that the more radical shake-up after 1989 was again technocractic in its origins. On the other hand, it can be argued that the health service hardly deserves to be regarded as a special case, or the only ideology-free zone in government. Experience in managing the NHS was the occasion for Sir Keith Joseph's revulsion against 'statism'. The health service was also regarded by Mrs Thatcher's Chancellor, Sir Geoffrey Howe, as a prime test case for the assault on collectivism. As a huge bureaucracy and one of the greediest mouths among the spending departments, the NHS was a prime symbol of the evils of the system that Mrs Thatcher was pledged to dismantle. Indeed, if the health service was not radically reformed, it would introduce a massive inconsistency into the government's programme, and block the crucial mission to roll back the state, reduce the scale of public expenditure, and expand the scope of the market economy. If the politicians were apt to backslide by making an exception of the health service, such well-appointed bodies as the Adam Smith Institute, the Conservative Medical Society, the Conservative Political Centre, the Institute of Economic Affairs, the Institute for Policy Studies, the Selsdon Group, or the zealots associated with the same institutions operating as official advisers were eager to supply evidence concerning the offensiveness of Bevan's NHS to market and monetarist convictions. As noted below, the high motivation and capacity of these groups to influence events was demonstrated during Mrs Thatcher's review of the health service.

The NHS was, therefore, a prime target for the ideologues of the right, and this group was assured for the first time of a more positive response from senior ministers. Among the widely accepted objectives among the marketeers were: reconstruction of health care on the basis of private insurance, with the NHS reverting to the status of a safety net for the poor; narrowing the range and scope of services provided under the NHS; privatization through compulsory tendering, beginning with support functions, but extending eventually to clinical services; increasing the range and level of direct charges for services, with the aim of shifting the burden of financing the health service from the taxpayer to the user; dismantling the current hospital administration and reconstruction according to different management and market criteria; and, finally, extensive deregulation and measures to increase competition in the FPS. This radical agenda was by no means confined to an unrepresentative fringe. Although for obvious reasons of political calculation these ideas were not committed to an authorized policy prospectus, these objectives were characteristic of the aspirations of Mrs Thatcher's most trusted senior ministers and policy advisers.

The Thatcher administration therefore represented what it seemed at the time: a reversion to a more ideologically determined approach to health policy. It ended a long period during which some kind of fragile consensus had predominated. Just as socialism had grasped its opportunity in 1945, so in 1979 it was the chance for Thatcherism to reconstruct a system still permeated by Bevanist assumptions.

From the outset there were good grounds for suspecting that the Thatcher team was committed to radical departure from the existing system; indeed, continuity was entirely inconsistent with the predominant political rhetoric concerning the intentions of the Prime Minister. In the event, the intervention of other policy priorities, political prudence, or indecision over policy options rendered immediate, root-and-branch reform of the health service impracticable. However, despite the complexity and sensitivity of the operation, the inertia of the system, and the weight of opposition to the government's thinking, there was every determination to take steps to bring the health service into line with the government's programme for reforming the welfare state, as and when the opportunity presented itself.

The problematical nature of this task is indicated by the anodyne character of the sections on the health service in Conservative general-election manifestos during the 1980s. The 1979 manifesto proposed to decentralize the service and cut back bureaucracy, not to reduce spending, to improve the situation with respect to hospital building, priority services, and under-provided regions, and to end the 'vendetta' against private medicine. All of this was in line with the recommendations of the Merrison Royal Commission, and not much at variance with Labour's own programme. The manifesto also indicated that the government would consider long-term changes in methods of funding the NHS, which was a coded but nevertheless potent reminder that, on policies of fundamental importance, the Thatcher team was willing to consider controversial solutions well outside the consensual framework previously observed.

Later manifestos from the 1980s tended to be called 'more of the same' by the press. The possibility of alternative funding of the NHS was discreetly dropped from the 1983 manifesto. In the Foreword contributed by Mrs Thatcher, she emphasized the Conservative pride over protecting the health service from the effects of the recession. The manifesto promised continuing improvements, making specific commitments concerning priority groups and community care. A positive role was encouraged for private medicine, and for competitive tendering for support services. The only mention of management issues was the promise to 'reduce costs of administering the health service', which even the trained eye was unlikely to detect as a reference to current radical policy reviews such as the Griffiths management study, which was virtually completed by the date of the election.

The 1987 manifesto repeated its predecessor's promise to continue to improve and give better value for money. Even more than on earlier occasions, in 1987 the Conservatives concentrated on their spending record and drew attention to various areas of growth within the service. The only area of policy review mentioned was community care, but no indication was given that ministers were actively considering a further major overhaul of the entire health service.

In view of the radical reforms of the health service announced in 1989 and implemented in 1991, the 1992 Conservative manifesto issued by John Major was inevitably concerned with the retrospective justification of the new market system. But the manifesto was equally concerned with giving reassurance to patients that the changes would be associated with a continuing year-on-year increase in expenditure, reduction in waiting lists, and other specified improvements in services.

The low-key and emollient messages emanating from the manifestos were backed by frequent affirmations of commitment to the NHS in ministerial and prime-ministerial statements, most famously at the Conservative Party Annual Conference on 8 October 1982, when, in her closing speech, Mrs Thatcher proclaimed that 'the National Health Service is safe with us'. Subsequently, she confessed to 'peppering' her speeches with favourable input and output figures in order to reinforce the impression of her government's commitment to the NHS.[3]

Understandably, the government's assurances were not taken at face value. Consistent with the policy imperatives mentioned above, frequent and obviously well-informed leaks concerning radical policy initiatives, and the experience of regular rounds of NHS cuts and increased charges, there was a constant state of public apprehension concerning the future of the health service. Throughout the 1980s, rumours of big shake-ups of the NHS were never far from the newspaper headlines. Indeed, the above Party Conference intervention by Mrs Thatcher was needed to dampen down public anxieties following leaks of Cabinet papers indicating that ministers were considering a transfer to health insurance and greatly enhanced health-service charges.

The Thatcher period continued to be plagued by rumours of draconian changes, necessitating reassurances from ministers they were loathe to issue, as, for instance, during the 1983 general-election campaign when rumours of a 'secret Tory manifesto' or 'secret agenda' caused Mrs Thatcher to promise that she would not institute hotel charges for hospital patients, charges for attending the general practitioner, or reduce the extent of exemptions from health-service charges.[4] In preparing for the 1987 election, reform of education and housing policy featured prominently in Conservative plans, but much-publicized proposals for equally radical health-service reforms were shelved, causing one ministerial observer to comment with evident disapproval that the Prime Minister 'still feared that the reform of the NHS was too sensitive a topic to expose to the electorate'.[5] Since proposals for alterations in the health service faced insurmountable presentational difficulties and were intrinsically unpopular with the electorate, they were best kept away from the public gaze and saved for introduction without electoral mandate.

Paying for Health Care

Since the very beginning, finding the resources needed adequately to support the health service had constituted a nagging source of policy difficulty. This dilemma was even sharper for the Thatcher administration in view of its determination to achieve absolute reductions in public expenditure and income tax. On the other hand, it was specifically pledged to maintain spending levels and continue advancement of the health service. The Thatcher administration was, therefore, faced with a difficult problem of squaring the circle, preventing the growth of spending, while maintaining public confidence that the health service was expanding and improving. This was particularly difficult in the wake of the previous government's legacy of retrenchment, which had created a substantial backlog of demand. The Conservatives managed tolerably well. In the face of persistent adverse criticism and evident signs of strain within the system, the government kept up a consistent effort to increase output and prevent collapse of public confidence.

Nevertheless, the public was never convinced about the government's claim that the service was adequately funded, improving on all fronts, and suitably adapted to meet the challenges of the future. The state of anxiety concerning the state of the health service that took hold under Labour in the mid-1970s persisted and became intensified. Central to this fear was the moral certainty that resources were inadequate to meet reasonable expectations concerning health care. Repeated ministerial assurances and inundations of figures concerning increases in 'real' expenditure, or impressive statistics regarding activity levels, succeeded in stemming the tide of alarm to only a limited degree. Understandably, the outlook of the public was influenced by the abundant evidence of adverse local experience, supported by the testimony of health authorities, the health professions, and outside experts, suggesting that resources were insufficient to meet the basic requirements of the service.

The government succeeded to a limited extent in its major objective to reduce the share of GDP absorbed by general government expenditure. In 1975 public expenditure reached its peak, accounting for nearly half of GDP, after which it fell slightly during the last years of the Labour administration. After initial adverse movement, taking government spending to 45 per cent of GDP, the Thatcher administration succeeded in reducing government spending to 38 per cent of GDP by 1988, which was the lowest level for twenty-two years, but afterwards there was a gradual climb in the first half of the 1990s, taking government spending back to 43 per cent, followed by a further decline to reach 40 per cent in 1997. The latter position was, therefore, almost the same as at the beginning of the Thatcher administration. Public-expenditure projections made during the last months of the Conservative administration and adopted by Labour anticipate a target of 38 per cent by the date of the millennium. The share of GDP absorbed by the health-service expenditure edged above 5 per cent during the 1980s; it averaged just below 6 per cent during the 1990s. As indicated in the next chapter, this long period of containment came to an abrupt end in the new millennium.

Contrary to the government's intentions, social spending increased after 1979, but only to a modest extent. All social commitments apart from social security were maintained within reasonable limits. Within the welfare state there were notable losers and gainers. Education lost some ground to health; education spending ran along the same lines as health after 1979, but, for the first time since the Second World War, health edged above its traditional competitor. The major losses were recorded in the field of housing, where spending fell by half. Spending on the personal social services remained constant, whereas the health service was a minor beneficiary, expanding its share from 18 to 22 per cent of the social budget, and from 11 to 14 per cent of general public expenditure. The dominating factor in social spending was the inexorable rise in social-security spending, largely on account of unemployment. In 1976 social security absorbed about one-quarter of all government expenditure; in 1996 this figure had increased to one-third. Using the government's favoured GDP deflator, expenditure on the NHS increased after 1980 at an average of about 3 per cent a year. As indicated by Table 3.1, although this average was just about maintained until the end of the Conservative administration, a distinct downturn was then predicted, even on the basis of this GDP deflator estimate most favourable to a government's spending record.

Of course, health-service expenditure is an aggregate composition, and a distinct shift of balance became evident after the 1970s. First, it took until about 1990 to recover from the setback to the NHS capital programme that occurred in the mid-1970s; then a further slump in capital spending took place after 1994. A notable development during the 1980s was the rising proportion of NHS funds directed towards the demand-led FPS, especially the pharmaceutical and general medical services, each of which maintained an average rate of growth more than twice that recorded for the HCHS.

TABLE 3.1. *Net National Health Service expenditure, England, 1991–2000*

Year	Expenditure (£m.)	Real terms change (%)
1991/2 (outturn)	25,353	—
1992/3 (outturn)	27,970	5.9
1993/4 (outturn)	28,950	0.6
1994/5 (outturn)	30,579	3.8
1995/6 (outturn)	31,968	2.1
1996/7 (estimated)	33,287	1.6
1997/8 (plan)	34,368	1.2
1998/9 (plan)	35,143	0.2
1999/2000 (plan)	35,883	0.1

Source: Department of Health, *The Government's Expenditure Plans 1997–2000*, Cm 3612 (London: The Stationery Office, 1997), table 2 1

Consistent with the findings recorded in the previous chapters, applying the specific NHS price index as a deflator suggests much smaller increases in health-service expenditure. On this basis the increase averaged at about 1.5 per cent a year since 1980 for health-service expenditure as a whole, but only 1 per cent for the HCHS, which is widely regarded as only half the rate of growth required to sustain services. The fluctuating and low level of increase in the purchasing power in the HCHS sector was widely cited as the basis for the recurrent financial problems facing health authorities. It is, therefore, evident that during the 1980s a substantial shortfall built up between target growth and the spending power of health authorities. In the course of the 1980s this latter argument was effectively developed by the House of Commons Social Services Committee, the National Association of Health Authorities, and the King's Fund, which evolved simple but effective graphic presentations of this conclusion, an early example of which is given in Fig. 3.1. Despite much ingenuity on the part of health ministers, they were unable to dispose of this argument. In the view of critics, the extent of underfunding steadily increased from 1980 onwards, until for the year 1990/1 it reached about 5 per cent of the total HCHS budget.[6] For the period after 1980 the House of Commons Social Services Committee estimated that the annual increase in purchasing power had averaged at only 0.6 per cent.[7] The issue was, of course, never cut and dried, and, as in other aspects of the welfare issue such as unemployment, the debate was complicated by changes in accounting methods and terminology. Whereas critics founded their argument on the NHS price index and input volume estimates, the government concentrated on the GDP deflator and economic cost estimates, which it attempted to endow with greater authority by christening indices based on these assumptions as indications of 'real' spending on the health service, with the implication that other indices were imbued with lesser authority as a representation of reality. This device failed to deter the experts, but it breathed fresh life into the campaign to endow government statistical popularizations with a new level of optimism. Sometimes the method fails, as, for example, in the 1997 edition of *Social Trends*, where table 8.1 inserted by error the volume figures for 'real growth in NHS expenditure', and the associated text accordingly

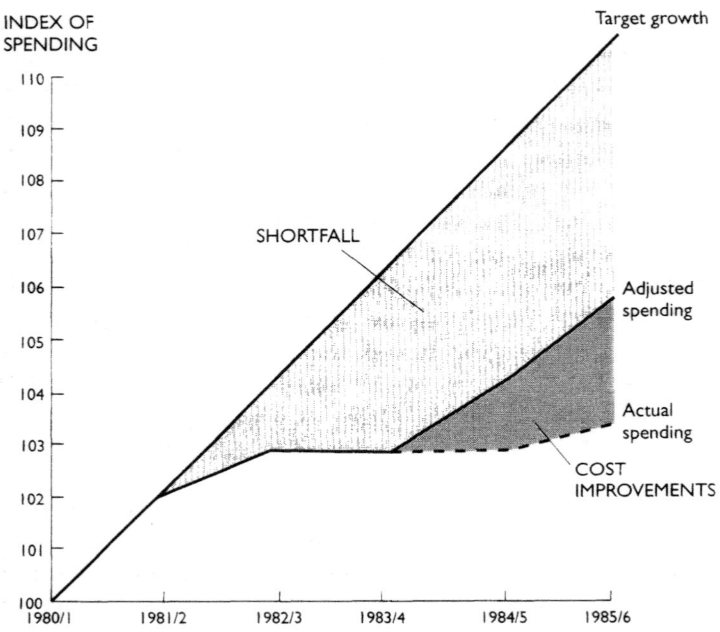

Figure 3.1. HCHS trends in current spending, targets, and shortfall, 1980–1986

Notes: Target growth = 2% compound increase over base spending
Adjusted spending = actual spending plus cash releasing cost improvements at 1985/6 input volume rates
Actual spending = spending at 1985/6 input volume prices

Source: *House of Commons Fourth Report from the Social Services Committee Session 1985–86 Public Expenditure on the Social Services*, HC 387-I (London: HMSO, 1986)

conceded that there had been an increase in health-service expenditure of only one-sixth over a twenty-year period.

The government's claims about sufficiency of resources depended on favourable outcomes with respect to all the factors influencing health authorities' purchasing power. Owing to the government's failure to meet its over-optimistic targets concerning holding down costs and increasing efficiency, and its inability to provide additional resources to meet the shortfall, the scope and quality of the service were inevitably adversely affected. An already stressed system was therefore likely to be overtaken by a creeping paralysis. This serious situation possessed the potential for damaging electoral consequences. It forced the Conservatives to search with ever greater desperation for means of extracting greater volumes of output from the limited available resources, or for means of defining the role of the health service more narrowly. Most of the policy initiatives of the Conservatives can be traced to this root. At every level, from routine house-keeping changes to large-scale reshaping of the service, there was a calculation that economies would either be forthcoming immediately, or were likely in the longer term. Although political prudence caused economy and cost containment to be played down in presentation, this objective was never far below the surface.

Insuring Health Care

Under Mrs Thatcher some of the most radical proposals for solving the funding problem, which had been considered briefly but rejected on previous occasions, were given more active and sympathetic consideration. The UK was clearly out of line with its Western partners in its reliance on general taxation as the main source of funding for the NHS. As already noted, among the Conservatives there had always been an undercurrent of opinion favouring reversion to insurance arrangements of the kind dominant in Western Europe or the USA. This was canvassed as a decisive means to rid the Consolidated Fund of the incubus of the NHS, which was a superficially attractive proposition. However, the argument in favour of insurance was perhaps even more unconvincing in the 1980s than it had been when it was considered at an earlier date. Insurance-based health care was notoriously expensive and heavily bureaucratic. Also the state would still be left with a substantial burden, since it would need to bear the cost of providing services for residual groups without access to insurance provision. Transition to insurance therefore represented a risky and potentially highly unpopular venture, which was likely to produce a two-tier system of health care without generating substantial savings in public expenditure.

Regardless of the known disadvantages, party activists and senior Conservative ministers persisted in their enthusiasm for health insurance. In connection with the 1979 general election, the Conservative Party Health Study Group advocated a universal system of item-of-service charges (specified payments for each item of service delivered), supported by compulsory health insurance set at a minimum level, with the government carrying unacceptable risks and providing support for those who could not afford to pay a competitive market premium. As already noted, Sir Geoffrey Howe had long been interested in the idea of insurance funding. Throughout his period as shadow spokesman on health and indeed after his appointment as Secretary of State, Patrick Jenkin was a vociferous advocate of health insurance. Lack of sympathy for this idea on the part of the Merrison Royal Commission lay at the root of his disdain for its report.

During the Thatcher administration there were at least three major appraisals of health insurance. Naturally, Jenkin gave high priority to an examination of this policy immediately after his appointment as Secretary of State; this departmental review evolved into a formal inquiry by an interdepartmental working party, which reported in January 1982, but news of its deliberations were known from leaks at the end of November 1981.[8] In the light of adverse publicity, Norman Fowler, the new Secretary of State, tried, not entirely successfully, to dampen down rumours concerning the government's intentions to abandon the existing system of funding the NHS.[9]

A more widely publicized episode occurred in the autumn of 1982, in the context of frightening predictions concerning the escalation of public expenditure. At short notice, the CPRS was asked to produce proposals for major savings in the fields of defence, social security, the health service, and education. Prominent among these think-tank proposals for health included consideration of transfer to health insurance, which under optimal conditions was thought to be capable of yielding substantial savings in public expenditure, although such savings were by no means certain. Leaking of the think-tank programme was embarrassing to the hardliners, but it represented a notable *coup* for Cabinet dissidents, causing the think-tank report to be disowned. The special sensitivity of this leak concerning the health service is indicated by the need for Mrs Thatcher's 'safe-in-our-hands' utterance at the

October 1982 Conference.[10] This fiasco conferred some degree of immunity on the health service against further consideration of alternative funding methods, at least in the short term.

Notwithstanding what it regarded as a tactical retreat in 1983, the press continued to regard health insurance as a live policy issue among ministers. As discussed more fully below, the most active discussion of the insurance option took place in the context of Mrs Thatcher's confidential review of the health service, but it was again rejected on account of the uncertainty of its benefits and its evident disadvantages.[11] Throughout 1988 rumours persisted about scrapping of existing funding arrangements. These were not finally dispelled until the Foreword by Mrs Thatcher to the January 1989 White Paper *Working for Patients* contained the unambiguous assurance that the 'National Health Service will continue to be available to all, regardless of income, and to be financed mainly out of general taxation'.[12]

As during the Macmillan administration, the positive atmosphere regarding the insurance principle facilitated greater exploitation of the NHS Contribution; during the 1980s this insurance share of health-service expenditure was increased from 9 to 17 per cent. It subsequently fell back to a level of 12 per cent in the mid-1990s. Thus, as in the case of direct charges, the later situation was not greatly different from that bequeathed by Labour in 1979.

Although wholesale transfer to health insurance was rejected, the Conservatives introduced minor incentives to assist the development of private health insurance. In 1980 tax concessions were introduced on employer-paid medical insurance premiums for those earning less than £8,500 a year. This gave a boost to private health insurance, with the result that by 1990 some 12 per cent of the population were covered by such schemes, compared with about 6 per cent in 1980. During the 1980s spending on private health care increased from 3 to 6 per cent of NHS spending.

A further incentive to the expansion of private health care was provided by the 1989 White Paper, which proposed tax concessions on non-corporate medical insurance for those above the age of 60. This provision was duly included in the 1989 budget, but with little enthusiasm on the part of the Treasury, which had consistently resisted tax relief on non-corporate medical insurance on account of the dangers of setting a precedent. It was feared that pressure would build up for extension of this tax relief to a wider age band and then into the sphere of school fees, with potentially disastrous loss of tax revenue. In practice, owing to the economic recession, the growth of private insurance slowed down during the 1990s. Indeed, it is likely that the numbers covered by private health insurance in 1997 were only slightly above the level for 1990. Private medical insurance has remained for the most part a disposable amenity, not supplanting the NHS, even for those groups who are its greatest users.

Although minuscule in scale, private health insurance has proved sufficient to sustain the growth of private providers to the point where they have attained a viable critical mass, under the market system introduced in 1991, able to take over services hitherto provided by the NHS. By the date of the fiftieth anniversary consortiums of private providers and NHS consultants acting in their private capacity were colonizing many services which had hitherto been entirely the province of the NHS.

Direct Charges

As already indicated, direct charges for FPS were by 1979 a fixed characteristic of the health service. Nevertheless, these charges had remained limited in their effect. There was considerable uncertainty about the extent to which they would be increased by the Thatcher administration. At the time of the 1979 election, Labour predicted that the right would greatly increase charges, while the Tories denied that this was their intention. Once in power, charges were increased, although political sensitivities inhibited the pace of the implementation of this policy.

In practice the Conservatives concentrated on increasing existing charges. They also regularly seriously considered but always rejected such old chestnuts as hotel charges for hospital patients, or a charge for attending the general practitioner, as well as many types of charge hardly considered previously. During the closing months of its existence, the CPRS produced a pessimistic analysis of the prospects for charges, which concluded that the only new charges with possibility for success related to treatment in hospital or by general practitioners, with an upper limit of £50. The latter was adopted as 'roughly the cost of a television licence', on the grounds that patients should be encouraged to 'put as high a value on their health as on watching television'.[13]

Immediate increases in prescription charges signified the direction of Conservative policy. The prescription charge had been pegged at 20p during the 1970s. It was increased on three occasions during the first eighteen months of the Thatcher administration, taking the level to £1 per item in December 1980. During the first ten years of the administration, the prescription charge was increased by more than 500 per cent in real terms.

Eye-service and dental charges were also increased at regular intervals under the Conservative administration. For the first time in the history of the health service, increases in charges became an annual ritual. The yield from these greatly inflated charges was not as great as might be expected on account of the maintenance of exemptions for the elderly, the young, and the poor. Indeed, in order to soften opposition to their actions, ministers regularly offered assurances concerning their commitment to exemptions. Chargeable prescriptions therefore declined from 25 per cent of the total in 1985 to 16 per cent in 1996. The wide scope of exemptions necessitated even higher increases in charges for other users in order to prevent a slump in the return. With some difficulty the Conservatives managed to increase the yield from FPS charges, which increased from about 2 per cent of the gross cost of the NHS in 1979 to reach a peak of 4.5 per cent in 1989/90, after which there was a steady decline to the 1997 level of 2.4 per cent. Thus, despite the great effort devoted to increasing direct charges, and the unpopularity associated with this policy, the Conservatives only marginally advanced upon the yield recorded under the previous Labour administration, which was, of course, ostensibly committed to low charges.

Increases in direct charges were associated with some important alterations of policy. Completing a long-running process of erosion of the NHS eye service, in April 1985 the supply of NHS spectacle frames was ended, except for restricted groups.[14] These changes were associated with the general deregulation of the optical profession. For children and those on low incomes, in July 1986 a voucher scheme was introduced to support the cost of spectacles.

When ending the supply of NHS spectacles, ministers gave assurances that eye tests, the one universal subsidy still available, would remain free. This policy was reversed in April 1989, when everyone except children and the poor, or those referred to hospital, were charged for eye tests. This policy, together with the reduction in the age limit for free dental treatment from 21 to 16, and removal of free dental examinations from January 1989, were heavily criticized, including from the government backbenches. It was urged that these charges would constitute a deterrent to early detection and treatment especially among the poor, thereby risking increasing the incidence of some serious defects and adding to morbidity levels and health-service costs. These fears seemed well founded in a situation where only one-third of semi-skilled and unskilled social classes attended dentists for regular checks, and where almost half of these social groups above the age of 55 possessed no natural teeth. As a consequence of restriction of the general ophthalmic service, there was an immediate reduction by two-thirds in the number of sight tests, and a fall of more than half in spectacles supplied under the NHS.

These policies also seemed inconsistent with the government's newly stated enthusiasm for screening in the FPS. The government was better able to withstand the tide of criticism over removal of free dental checks and eye tests owing to the clever timing of its measures, since its political critics and health-service professionals were heavily preoccupied with the even more controversial *Working for Patients* White Paper and with battles over the revision of the general medical practitioners' contract.

Patients First

The first couple of years of the Thatcher government were spent in responding to the Royal Commission on the NHS and drawing a line with respect to commitments entered into by the previous administration. The best remembered of these symbolic gestures was the dissembling response to the Black Report on inequalities in health. As an alternative to complete suppression, the report was published at the August bank holiday 1980, in a form normally reserved for in-house documents, and without the press conference or publicity that is normally associated with such events. The text was introduced by some largely unflattering remarks by the Secretary of State, to the effect that he was unable to endorse the report's recommendations. From his Regents Park citadel, as President of the Royal College of Physicians, Sir Douglas Black deftly turned this snub to advantage; he and his team made sure that the report was widely publicized; ultimately it was so much in demand that, unique among the policy documents produced by the Conservative government, it merited distribution in a commercial paperback edition, in which form it has remained in print, ensuring that the spectre of health inequality plagued Conservatives for the whole of their time in office.[15]

Arguably the weakest planning document of the early days was the *Future Pattern of Hospital Provision in England*, issued in May 1980. This fundamental shift in policy was described in a slender pamphlet, containing no effective justification. The document effectively brought to an end the building of vast district general hospitals, so enabling the government to gain breathing space and cut back its capital programme. The document was littered with other proposals designed to rule out capital developments, serving to cut back the demand for resources, although it was also conceded that the new policy was in certain respects a false economy, since it would preclude economies in scale of the kind envisaged in existing hospital-building schemes. *Care in Action*, issued in 1981 to assist the new health authorities in planning their priorities, was better looking than other planning documents of this vintage, but again was negative in its implications, representing the final retraction of expectations raised by Labour's priorities initiative of 1976. In revising their planning programmes, the new health authorities were instructed to abandon previously agreed norms for services and told that expansion of services for priority groups was expected to come from efficiency savings.[16]

Review of the 1974 health-service reorganization represented the most urgent policy task facing the Thatcher government. Following a tide of criticism, samples of which are cited above in Chapter 2, within the health service there was widespread resignation to further change. The Merrison Royal Commission Report, which was published shortly after the Conservatives' return, contained a balanced assessment of opinion, on the basis of which it offered specific proposals for change. In opposition the Conservatives had acknowledged the need for corrective measures to improve efficiency and 'cut red tape' within the health service, and this objective was reflected in their 1979 general-election manifesto. They were also known to be favourable to eliminating a tier of health service administration.

The government was therefore well placed to act promptly and its plans were announced in a short consultative paper, *Patients First*, published on 12 December 1979.[17] This modest package was relatively uncontroversial and was implemented without substantial alteration. The main effect of the reforms was to eliminate the area tier of administration and elevate the districts into statutory health authorities. The 192 District Health Authorities (DHAs) established in England in April 1982, although supposed to be 'natural' socio-economic units, in fact differed little from the district pattern bequeathed from the 1974 reorganization. On account of the simpler structure of their health administrations, Scotland and Wales were hardly affected by the 1982 reorganization.[18] Throughout the UK there was a new level of emphasis on devolution of responsibility to local units of management.

Abolition of the area tier raised the question of the future of FPCs, which were largely autonomous satellites of area authorities. Responding to the self-assertiveness of FPCs and animosity of the independent contractors to any kind of outside interference, the government allowed the existing FPC structure to continue, with suitable strengthening of its functions consequential upon the abolition of the parent AHAs. While the government's permanent commitment to regional authorities was left in doubt, in view of the authorities' immediate utility in overseeing the 1982 reforms, consideration of a substantial change in their role was postponed. The only significant point upon which the government offered a concession related to CHCs, the abolition of which was raised as a possibility in *Patients First*. Ministers anticipated that this would provoke demand for retention of CHCs, which is precisely what occurred. Perhaps learning from the events of 1973, the government gracefully retreated and allowed CHCs to continue, which was not inconvenient since, although sometimes troublesome, they were not particularly influential. CHCs therefore counted among the lucky survivors of Mrs Thatcher's much-vaunted assault on public-interest quangos.

The 1982 reorganization was rightly seen as a piece of fine-tuning rather than as a major shake-up. While eliminating ninety AHAs was consistent with the government's attack on unnecessary bureaucracy, it was not regarded as ideologically slanted, merely a means to achieve the widely accepted objective of taking decision-making to the level of the local community. In fact the government was reverting to the region–district model which, as already noted, had been widely favoured in NHS circles at the outset of preparation for the 1974 reorganization, but discarded on account of local-government susceptibilities. In 1979, this imperative no longer applied to nearly the same degree, although care was taken to avoid a confrontational presentation of changes that in a variety of respects were adverse to local government.

The 1982 reforms were less of a settled solution than seemed apparent on the surface. Disagreements among the Conservatives aptly illustrate their dilemmas over translating vague policy aspirations into concrete policies. With commendable modesty, *Patients First* accepted that the reforms were not a 'final and rigid blueprint to last for all time'.[19] This reflected a degree of uncertainty concerning the adequacy and direction of the changes, which even in government circles were regarded at best as a halfway house. Jenkin's speedy production of *Patients First* was widely seen as a pre-emptive strike designed to appease vested interests within the health service. In other respects also, Jenkin's policies were kind to the NHS establishment—for instance, by caving in to the consultants over the revision of their contract, which entailed concessions of a kind resisted by previous administrations in the course of negotiations that had dragged on for nearly a decade. The new contract especially benefited consultants with part-time contracts, and the same group was appeased by the abolition of the Health Services Board, established by the previous Labour government to oversee the phasing-out of private beds from NHS hospitals and supervise the private hospital sector.

Right-wing critics were concerned that, in significant respects, *Patients First* was even more timid than the Royal Commission

Report. Although abolition of the area authority was not actively opposed, it was feared that this would sacrifice many economies of scale achieved by AHAs, complicate relations with universities and local government, and obstruct the development and efficiency of community care. More important, since the *Patients First* scheme placed the HCHS administration at the district level, leaving the FPS at the area level, the two sectors could not be assimilated for the purpose of cash limits. The 1982 arrangements therefore constituted an obstacle to the extension of cash limits to the FPS, thereby preventing correction of a major anomaly and disrupting the government's drive for better value for money in the health service.

Even Jenkin's favourite ideas of decentralization and maximum local delegation ran into difficulties. It was felt that increasing the power of the district at the expense of the region was subversive to more effective management. Indeed, the devolution of power to some 200 local health authorities was regarded as a licence for inefficiency, a vice rendered more likely through rejection of management by chief executive, which 'was not compatible with the professional independence required by the wide range of staff employed in the Service'.[20] Despite the optimistic tone of *Patients First*, there was a widespread feeling that round one in the battle to implant market-oriented reforms had been decisively lost to the NHS power groups.[21] Sir Geoffrey Howe confided to a delegation of Conservative MPs that the 'attempt to create an independent and responsible lower tier organisation to administer health had in practice resulted in the worst of both worlds; the health authorities were not really independent or responsible yet neither were they under proper control from the centre'.[22] The 1982 changes therefore settled few of the long-standing ambiguities about department–region–district relations. *Patients First* was, therefore, even less of a stable blueprint for the future than the Secretary of State had anticipated.

The Management Revolution

Although *Patients First* was addressed to both 'structure and management', and throughout the document management improvement was frequently mentioned, it was in practice almost entirely concerned with structure. As in the case of Sir Keith Joseph's reforms, management by chief executive was decisively rejected; thereby *Patients First* perpetuated the increasingly criticized system of consensus management.[23] Understandably, although *Patients First* offered vague expectations of efficiency savings from the removal of the area tier, this was not seen as a fundamental contribution to improving management or increasing efficiency. In view of the cash crisis facing the NHS, there was an urgent necessity to explore other avenues for attaining efficiency objectives. Otherwise, health authorities would fall short of the higher output targets planned on the assumption of an increase in resources more than twice the level that actually materialized.[24]

The profusion of management initiatives instituted during the first term of the Thatcher administration belies any claim that the government was diffident about confronting the existing culture of the NHS. The measures undertaken varied greatly in the speed and extent of their impact, but this does not derogate from the scale of the effort, most of which represents application to the health service of initiatives originating elsewhere in the government services. The various management-policy developments were novel both in their character and in the manner of their formulation. Whereas all previous administrations had been reluctant to hazard even minor policy alterations without engaging in cumbersome and time-consuming routines involving expert committees and long spells of consultation with professional and NHS interests, the Thatcher team displayed greater self-confidence and faith in its own policy resources. When advice was needed, Mrs Thatcher relied on her levy of official and unofficial advisers; if wider enquiry was needed, this was delegated to some trusted individual or small team, usually drawn from the world of business, and the report was expected to be brief and expeditious. The extent of the Prime Minister's personal involvement in policy-making was itself without parallel. Because of her reliance on outside advisers, this gave a degree of power to certain business leaders that was itself exceptional. This manner of proceeding had some interesting consequences. For instance, it virtually eliminated the woman's voice, except of course for that of the Prime Minister. Social scientists were much less in evidence in ministerial entourages than previously. Also there was a great diminution in the power exercised by the BMA and its associates. The advice of doctors was taken to some extent, but these individuals tended to be drawn from the ranks of known political sympathizers. The medical profession remained a force to be reckoned with, but it was no longer able to exercise a stranglehold over the government's health policies.

Along with the new way of framing policy went new ways of presentation. The government responded to health-service and public suspicion concerning its policies by devoting more attention to persuasive methods of presentation, utilizing state-of-the-art methods of graphic design, and even introducing advanced audio-visual techniques as these became available. Beginning with such items as *Health Care and its Costs* of 1983, and the new-style *Health Service Annual Report* for 1984, health-department policy documents were refined to a minimum of text and maximum of visual display, the whole design possessing a thinly disguised propagandistic purpose.[25] As the decade wore on, the Thatcher camp became increasingly adept at exploiting the public-relations arts, mobilizing the media to spread alarm and build up disenchantment concerning the current state of the health service, and then to instil greater public confidence in the government's chosen market solutions.

Although the health service was not ripe for wholesale privatization, it seemed an ideal candidate for comprehensive application of the business methods associated with the New Public Management. The first steps in the long march of management upheaval were modest and uncontroversial and generally in line with the government's new Financial Management Initiative. An early intervention occurred in 1982, when ministers instituted an annual review of the performance of each region, while regions were ordered to monitor their districts with respect to a set of newly devised performance indicators. These reviews were partly designed as a defensive move against criticism by such bodies as the House of Commons Social Services Committee, which complained about absence of objective standards for assessing progress in reaching declared policy goals in fields such as community care, or lack of efficiency in the use of human and material resources.

This attention to monitoring the performance of health authorities spawned a variety of projects that constituted important preparatory steps towards the Griffiths reforms. Starting from a rather primitive baseline, active efforts were made to improve performance indicators, and further development work was undertaken on computerized financial management systems. Suggestions for simplification and standardization of basic data requirements and improved management information also emanated from a steering group on health-services information headed by Mrs Edith Körner, which was one of the government's earliest management initiatives, starting in 1980. The six final Körner reports were published in 1984. The Körner programme was wide-ranging, but its central feature comprised proposals for sets of standardized minimum data for each sphere of service activity, human resources, and financial information, with the general objective of improving the efficiency and effectiveness of management. Also relevant to the Griffiths reforms was the basic development work on clinical management budgeting that had been quietly building up since before the 1974 reorganization, without attracting much interest outside a small band of enthusiasts.

Beginning in 1981/2, health authorities were expected to contribute efficiency savings representing one-half per cent of their budgets annually. Although not much publicized, efficiency savings were expected to bear the cost of improvements in service associated with medical advance, which was ironical, since from the outset government scrutineers had suspected that the efficiency savings were being attained by cuts in services and reductions in standards of care, rather than in such areas as fuel efficiency, as was intended.[26]

Conservative Party activists regarded privatization as the greatest potential source of efficiency savings. This policy aimed to cut back domestic and ancillary staff, the numbers of whom had become swollen to about 240,000 in the early 1980s, which represented a threefold increase since the beginning of the health service. The increasing propensity of this group to industrial militancy had been demonstrated since the time of the Heath administration. Particularly fresh in the mind was the 1982 NHS national pay dispute, which had involved the greater part of the ancillary workforce and lost nearly 800,000 days of work, a total surpassed only by Labour's recent Winter of Discontent. Conservative enthusiasm for privatization therefore possessed the mixed objective of securing economies and offering opportunities for entrepreneurial gain, with the bonus of eroding the influence of health trade unions.

Much attention in Conservative circles was attracted by the claims of Michael Forsyth concerning the large scale of savings attainable from contracting out support services.[27] In 1982 only about 2 per cent of the spending on support services went to the private sector. The DHSS and health authorities were pessimistic about the prospects for savings and lethargic about entering into large-scale privatization without an extensive period of trials. Ministers nevertheless forced along the pace, and provided additional inducements to privatization through obstruction of capital schemes relating to support services. In September 1982 health authorities were instructed to engage in competitive tendering for support services. Although tendering was slow to develop and never resulted in wholesale privatization of support services, this policy had a marked effect on the health service. In the effort to compete with outside agencies, health authorities were forced to cut their costs to a minimum, so driving down wages and staff numbers; the ancillary and maintenance staff group experienced a dramatic and continuing fall in numbers down to about 100,000 in the late-1990s.

A further initiative dating from 1982 was the national inquiry undertaken under the auspices of Ceri Davies to identify surplus land and property, and devise incentives for health authorities to dispose of their surpluses. This issue had been addressed sporadically since the 1950s, without success. Among its effects, the Davies review resulted in the introduction of a system of notional rents for NHS property.

In 1982 the programme of efficiency scrutinies undertaken under the aegis of Sir Derek Rayner, joint managing-director of Marks & Spencer, was extended into the NHS and was applied to a variety of specific functions, most of them long known to be a source of inefficiency. The new Health Service Supply Council addressed another long-standing area of neglect and was expected to strengthen centralized arrangements for purchasing supplies, with the expectation of substantial gains from economies of scale.

Also in 1982 a full review of NHS auditing arrangements was conducted by a committee chaired by Patrick Salmon, which reported in 1983, and suggested a wide range of changes, including greater standardization and reference to value for money criteria. This initiative was associated with the introduction of pilot schemes for contracting out NHS auditing to private accountancy firms.

The cumulative effect of the review process and other changes listed above generally served to strengthen the role of the central department and the regions, increase uniformity, and reduce the latitude for independent action by the districts, which was, of course, in direct contravention to the devolutionist impulse represented by *Patients First*. Thus the government committed to rolling back the frontiers of the state found itself, in the health service as elsewhere, introducing a much greater degree of central supervision over field authorities than had ever before been contemplated.

Griffiths Management Reforms

The Griffiths Report of October 1983 represented the natural conclusion of the first wave of the government's campaign to reconstitute health-service management. 'Griffiths' soon became the dominant health-service eponym and the main defining influence on the health service of the Thatcher era. On the basis of this *coup*, Roy Griffiths, the main author of the report, shot into public prominence, became a major actor in health policy-making and a close adviser to Mrs Thatcher. As deputy chairman and managing-director of the grocery firm J. Sainsbury, Roy Griffiths was an obvious name to recruit for implanting sound business doctrine into a moribund public service. However, Griffiths was a more complex figure than his credentials suggest. His origins from a humble mining background and his experience of poverty in his early years engendered a positive attitude to the health service and the welfare state more generally. He was also directly acquainted with problems of the health service from members of his family who worked in the NHS. His interventions displayed an unpredictability, independence of outlook, and open-mindedness, not always attractive to the government, as demonstrated below with reference to his report on community care.

Griffiths' first report possessed both symbolic and practical importance. Somewhat unintentionally, it turned out to be the flagship of the reports produced by business teams advising the government. It drew together into a single document and consolidated into one programme a variety of only poorly coordinated antecedent management, manpower, and efficiency initiatives. Besides giving further incentive to existing policies, it struck a decisive blow at consensus management and revived the idea of disentangling NHS administration from Whitehall interference.

In its origins, the Griffiths initiative was more integrally related to preceding developments than seems evident at first sight. During the *Patients First* exercise it was appreciated that there was a strong argument for radical management reform in the health service. Sentiments expressed at this date not infrequently anticipated the *bon mots* of Griffiths himself—as, for instance, when Patrick Jenkin reported that 'It was recently said to me by a shrewd hospital head porter that there is too much administration and not enough management' in the health service.[28] However, there seems to be no obvious precedent for the even better-known and deservedly memorable lines from the Griffiths Report: 'if Florence Nightingale were carrying her lamp through the corridors of the NHS today, she would almost certainly be searching for the people in charge'.[29] Griffiths could hardly have been aware that his innocent historical allusion would set off further reverberations in the forthcoming management war.

At first, Jenkin applied the traditional nostrum to the management problem, by instituting yet another of the periodic campaigns to reduce the administrative and clerical costs. This action was consistent with the increasing sense of urgency concerning the more efficient use of human resources in the NHS. Given the dominant contribution of wages to the total NHS bill, it was clearly essential to place a brake on the seemingly endless growth in the NHS labour force and devise means for using existing human resources more economically. This problem drew attention to the primitive state of human-resources planning in the NHS. There was no uniform system of control and planning of staff numbers. Each sector was beset with argument concerning human-resources planning. As already noted, with respect to the large ancillary and domestic workforce, advocates of privatization held out the prospect of substantial reductions in their numbers. In connection with the Merrison Royal Commission, Maynard and Walker expressed scepticism about the Todd recommendations for a 4,000 annual intake into the medical schools, which they predicted was likely to have severe consequences for HCHS expenditure.[30] Both the medical profession and the government were uncertain over the wisdom of introducing controls designed to reduce the size of the medical workforce. Within the government, some believed that the competition of increased numbers would drive down costs; others argued that economies would not be attained without planned reduction in the expensive medical workforce. In nursing, which accounted for half of the NHS personnel, opinion was also divided over prospects for the future. The health departments believed that nursing staff were employed uneconomically and that improved planning would obviate the need for higher numbers of trained nurses.[31] The departments were also confident that any residual difficulties over recruitment would be corrected by the new review body for nursing pay modelled on the long-established review body for doctors and dentists. However, on the basis of continuing high levels of wastage and the anomalous status of student nurses, the Commission on Nursing Education, reflecting the views of nursing bodies, predicted that a disastrous shortage of skilled nursing personnel was imminent.

What was still called Manpower Planning therefore represented a problem of nightmarish proportions for health ministers. As a step to resolving this problem, in January 1983 ministers assumed central control of manpower numbers. In view of the need to speed up progress in dealing with this intractable problem, the government adopted its increasingly favoured device of an inquisition by a small business team, in this case headed by Roy Griffiths. This review began in February 1983; it proceeded with expedition, producing an interim report in June, and its final report in October. Initially it was not the intention to publish this report, and indeed somewhat unconventionally it was written in the form of a letter to the Secretary of State from Griffiths on behalf of his team. In the event, the government decided on publication and this occurred on 25 October 1983. The government's proposals for what amounted to full implementation of the Griffiths Report were announced in June 1984 after a period of agitated consultation, during which it became evident that there was little support within the health service for the Griffiths package, apart from among senior administrative staff.

The best-known recommendation of the Griffiths Report was for the scrapping of consensus management and for its replacement by a system of general management applying at all levels in the health service. This was indeed the most original, controversial, and far-reaching of the recommendations, but this bias of emphasis in the report was by no means predictable at the outset of the inquiry.

As rightly stressed by Harrison, the Griffiths terms of reference were vague and confused, but the common denominator of documentation relating to its inception was concern over the effective use and management of manpower; the committee was selected on this basis.[32] In March 1983, with characteristic imprecision, the health department described the Griffiths Committee as a response to concern about NHS *manpower levels*. To meet expressions of alarm by parliamentary bodies, the government was creating a special inquiry into NHS *management* that would be 'able to investigate NHS *resource use* as fully as its members think necessary, and advise on what further *management* action is needed'.[33] From the moment of its inception, the Griffiths team was known as the 'Management Inquiry', which itself was open to a variety of interpretations, and press comment on its activities found difficulty in locating a centre of gravity for its operations. This laxity over the remit of Griffiths rather suggests that this exercise was not regarded as possessing quite the degree of importance that it ultimately assumed.

Reflecting its vague remit, the Griffiths Report touched briefly and with approval on almost all the management and efficiency measures described above, including the trend towards devolution of management responsibility to the unit level. Among the special points of emphasis, it recommended the development of efficiency saving schemes into Cost Improvement Programmes, which would introduce efficiency without involving cuts in services. Also, in order to involve clinicians more closely in the efficiency drive, it was proposed greatly to extend the application of clinical management budgets. Since clinical management budgeting was in its infancy, this could not be extended without further trials and research into the various alternative systems of implementation. This attempt to involve doctors and nurses in using financial and other management information for the purposes of achieving more effective use of resources was given a new boost in 1986 with the official launch of the Resource Management Initiative.

In the course of the next few years, the Resource Management Initiative became what the Cogwheel initiatives on the management of medical work in hospitals had been to an earlier generation of the health service, and its experiments with such innovations as clinical directorates was anticipated by Cogwheel. Partly because of technical difficulties in establishing the experiments, partly on account of lack of conclusive evidence concerning benefits to patients, the Resource Management Initiative never fully commanded the confidence of clinician opinion-formers. As noted below, this unproven instrument nevertheless became accepted by the government and was extended on account of its utility in implementation of the internal market.

Despite its fussy radicalism, the Griffiths Report was circumspect in its proposals relating to the central department. The logic of its position suggested that Griffiths should have favoured hiving off the NHS to an independent corporation, an idea considered and rejected at every health-service reorganization. This idea had also been considered sympathetically by the Merrison Royal Commission Report, but this recommendation was rejected by the government. The Commission had also been favourable to granting regional authorities the status of mini-corporations. This idea was promoted by the regional authorities, led by one of their chairmen, who became a leading member of the Griffiths Committee; but this also was rejected by the government.

In deference to the known objections of the health departments to an independent corporation, Griffiths proposed a compromise arrangement, which led to the creation of a central framework intended to achieve some of the objects of a statutory corporation.

This comprised two central bodies, the Health Services Supervisory Board and the NHS Management Board; the former was charged with strategic oversight and control over the Management Board, which would be concerned with detailed implementation of agreed policy. The Achilles' heel of this arrangement lay in the ambiguity over distribution of power between the two boards and the civil servants in the health department, the problem that lay at the heart of the government's traditional objection to an independent corporation.

This artificial construct exactly epitomized the vices of overcomplexity and confused relations that Griffiths was supposed to be correcting. The Nightingale lamp was likely to search in vain for the true seat of authority within this labyrinth. To reduce the confusion, after a short trial the Health Services Supervisory Board was painlessly dispatched. This placed the onus on the second central body, the NHS Management Board. The awful ambiguity over the distribution of power loomed just as large, but the tension was now transferred to relations between the fledgling NHS Management Board and the entrenched interests of the health department, which represented an uneven contest in view of the subtle capacity of the officials to prevent erosion of their power.

As inheritor of the mantel of the central-board concept, the NHS Management Board failed to achieve anything like the degree of authority or autonomy originally envisaged. It is therefore scarcely surprising that the first businessman Chairman of the Management Board lasted for only eighteen months. He was then replaced by the Secretary of State's subordinate, the Minister for Health, which represented a further retreat from the idea of autonomy, and was a step towards drawing the board firmly back under the wings of the Whitehall Department.

Soon the Management Board became the target of precisely the criticisms that had been the downfall of the ill-fated Supervisory Board. The Management Board failed to engage with important issues upon which NHS authorities were desperate for guidance. The board was also impaired by virtue of its limitation to the HCHS sector. It was reported that the board oscillated 'between a committee which ministers want to run and one which they and their civil servants want to keep at a distance and even to criticise'. In the light of such lack of definition of purpose, the Management Board was judged by an informed source as a 'complete and utter disaster'.[34] Given the failure to resolve relationships between the Management Board and the central department, it was inevitable that the question of hiving off the health service to an independent corporation would be resurrected. This occasion arose sooner than expected, with the government's Next Steps initiative of 1988, which aimed to maximize the devolution of government activity to independent agencies. This ensured that the independent corporation idea would be reconsidered in the context of the Thatcher review and the associated internal market reforms.

As already noted, the most radical and contentious part of the Griffiths proposals related to the ending of consensus management and its replacement by a system of general management at regional, district, and unit levels. Consensus management was liked by doctors on account of the high degree of control that they exercised, and by nurses because it had elevated their status in the management structure. Neither looked forward to relinquishing this authority. Nurses in particular were sensitive to the loss of hard-won status gained as recently as 1974. Although in principle it was possible for these groups to gain appointment as general managers, it was appreciated that this was unlikely to be a frequent event in practice. This was rendered even more unlikely, since the new breed of general managers was employed on fixed-term contracts and pay was performance-related. Despite much talk of recruitment from business, as with the 1974 reorganization, most management appointments went to senior administrators or treasurers of the authorities in which they already worked. In the first waves of general-manager appointments, only about 10 per cent of posts went to nurses and 12 per cent to outsiders.

From the outset, the Griffiths reforms were suspect among all groups within the health service except administrators. However, the opposition was fragmented and ineffectual. The BMA made bellicose noises but offered no effective resistance. Action by the unions was inhibited by the recent fate of the miners and memory of their own ignominious humiliation during the 1982 industrial dispute. The Royal College of Nursing, whose members had much to lose, failed to take action until 1986, when it embarked on an expensive publicity campaign, employing the image of Florence Nightingale against Griffiths, but this came to nothing.

Although general managers were undoubtedly more authoritative and prosperous than earlier generations of senior administrators and were thereby liable to become an object of scorn and jealousy, they proved not to be quite the draconian force feared at the outset, especially with respect to their medical colleagues. The position of greater influence and accountability in the general-management hierarchy of senior managers altered their relationship with health authorities and their chairmen, who were gradually but perceptibly marginalized and reduced to the level of rubber stamps to an even greater degree than previously. The 1983 Griffiths management reform package therefore played its part in throwing doubt on the viability and necessity of the regional–district health-authority structure established in 1982.

The Griffiths management reform was accordingly not a stable arrangement. Within the health service it continued to be treated with suspicion by most of the workforce; even among its friends, it was regarded as a step to further change. Radicals on the right suspected that the new general managers were merely token rulers, with no effective power, owing to their habitual deference to the medical profession. Professor Enthoven, the government's new friend, complained that general management had not been tested scientifically and he urged that, in the absence of market incentives, general managers would be just as insensitive to improving efficiency as the consensus teams they had superseded.

Family Practitioner Services

During the 1970s the government's armoury of expenditure controls and management reforms had been effective in bringing the HCHS under a much stronger regime of containment. Any satisfaction at this achievement was offset by irritation and embarrassment over the failure to achieve anything like the same degree of control over the independent-contractor services. The purchasing power of the FPS sector increased at twice the rate of the HCHS sector in the course of the 1980s. Management reforms, manpower controls, and economy measures imposed elsewhere were noticeably absent among the independent contractors. The numbers employed in most parts of the FPS drifted upwards in an unplanned manner. The already inflated drug bill rose more rapidly than the cost of any other function in the health service. To add to the indignity of this situation, owing to forecasting errors, the FPS regularly exceeded their estimates.

The demand-led character of the FPS was advantageous to the patient, especially because it enabled general practitioners to take up functions laid down by the cash-strapped HCHS sector. The Treasury regarded this situation as an affront; it endowed its expenditure controls with the character of a leaking sieve. Independent contractors had successfully thwarted all previous attempts to tighten up the system. The arrangement under which the practitioners were employed as independent contractors greatly strengthened their position; other features, such as weak local management structures, or the diverse and complex contract system under which the various practitioners were employed, added to the difficulties of containment. The associations representing the independent contractors were also notoriously aggressive in the defence of their clients. In the health departments, negotiating with independent contractors was therefore a torment akin to grappling with Hydra.

The Thatcher government was more unsympathetic than its predecessors with the professional monopolies and it approached their containment in a determined manner. As already noted, success was encountered in deregulating the ophthalmic profession and ending the supply of spectacles under the NHS for the majority of the population. In the course of the 1980s, the government entered into discussions with all groups of independent contractors over their contracts. These were in every case renegotiated, but, in the case of pharmacists, dentists, and general practitioners, the result was much less spectacular than the government wanted and in the main ended in yet a further stalemate.

Higher health-service charges were calculated to depress demand and produce a small yield for the exchequer, but this expedient was always fraught with political difficulty and was a blunt instrument of control, effectively leaving the vices of unsound systems in place. The government was determined to prevent independent contractors from continuing to draw on public funds without more effective control.

The main anxieties of the government related to general medical practitioners and the pharmaceutical bill which these practitioners effectively determined. These items accounted for the major part of FPS spending. Ideally the government aspired to impose a joint HCHS–FPS cash limit, which would have ensured that continuing indiscipline on the part of the independent contractors would have entailed countervailing cuts in the hospital and community sector. This was clearly a difficult path to follow since it would have caused injustice, but the Treasury hoped that such a system would force the DHSS to tighten up on its management of the family practitioners and prevent them from exceeding their estimates. As already pointed out, this objective was effectively undermined by the administrative split between DHAs and FPCs introduced in the *Patients First* reforms.

Desperate for some early success, the government returned to the question of excess profits by the pharmaceutical companies. Without much expectation of victory, it launched into further negotiations with the industry with a view to tightening up the Pharmaceutical Price Regulation Scheme. As on previous occasions this turned out to be a time-consuming way of achieving very little, which exposed the health departments to yet further criticism from the Public Accounts Committee. In order to save face, the government retreated into attempting to control the expenditure of the pharmaceutical companies on sales promotion. It was not until 1994 that regulations were introduced to prevent general practitioners accepting the more blatant financial inducements from drug sales staff, but these controls were even then not effectively implemented.

A seemingly more feasible option was promotion of moves towards generic prescribing or generic substitution. In 1982 the press contained much speculation about the large savings that could be made if even a small number of widely used drugs were replaced by their generic equivalents. The press speculated that annual savings might be as high as £170 million; the Association of the British Pharmaceutical Industry urged that £50 million represented the maximum possible saving, while the health departments estimated an even lower figure. Even modest estimates rendered the exercise worth pursuing. In 1983 the Labour MP Laurie Pavitt introduced a Private Member's Bill to promote generic substitution. Evidence that this substitution practice was already widely applied in hospitals and in a few local cases of cooperation between chemists and general practitioners gave hope to the reformers. The report of the Greenfield working group on effective prescribing published in February 1983 provided a further boost to this idea. Having prepared itself for a fight, the government suddenly dropped its case, partly on account of opposition from the BMA, but more likely because the price-regulation scheme contained nothing to prevent the companies from restructuring their prices to compensate for any reductions in profits due to imposition of generic prescription or substitution.

The next idea was to revive the old proposal for a limited list. The medical profession was opposed to this idea for very much the same reasons that it had fought obligatory generic prescribing or substitution on account of alleged restriction of the traditional freedom to practise. Under pressure to achieve some tangible saving, in November 1984 Norman Fowler announced that minor limitations in prescribing would be introduced, with the effect of excluding remedies for minor ailments. The BMA and pharmaceutical industry again joined forces to spread alarm concerning the dangers of the limited list. Under duress the government compromised and reduced the prohibited list, so cutting the anticipated saving by about a quarter when the measure was introduced in February 1985. The savings were insufficient to make more than a minor indentation in the drug bill, which continued to grow, now at the rate of about 6 per cent a year, which was even higher than in the previous decade. This necessitated a further drive to achieve more economic prescribing by the traditional method of exhortation. This was itself merely a brief intermission pending the imposition of an indicative drug budget in connection with the 1990 contract.

In the effort to avoid ignominy and regain the initiative in its efficiency drive, the government turned for inspiration to outside consultants. On this occasion, the chosen instrument was a team from the accountants Binder Hamlyn. In July 1982 it was announced that the accountants would conduct a review of forecasting and controlling expenditure on the FPS, which seemed like a largely technical exercise, although in fact it was designed for the important purpose of preparing the ground for imposition of cash limits. The Binder Hamlyn Report was completed in the summer of 1983. This report proved less helpful on cash limits than had been expected, but it produced a wide range of other proposals for management and financial controls relating to each part of the FPS, most of which were expected to be controversial, while many of them had legislative implications.

After a great deal of equivocation, it was decided that the Binder Hamlyn Report required careful packaging in order to avoid inflaming feeling among the independent contractors. The accountants' work was therefore quietly buried and it was replaced by government planning documents, the main aim of which was to institute renegotiation of the contracts of the independent contractors, a policy which seemed to offer the best prospects for efficiency savings, but only in the long term.

The effect of this change of tactics was greatly to slow down the efficiency operation and cause the steady erosion of the more radical ideas derived from the Binder Hamlyn exercise. The tentative thoughts of the government were expressed in the Green Paper *Primary Health Care: An Agenda for Discussion*, published in April 1986; these proposals reappeared in further watered-down form in the White Paper *Promoting Better Health* in November 1987. The government's public-relations machine made the fullest effort to present these planning documents in the most altruistic light—for instance, by drawing on the most recent internationally inspired thinking on the development of primary care, especially the World Health Organization's 'Health for All by the Year 2000' initiative. The design of this model for the Developing World context made it also appealing to a Western government looking for a means to cut expenditure and legitimate its campaign to bring independent contractors under more effective regulation. The idea of 'general-practitioner-led' primary care was also a useful holdall for other purposes—for instance, indicating the government's commitment to filling the vacuum left by the collapse of the public-health medicine speciality, many of the functions of which, from dealing with

HIV/AIDS to health education, could be designated as part of the expanded scope of the primary-care team. Reflecting further response to WHO stimulus, the primary-care team was coopted to play a leading part in the five areas of action for health improvement announced in the government's *Health of the Nation* strategy launched in 1991 and designed to display to the international community the soundness of the government's credentials in the field of prevention.

Needless to say, the primary-care veneer was thin and selective in its content, but it at least conveyed the impression that the government was making an effort to shift the independent contractors to centre stage in the health service. The government also instigated token inducements to assist with consumer satisfaction, such as improvement of information available about practices, a simplified complaints procedure, and allowing patients to change doctor more easily. Naturally, the government's intention to end free eye tests and dental checks was less attractive to the consumers, not consistent with enlightened thinking on primary care, and unlikely to be helpful in improving the preventive record. Significantly, dental and eye health were excluded from the target areas for improvement in the *Health of the Nation* exercise.

The central core of the government's primary-care proposals was self-evidently related to its wider drive for management reform and greater value for money. The Green Paper, and, to an added extent, the White Paper, proposed substantial strengthening of the management functions of FPCs. These were notoriously weak organs of administration, even after the legislation of 1985 giving belated effect to the *Patients First* family-practitioner reforms. Their inferiority was even more evident when the Griffiths reforms took effect in the HCHS sector. The government insisted in strengthening their power to manage the service and monitor the performance of the independent contractors. This evolution to a new level of management authority was finally confirmed when the FPCs were converted into Family Health Service Authorities (FHSAs) in September 1990 in the course of implementation of the *Working for Patients* changes.

The central proposals of the primary-care planning documents related to contractual issues, most of which had been under negotiation for many years. In the case of the dentists there was a long-running controversy that was not finally resolved until 1997. An influential minority of dentists remained convinced that the agreed contract was completely inappropriate, while the new arrangements also contained some nasty punitive measures directed at the patient.

Although presented as an exciting concept and a new deal, the government's proposals for the general medical practitioner contract remained tied to the conceptual framework of the 1966 contract, and indeed in some respects they looked back to 1948. Having in 1966 shifted general practitioners' remuneration away from the capitation system, the government now reversed this trend. By scaling down the salary components and proportionately increasing the payment based on numbers on the list, the government aimed to give inducements to greater activity and increased competition. Capitation was also attractive to the government on account of being the form of payment most subject to cost control. On the other hand, it was insensitive to the amount or quality of care, which was the reason for its dislike among progressive doctors under the panel system and during the early NHS, when large-list doctors collected big incomes for little work, while conscientious practitioners with small lists were poorly remunerated. Capitation was a move towards the fashionable Health Maintenance Organization (HMO) model, but it also threatened to shift general practice back to the dark ages of big lists and impersonal service.

The switch to capitation necessitated measures to counteract any temptations to laxity in performance. In a few instances where monitoring was easy, it was proposed to relate rewards to direct or indirect measurements reflecting the quality of care. The payment system was designed to encourage partnerships and discourage deputizing services. Population targets were adopted for certain preventive services such as immunizations and cervical cytology. Fees were offered for examination of new patients, for regular checks on the over-75s, and for clinics of various types.

After the earlier largely unsuccessful attempts to contain the drug budget described above, the government proposed the more radical option of moving towards limits on spending by means of an indicative budget. Not only this, but other aspects of the new contract were made easier to implement by advances in information technology.

On account of the alien origins of the contract and in accordance with its habitual robust negotiating style, the BMA insisted on substantial modifications, especially with respect to the powers of FPCs, capitation, population targets, and the indicative drug budget. Negotiations extending from March 1988 to May 1989 hammered out an agreement involving some minor concessions. However, the new contract was rejected by the rank and file, who demanded further concessions, but these were not granted and the new contract was imposed in April 1990. The profession expressed noisy antagonism, but the members were unwilling to take action in defence of their position. This was ostensibly a humiliation for the BMA, and implied that the government would be emboldened to impose further unpalatable changes on the health service in the face of professional opposition.

In the mode of its genesis and implementation the new contract was a contrast with the 1966 exercise, but the extent of disadvantage to the profession was less than suggested by its rhetoric. Most of the government's more radical ideas were scrapped even before the Green Paper was published and were replaced by proposals thought to be congenial to the profession. Consequently, rumours that controls would be placed on the numbers of general practitioners or subsidized practice staff proved to be unfounded. The initial idea of 100 per cent capitation was replaced by 60 per cent. The balance of advantage of the new contract therefore rested firmly on the side of the general practitioners.

In the event, the new contract served a similar function to the 1966 contract; it was a boost to both the status and the income of general practitioners. Their position was strengthened in other respects. The Cumberlege Report, *Neighbourhood Nursing—A Focus for Care*, published in April 1986, seriously questioned the dominance of general practitioners in the primary-care team, promoted the idea of independent neighbourhood teams of community nursing professionals, and advocated a more pluralistic concept of primary care. This approach had been developing since the 1970s, but it was not actively encouraged by the government, and the

Cumberlege philosophy was not allowed to become an impediment to the dominance of general practitioners.

Although the government wished that general practitioners were cheaper, their role as gatekeepers to the hospital service was recognized as an indispensable means to economy in the British system of health care. On this account the gatekeepers were deemed deserving of generous treatment and they were destined for even more substantial rewards as a consequence of the *Working for Patients* reforms.

Working for Patients

Although the management changes described above amounted to a formidable programme of action, they completely failed to generate a sense of well-being within the health service. This was due partly to the intrinsic limitations of the changes themselves, and partly to the worsening resource situation. Even the new general managers accepted that the limited economies and gains in efficiency derived from the management changes were nothing like sufficient to compensate for the estimated funding shortfall.

There were only two ways to resolve this dilemma, either release of additional resources, or a further and more radical overhaul of the service. After much vacillation the Thatcher administration fell back upon the option of further structural change, the proposals for which were announced in the White Paper, *Working for Patients*, published in January 1989. However, this failed to extricate the government from its dilemma over funding; the proposals for overhauling the health service merely reinforced the case for more resources. A further substantial increment in expenditure was incurred, but without any tangible prospect that the new system would yield economies even in the medium term.

As with the management and family-practitioner reforms described above, the market changes came about by a more unpredictable and indirect route than might have been anticipated. The main source for the Thatcher review was the increasing state of turmoil over the funding of the health service. This problem was already looming up during preparations for the 1987 general election. As already noted, the more radical element in the Thatcher camp was irritated that the 1987 general election was not taken as an opportunity to announce sweeping alteration of the health service, consistent with the ambitious changes proposed for education and housing. The innovators were especially keen on abandoning the current method of funding in favour of transfer to an insurance alternative. For four reasons Conservative Party managers firmly rejected plunging into a major review of the NHS, even in a third term of office. First, it was hoped that policy measures already in train would prove sufficient; secondly, the party lacked any agreed policy on the way forward to improve the situation; thirdly, the commitment to reform of education, housing, and local government left no space for further efforts on the welfare-state front; finally, since their suggestions for change were likely to be contentious and unpopular, they needed as much advanced preparation as possible. Therefore this toughest of assignments was best left to the fourth term.

Unfortunately for the government, the funding problem resurfaced immediately after the election, when in July 1987 the House of Commons Social Services Committee produced a compelling critique of the government's spending record, and demanded steps to make up for the shortfall in that year estimated at about £450 million, and thereafter ensure that resources were increased at a rate of 2 per cent with reference to the NHS price index. The Social Services Committee insisted that Whitley settlements should be met in full with addition to the cash limits where necessary and that additional resources should be provided to safeguard medical advances and teaching commitments, and it also asked for correction of the slippage in the hospital construction programme. The Social Services Committee was not entirely flattering about the government's management and efficiency innovations; it also used the sudden and unexpected resignation of Mr Victor Paige, the first Chairman of the NHS Management Board, to rub salt into the government's wounds.[35]

There is every reason to believe that John Moore, the new Secretary of State, was aware of the need for action. On the basis of the UK's low level of expenditure on health care compared with its OECD neighbours, he was convinced that only greatly increased investment of resources would resolve the crisis within the health service, which inevitably implied consideration of major policy initiatives, including alternative funding options. As early as July 1987, it seems as if Moore's suggestion for a review of health-service policy was rejected by the Prime Minister.[36] Discussions between the Treasury and the DHSS concerning the feasibility of policy reviews continued at a lower key, and the No. 10 Downing Street policy unit also became engaged in this operation.[37]

Continuing vacillation on the part of the government attracted adverse comment at the time of the 1987 Conservative Party Annual Conference. Moore's performance angered both left and right. The likelihood of disaster was increased by evidence of Moore's acceptance of an adverse financial settlement for the year 1988/9. The effect of the existing squeeze on resources and suspicions about even greater expenditure constraints in the future engendered an atmosphere of alarm, unprecedented even by the crisis-prone standards of the health service. Throughout England, NHS authorities began folding up their services; for the first time even emergency care was under threat. The media reported these events in full and publicized alarming examples of individual distress, the best known of which related to the death of the Birmingham baby David Barber, after repeated cancellations of surgery for a cardiac condition. The government exacerbated public rage by the poor timing of publication of its primary-care White Paper, which announced the introduction of charges for dental checks and eye-sight tests. To the applause of the public, health workers took to the streets in protest; both nurses and blood-transfusion workers began strike action over industrial-relations grievances. In a rare expression of united action, the Presidents of three Royal Colleges issued an urgent call for additional resources for the health service. These alarming developments were reflected in parliament, where unrest spread to the government backbenches. All the relevant parliamentary investigative agencies began preparations for fresh inquiries into the NHS financial situation. Finally, the government's plight was compounded by the illness of Moore, which impaired his performance at the height of the crisis.

The government's response to this crisis was inadequate and counterproductive. Embattled ministers fluctuated between token concessions and bad-tempered attacks on health-service managers and consultants. With increasing difficulty, health ministers tried to maintain the line that neither additional funds nor policy changes were required. Given the collapse of public confidence, it was unrealistic to persist with the administration's preferred course of deferring action until a speculative next term of office.

There is every indication that Mrs Thatcher was a late and reluctant convert to the idea of radical interference with the health service. This was one of the few areas of policy where she judged that it was best to leave well alone. Even with a strong electoral mandate, especially in the light of warning signs concerning such policies as the poll tax, Mrs Thatcher was apprehensive about handing the opposition a golden opportunity to regain its legitimacy.

As suggested above, Mr Moore and his allies were in favour of grasping the nettle of alternative funding at the outset of the third term. By mid-December 1987 the press was awash with stories that senior ministers were convinced that it was not practicable to delay a review of funding. Ambiguities in the representations made by the Presidents of the Royal Colleges suggested that the medical profession was at last ready for radical expedients. Sensing that their time had come, Conservative think-tank activists polished up their draft pamphlets in preparation for a grand assault, and advanced information from these, couched in suitably ominous tones, was liberally sprinkled about in the press.

In December 1987 the No. 10 Downing Street policy unit became more actively involved in preparations for a review. The final decision to upgrade interdepartmental discussions into a full-scale review of the health service was taken in January 1988. In the campaign to bring Mrs Thatcher on board, the *Spectator* included a prominent piece by a doctor calling for a new Florence Nightingale to save England's hospitals from dereliction. The author mused rhetorically whether 'she is already in Downing Street'.[38] This entreaty was reinforced by a front-cover cartoon in which a ghostly figure, putatively evocative of both Nightingale and Thatcher, hovered expectantly in the dirty corridors of a NHS hospital.

By 23 January the press was alert to the imminence of an announcement concerning a high-level review, which it speculated would be confidential and comparable to the Griffiths management exercise in its importance.[39] On this date the *Spectator* urged the Prime Minister to eschew the role of cautious caretaker for which she was ill suited. Her committee needed to expose the full bankruptcy of the existing conception of the NHS. Mrs Thatcher was also advised to conduct the argument of her review in public in order to prove how flimsy was the case for the existing form of health service.[40]

The final decision to hold a high-level inquiry into the NHS was announced by the Prime Minister on 25 January 1988 in the somewhat unconventional context of the BBC television programme *Panorama*. The mode of inquiry was also unusual, the form adopted being a small group of ministers, together with a few others, including Sir Roy Griffiths, and headed by the Prime Minister. This formula was designed to allow examination of the problems of the NHS in conditions of strict secrecy, avoiding embarrassing leaks of the kind that had occurred in 1982 when the NHS funding issue had been referred to the whole Cabinet. An important change in the review team occurred in July 1988, when the DHSS was split into its component parts; Kenneth Clarke entered discussions as Secretary of State for Health, which helped to breathe new life into the review, and shed the reputation for failure that overhung Mr Moore. Ministers representing Scotland, Wales, and Northern Ireland were not consulted until near the end of the exercise.

The Thatcher review was tolerably confidential, but evidently well-founded rumours enabled its course to be charted. The exercise was accompanied by pamphleteering on a level of intensity unprecedented since the debate surrounding the establishment of the NHS. However, on this later occasion the stage was entirely dominated by the political right.

Naturally the funding issue dominated early deliberations and pamphlets from the think tanks initially concentrated on this issue.[41] Some of the alternatives, such as extension of direct charges or increasing the NHS Contribution, were old favourites capable of immediate implementation, but limited in their scope for well-known political and practical reasons; others, such as voluntary insurance, were at best a distant prospect. The ministerial team religiously examined all options, ploughing through the rich assortment of plans for a hypothecated health tax, extension of vouchers, topping-up payments, tax credits, opting out, etc. emanating from the petitioners. By a laborious process of attrition the options were whittled down to almost nothing. Mrs Thatcher and Mr Moore continued to advocate extending tax concessions to encourage private insurance, but, as already noted, this was unacceptable to the Treasury. In the final recommendations, the only trace left by this reappraisal of funding was the tax concession granted to the elderly investing in non-corporate health-insurance schemes.

The entry of Kenneth Clarke put a final end to gossip about alternative funding or tax concessions to boost the private sector. Clarke reverted to the thinking that had been dominant during his term as Minister for Health between 1982 and 1985, the era of the management reforms. Even before Clarke's arrival, realists among the radicals had appreciated that alternative funding represented a blind alley. They therefore deftly shifted their ground and trawled around for alternative ways of retrieving their reformist objectives.

The unlikely source of rescue was a social scientist, but in this case the maverick American systems analyst, Professor Alain Enthoven, who, after cutting his teeth on the military disaster of the Vietnam War, turned to health care, became an advocate of managed competition and passionate publicist for HMOs. UK observers were by no means ignorant of HMOs; indeed in 1985 the DHSS had sponsored a visit to the USA to appraise their relevance for the UK situation. The model was regarded as an advance on some alternatives in the USA, but HMOs were not regarded as transferable to the UK. Accumulation of adverse reactions concerning HMOs in the American literature further dampened down enthusiasm for this idea. However, Enthoven managed to attract some support in the UK, especially among those inclined to reach across the Atlantic for salvation. An early lay enthusiast was Norman Macrae, whose long and pessimistic account of the NHS concluded that, for the purposes of reform, 'the key is Enthoven'.[42] Enthoven was given a chance to shine when he was brought over by the NPHT for an extensive visit to St Catherine's College, Oxford, which incidentally had earlier acted as host to Ivan Illich. Enthoven's practical proposals for reconstructing the health service were much less radical than his reputation or rhetoric implied. He advocated a gradualist approach based upon experiment and he even complained that changes like the Griffiths reforms had been introduced without prior experiment. He echoed the common call for increased incentives to encourage good performance or improvements in productivity. His original contribution was to call for development of an 'internal market' in the NHS, although the changes he suggested were relatively modest and again subject to trial. He suggested that a DHA might purchase care for its residents outside the district where cost-effective services were provided, or a lesser option of trading between districts. Enthoven also called for introduction of greater efficiency incentives for medical staffs and specific hospital services.[43]

Although his plan was taken up by the Social Democratic Party, the immediate impact of Enthoven was slight on account of many politically objectionable features of his scheme and doubts as to whether it would in reality embody sufficient incentive for DHAs to seek out more cost-effective services.[44] The Enthoven plan was, for instance, decisively rejected by the NHS Management Board.[45] A parallel, more radical, and rigorously defined proposal for an internal market operated through budget-holding general practitioners, who would secure services on behalf of their patients from hospitals of their choice, emanated from a group of prominent general practitioners and health economists.[46] Various permutations of the internal market idea were discussed in the run-up to the Thatcher review. This idea was also known to be attractive to Mrs Thatcher since it represented a way of ensuring that 'money would follow the patient', which became a favourite catchphrase of reformers.

Once the Thatcher review threw its funding exercise overboard, the internal market assumed centre stage. Although this concept had altered considerably since Enthoven, his name remained attached, possibly in line with the Thatcher partiality for good ideas with American credentials.

The internal market was naturally attractive to the government's advisers, who were being pressed hard to come up with management and structural reforms capable of yielding big efficiency gains. On this occasion they had stumbled upon an idea capable of attracting support in medical circles among groups frustrated with limitations imposed by the NHS bureaucracy. Many general practitioners aspired to break free of FPCs and control their own budgets; consultants, especially in teaching hospitals, resented the intrusion of district and regional authorities, and looked back with affection to the days of independent Boards of Governors, indeed even to their voluntary hospital precursors. The radicals and their fifth column in the health service had therefore hit upon a device that was capable of unscrambling the entire structure of health-service bureaucracy and reducing the NHS to a disaggregated market containing a diversity of purchasers and providers, whose competitive transactions would generate economies in public expenditure, without detracting from the financial rewards of the successful entrepreneurs.

In order to promote this audacious plan, Nightingale iconology was yet again mobilized. On 30 April 1988 *The Economist* included an article headed 'Set the Hospitals Free', which promoted a scheme containing most of the elements in the plan subsequently adopted by the government.[47] The front cover of *The Economist* reproduced the famous Scutari engraving showing Florence Nightingale with her lamp surrounded by desperate wounded soldiers, but the face of the nurse was that of Mrs Thatcher.

The pamphleteers now devoted their main energies to promoting the internal market, under the banner of 'separating the running of hospitals from their financing'. This purchaser/provider split was also accepted as a feasible option by The Institute of Health Services Management.[48] Indeed, the East Anglia region already had information systems in place to permit operation of an internal market under the existing mode of organization. It therefore seemed quite possible that the health service would move in this direction of its own volition under the impulse of existing management changes.

The outlines of the scheme eventually adopted by the government were therefore evident even before Clarke became Secretary of State. The last half of 1988 was spent in fine-tuning this scheme, a process itself fraught with difficulty owing to the wide range of options available, the technical complexity of the market system, and the political sensitivity of the issues involved. Residual arguments about tax relief for private health insurance also continued up to the last moment. Although many of the press rumours about the outcome of the Thatcher review were off the mark, the better-informed sources gave accurate advance warning concerning the outcome.[49] The leaks achieved certainty when the draft White Paper was widely and repeatedly leaked during the month before publication.

The fruits of the health-service review emerged in the form of the White Paper, *Working for Patients*, published on 31 January 1989.[50] These proposals were described by the Prime Minister as the 'most far-reaching reform of the National Health Service in its forty year history'.[51] Indicative of the importance attached to this policy statement, this was the first occasion upon which a Prime Minister had written an introduction to a health-service planning document.

Despite the lurid headlines, where friends and foes alike represented the White Paper as a fundamental turning point in the history of the health service, the package itself was an odd amalgam of the cautious, the evolutionary, the radical, and the ambiguous, therefore giving opportunity for a variety of constructions regarding the likely outcome of the new policy document. At the opening of his parliamentary statement, Kenneth Clarke placed the emphasis on continuity rather than upheaval; the proposals were built upon and evolved from improvements over the last ten years. They therefore reflected 'a change of pace rather than any fundamental change of direction'.[52]

Although *Working for Patients* promised radical changes and is remembered as the unveiling of proposals for an internal market, this term and its synonyms were noticeably absent from the text. Instead, the document discreetly advertised the benefits of local delegation (more rarely 'competition'); these changes, it was promised, would bring about both efficiency and greater consumer satisfaction.[53]

By contrast with all previous reorganizations, the 1989 proposals operated within the existing statutory framework. The hierarchies of NHS administration were left basically untouched. The regional and district health authorities, the family-practitioner administration, and the CHCs were expected to continue as before, albeit with subtle alterations in their relationships and a radical reduction of functions in the case of district authorities. Some of the changes relating to health authorities reinforced ongoing evolutionary trends—for instance, in the case of emphasis on the monitoring role of the regions, the increasing management role of the FPCs, or the adoption of a business model of executive and non-executive membership for health authorities, with virtual elimination of local-authority and professional representation. Mrs Thatcher, having begun her administration with an onslaught on advisory and protective quangos, ended her prime-ministerial career by placing a new generation of quangos at the heart of the administrative system.

Other proposals in the White Paper represented a continuation of existing management initiatives, such as the acceleration of the Resource Management Initiative, the universal application of medical audit, and the improvement of general audit arrangements by giving the Audit Commission access to all parts of the NHS. Ideas about expanding consultant numbers, reforming the distinction award system, reducing the hours of work of junior hospital doctors, or tightening up on the contract of consultants, were addressed to old problems that had defied solution for decades. Finally, the changes applying to family practitioners were consistent with proposals in the recent *Promoting Better Health* White Paper.

Continuity was also evident with respect to proposals concerning the central department, where there was an attempt to restore the structure envisaged by Griffiths, with a new NHS Policy Board chaired by the Secretary of State fulfilling the functions originally envisaged for the defunct Supervisory Board, and an NHS Management Executive chaired by a chief executive replacing the existing Management Board chaired by a minister.

In a highly significant departure from existing policies, major hospitals were offered the possibility of opting out of DHA control to form self-governing 'NHS Hospital Trusts', which would be given considerable discretion over their own affairs. The remaining hospital and community health services would remain under direct DHA administration. It was proposed to replace RAWP by an alternative formula for distributing resources to regions and districts; the latter would then purchase services directly for their populations from providers in the public or private sector.

In a second important departure from existing policy, general-practitioner groups with lists of at least 11,000 were promised the opportunity to become holders of 'GP Practice Budgets', in which case they would receive a top slice of the DHA allocation for purchasing a selected range of non-emergency services for their patients from providers in the public and private sectors. It was envisaged that budget-holders would receive their budgets from the region, but that their contracts would continue to be held by the FPC, which would also monitor the budget. In the 1990 legislation the Family Practitioner Committees were transmuted into Family Health Service Authorities and in the process granted additional management functions in line with the government's intentions concerning the 1990 contract.

Opting out of hospitals, general-practice budget-holding, and the introduction of the purchaser/provider split possessed profound consequences for health authorities, especially district authorities, which faced the prospect of a severe attenuation of their functions. In the future they seemed likely to be mainly purchasing agencies, controlling only that part of their budget not deflected to general-practitioner budget-holders.

As already mentioned, the White Paper stressed that the existing funding arrangements for the health service would continue. Little reference was made to private medicine, but the White Paper anticipated greater private-sector involvement, and, of course, it included the token tax concession for the elderly.

Naturally, the purchaser/provider system required the evolution of completely new contractual arrangements. To encourage the efficient utilization of assets, the new system also envisaged charging NHS providers for the use of their capital assets.

The government promised that the purchaser/provider split, moves towards a disaggregated structure involving self-governing hospitals and general practitioner budget-holders, together with general management devolution and hiving off to trading agencies would produce a health service that would benefit the patient and give better value for money. The timetable envisaged a target date of April 1991 for the introduction of the new scheme, which, it was promised, would be suitably adapted to the administrative situation in each part of the UK.

Unto Market

Working for Patients was a less weighty and precise document than White Papers of comparable importance from the past. In more leisurely circumstances, it might have been issued as a Green Paper. The provisional character of the White Paper left a degree of obscurity about the exact nature and scope of the portentous changes that it described. The glossy brochure mode of presentation enabled the authors of the White Paper to evade the kind of reasoned argument conventionally included in major policy documents. The absence of detail concerning policy intentions was excused on the ground that this information would be contained in a series of forthcoming detailed working papers. In the event, these working papers were not much of an advance on the White Paper. It was therefore evident that many basic proposals were only incompletely formulated. These limitations were a consequence of the unplanned nature of the government's entry into its overhaul of the health service. Owing to a late start, the government was faced with telescoping its planning operation in order to have the new system in operation by April 1991, since a general election was by that date imminent and its latest date was 1992. It will be recalled that the last complete reorganization in 1974 had taken more than six years to plan and execute. The new upheaval was compressed into half that time.

It was clear from the outset that promotion of *Working for Patients* would be an uphill struggle. The government compensated for the weaknesses of its White Paper by mounting a lavish and expensive promotional exercise, aimed particularly at the health professionals. Like Lloyd George in 1911, or Bevan in 1946, Clarke proved equal to the occasion and adopted a buccaneering style, employing weapons that penetrated the skin of his critics and indicated that there was no real prospect of compromise on central issues of the new policy.

The debate over *Working for Patients* was as much connected with ideological symbolism as with the specific reform proposals. This was evident in the very first salvo fired in parliament, which emanated from David Owen, who was himself sympathetic with the internal market. Nevertheless he castigated Mrs Thatcher on account of her non-use and alleged non-understanding of the health service; the NHS was not 'safe in her hands because there is no place in her heart for the NHS'.[54] This emotive outburst set the tone for the entire political confrontation. Klein has described these events as the 'biggest explosion of political anger and professional fury in the history of the NHS'.[55] Although the medical profession had been given to violent outbursts against Labour, as witnessed, for instance, by the events of 1946 or 1975, it had never before confronted a Conservative government with such ferocity, or allied itself with Labour in defence of the Bevanite conception of the health service.

At first Clarke's promotional exercise went badly wrong. For the first month the press largely ignored White Paper propaganda owing to its preoccupation with the recently resigned junior health minister, Edwina Currie, and her part in the Salmonella contamination controversy. In their important reports, the House of Commons Social Services Committee and the Audit Commission were far from supportive.[56] As with the Griffiths reforms, the only groups within the NHS enthusiastic for the changes were the senior administrative staff. Most other groups were sceptical or actively opposed. With the help of the health-service trade unions, Labour mounted a spirited campaign against the government's plan, efficiently led by Robin Cook. The representative bodies of the BMA expressed outright opposition, and a Medeconomics survey revealed that 80 per cent of general practitioners were sceptical about the proposals. The BMA replied to Clarke's propaganda by launching its own big and expensive campaign against the changes. Support for the embattled Clarke was even limited on his own side. He gained little enthusiastic support. He was censured from the right for having been too cautious in his reforms, which were regarded as an untenable compromise, embodying too many of the weaknesses of the earlier system. Conservative moderates criticized Clarke for his unconciliatory attitude to the doctors and for his insensitivity to the flood of anxieties emanating from the constituencies.

Following the example of the tough Celtic fighters who had been his predecessors, Clarke stood his ground and allowed the opposition campaigns to burn themselves out, permitting the democratic process to take its natural course. He was helped by the fact that many of his proposals represented an established course of development; in the case of the arrangements for general practice, they had been under negotiation for years with the profession. A substantial body of consultants and general practitioners appreciated that the changes were likely to be in their professional and financial interest, which was a strong inducement to eventual conformity, although they did not like being taunted by Clarke about 'reaching for their wallets' whenever policy change was in prospect. This equivocation within the medical profession, and the refusal of such prestigious bodies as the Royal College of General Practitioners to align themselves with the BMA, effectively undermined the latter's campaign of opposition, which was eventually called off in June 1992, without having achieved any of its objectives. The BMA leadership prudently observed that its contest with the government was likely to follow the same course as the government's earlier confrontation with the National Union of Mineworkers. There seemed little point in courting martyrdom over a cause that may have involved fine principles, but was not detrimental to the livelihood of BMA members.

The Secretary of State was also assisted by a generous public-expenditure settlement in the autumn of 1988, which was taken as an indication that his reforms were likely to be accompanied by substantial additional resources. Although the wider public remained apprehensive, the government's scheme was not self-evidently threatening. It seemed less pernicious than the notorious poll tax and perhaps not more unpalatable than analogous programmes being pursued in other fields like education.

The most evident weaknesses of *Working for Patients* related to the unbalanced nature of the exercise. Although presented as a programme for modernizing the entire health service, the government's proposals were heavily slanted towards the problem of funding acute hospital services, the issue that had originally sparked off the Thatcher review. All other sides of health care were treated as adventitious to the mechanics of funding hospital services. Without any explanation, policies relating to such high-priority areas as prevention and community care were left in abeyance. Although *Working for Patients* assimilated many recent planning documents, it maintained a studied silence about *Community Care: An Agenda for Action* dating from March 1988, which was particularly unfortunate considering that Sir Roy Griffiths was the author. Griffiths had once again been summoned to the government's rescue on account of the escalating cost to social security of subsidies for old people residing in nursing homes. By 1990 some 300,000 were in receipt of these payments. In view of this distortion in the hard-pressed social-security budget and limitations which this Speenhamland system exposed in community-care provision, Griffiths was asked to provide a solution. However, on this occasion, his approach ran contrary to the thinking of the government, owing to the recommendation that responsibility for community care should be concentrated in the hands of local government. This was, of course, anathema to a government committed to stripping local authorities of their functions. Ministers had not resolved this dilemma at the date of the publication of *Working for Patients*. The case was examined for transferring responsibility for community care to a new Community Care Agency, which was found to be impracticable; reluctant and extremely qualified acceptance of the Griffiths proposals was belatedly announced in November 1989.[57]

Despite all the impediments, the timetable outlined in *Working for Patients* was achieved. The National Health Service and Community Care Act became law in June 1990 and most of its provisions became effective from April 1991. Controversially, the government introduced a two-year delay for the introduction of the new community-care arrangements. This was excused on technical grounds, but it was also connected with resource considerations and confusion in local-government finances generated by the fiasco of the poll tax.

The health-care reforms of 1948 and 1974 had been impressive planning operations. On each occasion there had been a remarkably smooth transfer from the old system to the new. Special care had been taken to reassure all categories of staff about protection of their interests well in advance of the appointed day. By contrast, not only *Working for Patients* but even the 1990 Act left an element of doubt about the extent to which the health service would be affected by the new provisions. Statements by ministers merely added to this uncertainty. Sometimes they spoke as if the reforms were merely a logical continuation of the government's rolling programme of housekeeping measures; at other times they insisted that the changes would constitute the biggest shake-up the health service had ever seen. The extent of the change was largely dependent on the exercise of discretion by general-practice groups and potential opting-out hospitals. In view of the huge extent of opposition to the proposals, at the outset it was widely felt that there would be very little take-up of either route to independence. It was rumoured that the government, even the Prime Minister, would not be sorry to see the reforms limited to the margins. In that case, DHAs would remain dominant players in the system, but, in place of the existing hierarchical management system, the authorities would enter into contractual relationships with their directly managed units. In this case the government's review would have been a largely cosmetic exercise to defuse a crisis in funding that was to some extent already eased by the arrival of a more assertive Secretary of State.

The possibility that the internal-market reforms might be less draconian than feared brought little comfort to health-service personnel, who predominantly remained uncertain about their future and in a state of demoralization. Sensitivity to this problem of staff morale had prompted Bevan and Joseph to spell out their intentions with precision. The reforms of 1991 paid little regard for the sense of insecurity experienced by staff groups. This added to their alienation and to the feeling that they were being reduced in status to insignificant elements in the market mechanism and that the health service was being further caught up in the process of proletarianization. Imposition of local pay determination and further privatization also heightened the insecurity of NHS staff. The promises of the White Paper that the market reforms held the prospect of greater job satisfaction took on a hollow ring.

As indicated by Fig. 3.2, authority at the centre for implementing the market reforms was exercised by the NHS Policy Board and the NHS Management Executive (later abbreviated to NHS Executive). Unlike its predecessor Supervisory Board, the Policy Board at least managed to survive, but it remained a shadowy and insignificant body, serving functions such as hosting meetings of the non-executive regional chairpersons of the eight regions, who fulfilled a role in the health service similar to that of Balkan princelings after 1945. The centre of gravity of power and initiative firmly shifted to the NHS Executive and its eight regional offices. It was this body which effectively spearheaded the development of the internal market way beyond what the sceptics regarded as likely. Collectively, the changes taking effect after 1991 drew the health authorities closer than ever before to control by central government, marking a further decisive shift away from the *laissez-faire* policy that had been tried during the first term of the Thatcher administration. The health authorities perhaps became more effective management bodies, but, like other limbs of the Thatcher Quango Polypod, were remote, secretive, and subject to political manipulation, features which brought them under scrutiny by the Nolan inquiry, which caused minor and mostly cosmetic changes in their method of constitution.

The NHS Management Executive made sure that the balance of incentives favoured wholesale implementation of the market reforms. In *Working for Patients*, the government expressed only modest expectations concerning opting out. It recognized the eligibility of 320 major acute hospitals in UK. The government eased the conditions for opting out and maximized incentives for this course of action. The range of eligible units was increased and the option was extended to ambulance and community services. The title NHS Trust was therefore adopted to cover all these eventualities. The first wave of Trusts was dominated by larger acute hospitals, a total of fifty-seven, containing just over 10 per cent of NHS beds. By the date of the fourth wave of opting out, only 5 per cent of services remained directly managed. In 1997, provision of services in the HCHS sector in England was divided between 429 Trusts.[58]

In *Working for Patients* it was estimated that there were 1,000 practices with 11,000 patients in UK eligible to hold GP Practice Budgets, but the possibility of including smaller practices was mentioned if it was established that their budgets would be sufficiently large to support this exercise. To increase the range of practices eligible for opting out, the government quickly revised this maximum to 9,000, then 7,000, and finally 5,000; it also offered substantial financial inducements for participation. In addition the title of the scheme was changed to 'fundholding' to remove the connotation of a cash limit. The first wave of fundholding in England was supported by 291 practices, representing about 7 per cent of general practitioners, and covering about the same percentage of the population. With the 1996 wave of fundholding the scheme embraced about half of general practitioners in England, and a slightly greater percentage of the population. This slightly overstates the scale of the fundholding operation, since fundholders controlled only part of their budget (relating to elective surgery, outpatient attendances, pathology, and community care), originally accounting for a maximum of about 20 per cent of the hospital budget if all eligible practices participated. In order to develop fundholding still further, the system was modified to allow very small practices to participate to a limited extent, while in England about fifty groups

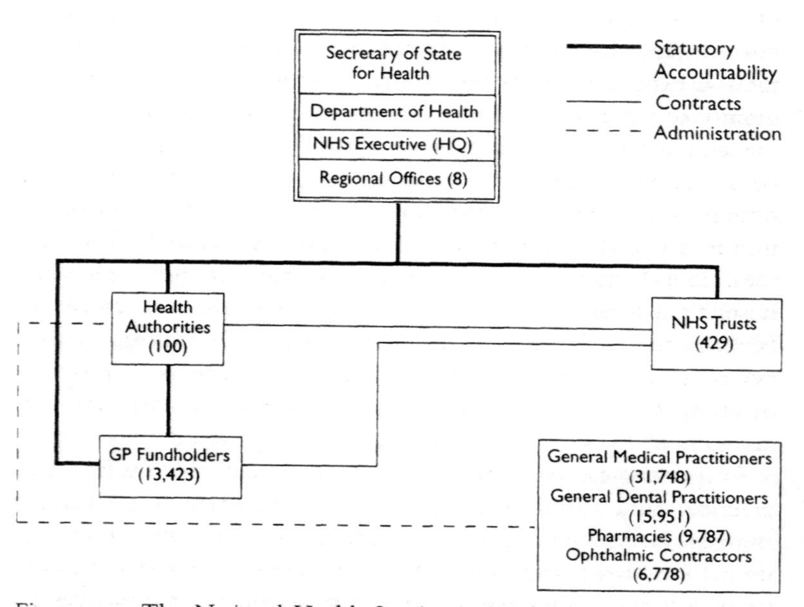

Figure 3.2. The National Health Service in England, 1997
Source: Department of Health, *Departmental Report*, Cm 3612 (London: The Stationery Office, 1997), annex E (adapted)

became involved in a pilot scheme for total fundholding.[59] The drift to fundholding was by no means over. The queue of aspiring fundholders hoping for recognition in April 1997 amounted to about 1,000 practices, which would have firmly tipped the balance of power in the interest of the fundholders. However, the election intervened and Labour immediately took steps to stem this fundholding tide.

Transition to the system favoured by the government was smoother than the sceptics predicted. The approximate state of play in 1997 is indicated in Fig. 3.2. The almost complete disaggregation of district services into Trusts avoided the anomaly of the directly managed unit and it created a tidy divide between purchaser and provider. However, this supply-side structure had not proved to be entirely stable. The NHS Executive, having given every inducement to breaking down the system into its most basic units, altered course and decided that the process of fission had gone too far, creating units that were too small and uneconomic. At the time of the 1997 election, as an alternative to bankruptcy and closure, providers were busily reamalgamating with partners from whom they had been only recently divorced. Naturally, both fission and merger were defended on grounds of their contribution to efficiency.

The demand side of the equation was not amenable to a stable equilibrium. DHAs, non-fundholders, and fundholders existed in an unstable relationship. Since the fundholding bandwagon became stuck at the halfway mark, there were two evenly balanced forces of general practitioners. For the first time in the history of the NHS there was a real risk that the frictions and divisiveness generated by this competitive arrangement would boil over into fratricide between the two types of general practitioner. Planners experienced the greatest difficulty in balancing the interests of these two types of general practice. The attractive inducements required to establish a viable body of fundholders risked generating a two-tier health service, to the benefit of the middle classes, leaving health authorities and non-fundholders operating a residual service for the poorer sections of the community. Any attempt to redress the balance in favour of non-fundholders sparked off the accusation that fundholding was a trap to impose cash limits and a punitive assault on the most efficient, successful, and innovative practices.

In the event the Conservatives' fundholding initiative remained in such a state of flux that no settled lines of division emerged on the demand side. Both fundholders and non-fundholders banded together into larger groupings, and cooperation even extended across the fundholding divide. Non-fundholders became drawn into close advisory relationship with their health authorities to determine policy over commissioning, and in some cases fundholders were also drawn into these negotiations. At the fall of the Conservative government the variety of collaborative arrangements was so great that no one place was like another. The Conservatives' NHS (Primary Care) Act of 1997 further facilitated experiment with various forms of locality commissioning.

It was perhaps naive of the government to believe that it was possible to retain the existing top-down hierarchical structure of health-service administration in parallel with a market system placing the centre of gravity at the level of field agencies. Once the 200 district authorities had lost administrative control over their hospital and community services, and reverted to the status of purchasers, responsible only for that part of the budget not creamed off by fundholders, it was evident that they were too small and weak to merit preservation in their existing form. There was the further anomaly that, after 1982, in any one locality, primary-care services were partly administered by DHAs and partly by FPCs/later FHSAs, the boundaries of which were not coextensive. The government accepted the folly of the situation it had created and set about reversing the changes of 1982 by linking FHSAs and DHAs into 100 Health Authorities. This amalgamation took place in April 1996 as a consequence of the Health Authorities Act of 1995.[60] This legislation also provided for the elimination of RHAs. The need for these authorities had often been questioned, but since 1982 it had been especially evident that they were living on borrowed time. In 1994 the RHAs were reduced from fourteen to eight, and in April 1996 their functions were taken over by eight regional offices of the NHS Executive. At this point the entire administrative hierarchy established by Sir Keith Joseph in 1974 had been disbanded. Almost accidentally, the

Conservatives ended up with something like the structure contained in the first Labour Green Paper of 1968; on the same account, to some extent they reinvented in 1996 the AHAs that they themselves had disbanded in 1982. However, the new Health Authorities were slightly more numerous than the AHAs and also considerably more restricted in their functions, which suggested that they were destined to be further reduced in number. Authorities established at this level were also vulnerable to the criticism that they were too small to relate to the local community but not large enough for planning purposes.

Although *Working for Patients* was designed to bring about an internal market in the NHS, reticence over the use of this term indicated doubt over its suitability to describe what was being undertaken. Subsequent literature introduced such alternatives as quasi-market, or planned market, but the guidelines issued by the NHS Executive gave continuing currency to the term internal market and its use was not entirely discontinued.[61] In fact, the new system was not internal nor was it a market in more than a restricted sense. 'Internal' was clearly inconsistent with the aspiration to maximize the involvement of outside agencies and the private sector. The 'market' analogy was obviously imprecise, since the consumer was unable to exercise choice of services; health authorities or fundholders acted as their surrogates. It was not so much a matter of the patient dictating where the money went, but the patient following whatever channel the professionals dictated. The residual capacity of the patient to influence the market and exercise choice lay in such expedients as changing doctor, petitioning commissioning authorities, or making complaints, none of which was particularly practicable or likely to exercise more than marginal influence.

From the outset it was appreciated that unrestricted operation of the market would reduce the health service to chaos. Indeed, even the limited application of the market immediately precipitated a crisis in the weakest parts of the system, especially London, which necessitated emergency action in the form of the Tomlinson review of the London health services. Like earlier such reviews Tomlinson drew attention to a profoundly unsatisfactory situation without producing a solution capable of commanding more than limited support.[62]

London graphically illustrated the disasters that would flow from unhindered application of the market model. Political and prudential factors, as well as inertia within the system, operated to place severe restrictions on competition and on the structure of the market. At first purchasers were instructed to maintain a 'steady state', or 'measured change', with the idea of achieving a 'soft landing'. Later, the terminology was altered to play down market and competitive connotations. The 'purchasers' were rapidly replaced by 'commissioners'. Although the NHS Executive clung to the idea of 'competition', at the field level the contracting process has increasingly become described in terms of mutual dependence between commissioners and providers, whose constructive negotiation aims to achieve optimal satisfaction for all parties, which in fact represents a revival of a consensusal approach to decision-making at the heart of health-service resource management.

The question naturally arises whether the improvements brought about by the market changes justified their expense. Substantial costs were incurred in introducing the internal market—for instance, with respect to information systems—and this mechanism added greatly to the routine transaction costs of health care. In all international comparisons the NHS has traditionally scored highly on account of its low cost of administration, which until the 1980s amounted to about 5 per cent of health-service expenditure. After 1981 administrative costs soared; in 1997 they stood at about 12 per cent; managers talked of 17 per cent as an eventual target. In the run-up to the general election Labour claimed that the internal-market changes had added £1.5 billion in total to management costs. In a situation where available bed numbers declined sharply and staff levels were falling, administrative and clerical staff increased by 18 per cent between 1981 and 1991, and by a further 10 per cent after that date. The rise in numbers of top management was particularly striking. In England there were just one thousand officially classified general or senior managers in 1986, 16,000 in 1991, and 26,000 in 1995. The emergence of this super-league of managers was accompanied by the infiltration of sleaze into the health service on a scale unknown previously, indeed sufficient to merit the distinction of a regular column in *Private Eye*. The ratio between nurses and administrative staff fell from 3.5:1 in 1981 to 2.5:1 in 1996.

The market was an expensive undertaking and assessment of its value was rendered more difficult owing to the government's decision to embark on wholesale implementation rather than follow the advice of experts to engage in controlled trials. This haste undoubtedly added to the cost of the exercise, and it meant that mistakes were needlessly replicated across the system. It is a strange paradox that, having in the interests of economy insisted on rigorous evaluation of clinical or management innovations, the government failed to observe this rule when it came to its market reforms. However, the market reforms did not go unmonitored. The early research findings tended to follow a pattern, suggesting that the market changes were marked by some beneficial results, but also by others that were adverse.

Judgements on the market system incline to be guarded and provisional, partly on account of the relatively short history of the reforms, also because of the continuing state of flux. Considering that research undertakings have been generally designed to show the market system at its best, their conclusions convey a remarkably lukewarm impression. Overviews by experienced commentators are also guarded in their conclusions. In his general verdict, Rudolf Klein concluded that 'if no great improvements in performance can be deduced from the post-1991 statistics, neither do these suggest any sudden deterioration as a result of the reforms either quantitatively or qualitatively'.[63] The Chief Economic Adviser to the Department of Health, who was at the middle of implementation of the reforms, admitted that, in the light of lack of conclusive evidence concerning the advantages of the market system, 'it is the nature of major organisation and management changes that they can rarely be proved to be more effective than those they replace'.[64] Such Pyrrhonic endorsements are rather less than the public was led to expect when the *Working for Patients* revolution was launched. The prevailing note of reservation in these judgements suggests that, in their positive benefits, the internal-market reforms compare unfavourably with the discredited 'command-economy' structure introduced in 1948, for which considerably bolder claims could be made about the advances in output, performance, consumer satisfaction, and morale of health-service personnel.

The contribution of *Working for Patients* is further diminished when it is appreciated that some of the more positive changes with which it was associated would have come about regardless of the internal market. Also, the decision to embark on an overhaul of the health service automatically triggered an injection of additional resources beyond what would otherwise have been available. Therefore, regardless of its merits, *Working for Patients* helped temporarily to alleviate the funding crisis that had been simmering throughout the 1980s. Immediately the NHS was resubmitted to restrictive public-expenditure targets, the system plunged into crisis. The fact that danger point was reached even more quickly than in the 1980s highlighted the marginal relevance of the *Working for Patients* reforms. The sense of crisis surrounding the health service in the period before the 1997 general election was therefore reminiscent of the autumn of 1987, when the Conservatives had been forced into their major review of the health service. This rather suggested that a decade of turmoil had failed either to address or to solve the basic problems of the NHS. Mr Blair's inheritance was, therefore, just as unenviable as the awful legacy picked up by Mrs Thatcher after the Winter of Discontent.

The Conservatives paid a big price for tying their fortunes to the internal market and adopting this as their flagship policy for the NHS. New Labour became adept at laying all the problems of the NHS at the door of the internal market. The public was instinctively sympathetic to the Labour message. The idea of making health care dependent on the vagaries of markets and competition was instinctively repulsive.

Mr. Major's government awoke to the dangers of this situation. During his short tenure as Secretary of State for Health, Stephen Dorrell worked hard to play down the market idea. Documents issued by the government largely expunged market vocabulary from their texts. The *Working for Patients* changes were now discussed in terms of raising quality, increasing responsiveness and improving the accountability of public services. The new approach emphasised that all recent reforms lay within the boundaries of the New Public Management, which represented a technical and pragmatic response to improving the value for money invested in the public services. This message was conveyed in Mr. Dorrell's 'Millennium Lecture' delivered in January 1996, which became the basis for his White Paper, *A Service with Ambitions*, issued in November of that year.[65] His lecture hardly mentioned the key elements of the internal market reforms. His main emphasis was on continuing support for the basic principles of the NHS. He described the NHS as a great public service, built on simple but powerful ideas, which had overwhelming support. He was confident that the NHS represented the soundest basis for provision of high quality, equitable and efficient services. The prestigious primary care system was identified as the nucleus for further development. Assurances were provided that wholesale management change and structural upheaval were things of the past. The NHS was promised a period of consolidation and stability. Mr. Dorrell promised that local NHS personnel would be allowed to develop a pattern of services appropriate to the needs of each district. The government would no longer enforce change according to a single formula. He expressed a determination to address problems of inequalities and unjustifiable variations in the quality of care that had opened up between one place and another. The service provided by clinicians would be improved by the more rigorous application of clinical audit and the dissemination of information about the best 'science based' practice.

A Service with Ambitions followed the same lines as the lecture. It reasserted the government's support for the founding principles of the NHS. Its five points of emphasis were: a well-informed public; a seamless service; evidence-based clinical decision-making; a more highly trained workforce; and responsiveness of services to patients' needs. The internal market reforms were relegated to almost adventitious status in this plan for long term development of the NHS. This new perspective was difficult for the opposition to criticise. Chris Smith, the Labour spokesperson, ridiculed his rival's work as 'fairy tales' or 'woolly aspirations'.[66] In fact the expositions about the fundamentals of health policy by Stephen Dorrell and Chris Smith were virtually interchangeable.

New Labour had every reason for gratitude to the Conservative government, especially in its later manifestations. The Conservatives had acted as the experimental animal for New Labour's programme of modernisation, only to witness the indignity of the opposition making political capital from attacks on a caricature of the internal market that no longer existed.

In the run-up to the May 1997 general election, on account of factors such as sleaze and wrangling among Conservatives over Europe, the public was in no mood to listen to Mr. Dorrell or any of his Cabinet colleagues. On health care Mr. Dorrell also had the misfortune for his message to be drowned out by events associated with another winter crisis, which filled the press with negative reports such as harrowing accounts of patients dying in hospital corridors. The accumulation of adverse media coverage about the health service suggested that the NHS was heading in the same disastrous direction as the privatised railways. Shortly before *A Service with Ambitions* was published, the media fastened on to the first scientific evidence of links between human disease and mad cow disease. This shock to public confidence was confirmed just before the 1997 general election, when Mr. Dorrell was forced to announce that BSE was in all probability implicated in human deaths from vCJD. If this was not enough, in the winter before the 1997 general election, an E. coli outbreak in Scotland was responsible for the deaths of 27 elderly people. The subsequent report by Hugh Pennington on this episode of meat contamination provided further bad news for the government at the time of the general election. Accordingly, bad publicity on many fronts ordained that Stephen Dorrell's tenure as Secretary of State was unlikely to be remembered for the enlightened aspirations of *A Service with Ambitions.*

4

NEW AGE OF LABOUR

> It is, in a very real sense, our chance to prove for my generation and that of my children, that a universal service can deliver what the people expect in today's world For all of us it is a challenge. But it is one we intend to meet.[1]

Befitting its centrality in Labour's heritage, the National Health Service held the key to the party's political rehabilitation. However, it was not until the appointment of Tony Blair as leader that the value of this asset was realised. Indicative of Labour's ineffectiveness as a party of opposition after its 1979 election defeat, Labour's health policy amounted to little more than empty rhetoric, trading on the residual fund of positive public sentiment left over from the distant past. The squandering of the NHS legacy under Neil Kinnock was all the more surprising, given that his political reputation depended on affiliation with Bevan. This was emphasised by the new edition of the Bevan's *In Place of Fear* issued by Kinnock in 1978.

Labour's failure to evolve a constructive policy for health care left the Tories with a clear field. Labour mounted only feeble resistance to the Thatcher government's first wave of management reforms and privatisations, with their obvious deleterious consequences for the health service workforce and union movement. Eventually the prospect of the massive internal market reforms exercised a cathartic effect. Labour politicians appreciated that they were not likely to regain their credibility as a future party of government unless they could convince the electorate that they too were agents of reform and modernisation. This awakening also reflected pressure from the unions, who recognised the internal market as yet a further threat to the interests of their members.

Fired by the catalyst of the Conservative government's *Working for Patients*, Labour embarked on a policy review, which generated a series of minor policy documents (*A Fresh Start for Health*, 1990; *Your Good Health*, 1992; *Health 2000*, 1994; and *Rebuilding the NHS*, 1995), in the course of which an entirely new policy standpoint became evident. Tony Blair and his advisors recognised that the NHS constituted an electoral winning card. From the outset of his leadership, the health service was central to the New Labour project. Tony Blair proved adept at soliciting sympathy from unlikely quarters, as for instance demonstrated by his widely noticed speech 'A One Nation NHS', delivered in June 1996 to the annual conference of the National Association of Health Authorities and Trusts. This audience was the main agent of the market reforms, but it was suitably placated by the emollient message of Labour's new leader, who seemed set to accomplish the revival of One Nation Conservatism. By such shrewd confidence-building measures, the entire NHS establishment was won over to Labour.

New Labour Project for Health

As a fresh opposition leader, Mr. Blair's mission to extend his constituency was eased by the general collapse of confidence in Mr. Major's government. The Conservatives were consumed by their own civil war, hardly noticing that Tony Blair's 'New Labour project' involved audacious colonisation of the government's hard-won political territory. With respect to health, as other areas of policy, the Conservatives failed to exploit the vulnerabilities of the Labour position or indeed to mount a credible defence of their own record.

On the NHS, New Labour was indeed open to criticism. At this time of rapid transition the party could be censured for pursing irreconcilable objectives. It kept up Old Labour's attack on the internal market and advocacy of the traditional concept of the NHS. At the same time New Labour stood for modernisation, which in practice entailed a retreat from its long-standing policies and even adoption of much of the internal market programme.

Tony Blair and Gordon Brown shook themselves free of older

Labour thinking and moved closer to the Conservatives on three important fronts. First, they emancipated themselves from Labour's image as the 'tax and spend' option. Secondly, they softened Labour's antipathy to the private sector, eventually even embracing the Private Finance Initiative that their colleagues had hitherto been busily demonising. Thirdly, although nominally committed to totally dismantling the internal market, in the event they opted for a policy of continuity.

Labour's policy presentations confirm the shift in perspective during the transition to New Labour. The most striking change related to the elimination of commitments to higher spending. In 1992 the Labour manifesto made lavish spending promises, well exceeding the generous levels of funding agreed on a short-term basis by the Conservative government at this date to smooth implementation of the internal market reforms. Labour's spending pledges were mercilessly exploited by the Conservatives to generate fears among the electorate about higher taxation and general economic profligacy. This cost Labour the 1992 election. After this humbling experience, in 1997 Labour retreated to the opposite extreme, on health committing itself to the draconian spending plans announced by the Conservatives, with the only promise of additional spending relating to trivial savings on bureaucracy through reform of the internal market. Labour therefore entered the 1997 election with the meanest spending package on health ever presented to the UK electorate since World War II. Given the moribund state of Mr. Major's government, this caution on spending may look excessive, but it was perhaps understandable given the priority of avoiding yet another election defeat.

Labour's sudden and enthusiastic adoption of the Private Finance Initiative on its return to government came as a surprise. In line with Labour's consistent attack on all manifestations of privatisation, it was natural that the new Private Finance Initiative was viewed with the greatest suspicion. The moment that the Conservatives extended the PFI idea to the NHS, Labour rose to the attack. In her capacity as health spokesperson, Margaret Beckett declared that PFI was totally unacceptable to Labour.[2] PFI was identified as a notable point of difference between Labour and Conservative, an exception to the convergence that seemed to be taking place in most other areas of health policy.[3] PFI remained in the firing line at least until the end of 1996. Chris Smith embraced the anti-PFI policy with gusto. At the Labour Party Conference in October 1996 he attacked all forms of commercialisation and privatisation in the NHS. He specifically criticised the decision to build a PFI hospital at Dartford and Gravesham as proof of the Tories' 'privatising agenda'.[4]

Evidently, by Christmas 1996, Gordon Brown decided to abandon Labour's opposition to PFI, after which he pursued the reverse policy with vigour. This change of heart was not signalled loudly, but Chris Smith's comments were suitably tuned to the new thinking. In February 1997 he declared that the only way to reverse drastic Tory cuts in capital spending was to employ the private sector to breach the gap. Now the Tories were criticised for their inefficiency in promoting PFI.[5] The 1997 election manifesto duly declared that Labour would sort out the problems that had plagued PFI and indeed develop other forms of public/private partnership that might benefit the NHS. Labour's sudden summersault over PFI is easily explained. Adherence to Conservative spending plans implied further cuts in capital investment on hospitals, which would fatally impair Labour's image as restorer of the NHS. To Labour, PFI took on the character of some kind of philosopher's stone, the value of which had not been fully understood by its Conservative inventor. PFI offered a way to spread out the burden of capital investment, thereby permitting an immediate hospital building spree of limitless proportions. PFI and further public/private partnerships therefore presented an expansionist opportunity that New Labour found irresistible.

Given New Labour's moratorium on spending, the whole weight of expectation for improvement in the NHS turned on its 'Modernisation' platform, which embodied Labour's alternative to the internal market. Labour had been developing its ideas about modernisation for some time. The section on health in its 1992 manifesto was boldly headed 'Modernising the NHS'. However, Modernisation assumed an altogether higher profile under New Labour. As illustrated by Labour's verdict on the internal market, this flexibility of meaning was essential to the continuing attractiveness of this concept. In the early 1990s Labour's modernisation policy denoted antagonism to the internal market. Under the New Labour project this opposition was progressively watered down. Eventually, modernisation fully embraced the New Public Management ethos that lay at the core of the internal market changes as they were actually implemented.

For reasons stated in the previous chapter, the internal market remained an attractive soft target for attack by Labour, but it became increasingly clear that in practice most of the basic elements of the internal market would be retained. Even GP fund-holding, which was the most criticised aspect of internal market changes, was acknowledged as a source of improvement. This tendency to criticise the internal market as a whole, but support retention of most of its constituent elements, reflected the caution that emerged in Mr. Blair's statements regarding the NHS in the period before the 1997 election. He appreciated that the NHS workforce was demoralised after exposure to more than ten years of major management changes, many of them unwelcome and imposed without consultation or the agreement of those concerned. Accordingly, New Labour shifted the focus of its criticism of the internal market reforms. It was not the individual reforms themselves that were necessarily at fault, but their monolithic character and the manner of their imposition, without evidence of their proven effectiveness or consultation with the expert personnel involved. Mr. Blair therefore promised that New Labour's 'One Nation NHS' would advance by 'reform not upheaval'; there would be no more 'permanent revolution'. Labour would avoid 'structural upheaval' to the maximum extent. Modernisation would therefore proceed incrementally, in an atmosphere of basic stability, with change being introduced after full consultation with those involved and only after prior experimentation. Labour would break free from the uniformity imposed by the Conservatives and allow for diversity within the system, in response to the requirements of local circumstances.[6]

Such pragmatism was a useful electoral asset to New Labour; it suggested a refreshing spirit of humility and emancipation from the ideological dogmatism of the Thatcher years. Thereby Mr. Blair became poised to gain the full electoral benefit from opposition to the unpopular internal market, without having to tie himself to any alternative. Labour's position was difficult for the Conservatives to criticise, and it was conveniently free from expenditure implications. With this new policy alignment, Mr. Blair was well placed to face the electorate.

Labour in Power

The health card was played with consummate effect in the 1997 general election campaign, when Mr. Blair's eloquent advocacy successfully persuaded the public that a vote for Labour was the only means to prevent the health service from imminent collapse. His reward was a landslide House of Commons majority, creating a parliamentary situation reminiscent of 1945. The scale of this success was testimony to Mr. Blair's personal achievement in generating enthusiasm for the New Labour project. In the process the Labour Party became rebranded as New Labour. For some time health policy statements were emphatically labelled as the product of New Labour, but gradually the government became more comfortable about its old party name. The following account approximately reflects this shift in terminology.

By the date of the 1997 general election Mr. Major's party had ceased to be a viable political force, impotent to contest Labour's programme on health or anything else. Fortunately for New Labour, after 1997 the Conservatives failed to capitalise from the government's failures in the public sector. After a further electoral humiliation in June 2001, the Conservative Party frankly accepted that its inability to project an image of trustworthiness with respect to the health service contributed to the party's lack of electoral appeal. Correction of this weakness was identified as an important priority for the new leadership in the first decade of the new century.

In May 1997, the choice of Frank Dobson as Secretary of State for Health came as a surprise. Perhaps it was thought that this Old Labour veteran would instil confidence among the public that Bevanite values would be observed. As a counterbalance, the appointment of Tessa Jowell and Alan Milburn as junior ministers ensured that the actual work of the department would be delegated to sworn advocates of modernisation. Frank Dobson bustled about noisily, but he was no match for the Treasury and was never more than a nightwatchman. When it became evident that the NHS was drifting in to deep trouble, Dobson was sacked and fed to the wolf in the form of Ken Livingstone at the first London mayoral election. In the autumn of 1999, Alan Milburn, who was fresh from a short apprenticeship as Chief Secretary to the Treasury, replaced Frank Dobson. Given his youth and newness to his appointment at the date of the 2001 general election, it was no surprise that he was one of the few Cabinet ministers left in post for a further term after Labour's second general election success.

The 1997 general election manifesto on which Labour was returned to power was an amalgam of Old and New Labour. Reflecting the tenor of Mr. Blair's pre-election speeches, much was made of the evangelistic cry to 'save' or 'rebuild' the NHS in consistency with its 'historic principles'. In terminology reminiscent of Bevan, Labour was pledged to the revival of a 'public service working co-operatively', which entailed rejection of the Tory idea of the NHS as a 'commercial business driven by competition'. Undoubtedly the passionate rhetoric of Mr. Blair's speeches, suitably echoed elsewhere, heightened public expectations that the health service was about to emerge from some kind of dark age and recapture the spirit of emulation that had been characteristic of the time of Bevan.

Even after the sobering experience of government, Bevan's imagery has not been entirely discarded. Even Mr. Milburn's NHS Plan and the Wanless Interim Report characterised the government's current programme in terms of Bevan's aspiration to 'universalise the best'.[7] Such expressions of high ambition have inevitably set a standard for public expectations against which the government's record is constantly assessed.

Initially the New Labour administration was resilient with optimism. The government was satisfied that it had comprehensively diagnosed the problems of the NHS and set in place appropriate remedial measures. Discordant voices were dismissed with impatience. Claims that the NHS was being fatally damaged by adherence to Conservative spending plans were treated with particular scorn. Adverse media coverage concerning staff shortages or failures across the hospital system, were apt to be dismissed by ministers as irresponsible scaremongering. Ministers were deluded by their own rhetoric into thinking that Labour's programme of modernisation possessed some kind of magic that permitted miracles to be wrought without the application of resources.

Inevitably the nostrums applied were insufficient to address the scale of such problems of crumbing infrastructure, obsolete technical facilities, or to arrest the melting away of the skilled workforce. Quite quickly modernisation was exposed as the recipe for fool's gold. Overconfidence at the outset risked generating disenchantment with the whole programme.

In the event, the government awoke to the catastrophic consequences of its myopia. Its own reappraisals gradually converged with universal experience. It was accepted that shortcomings in services were not isolated and unrepresentative events, or confined to short periods during the winter season. The tone of the government's annual reports gradually became noticeably more circumspect. At the launch of the second annual report in July 1999, it was claimed that every pledge had been fulfilled or was 'on course'. No doubt to underline Labour's success on the health front, the Prime Minister launched this report at the Homerton Hospital in East London. This public relations exercise misfired; the limelight fell on complaints from a disgruntled pensioner that patients were seeing no benefits from the government's NHS policies. The Prime Minster frankly conceded that he was frustrated by the slow rate of progress in the improvement of public services; he now admitted that it would take ten years to 'turn round' the ailing NHS.[8]

From the outset of his appointment Alan Milburn tended to be sanguine about the successes achieved; he candidly acknowledged the magnitude of the problem that he was confronting. In a well-publicised leaked personal memorandum, Philip Gould warned the Prime Minister that 'we have got our political strategy wrong. We were too late with the NHS. We raised expectations that could not be met in our first two years'.[9] In July 2000, the government's third annual report reflected this cautionary note. The vision statement conceded that 'people's day-to-day experience of the NHS often falls short'; it was accepted that they were habitually forced to wait too long for treatment; the quality of treatment varied enormously; appointments were inconvenient to obtain; hospital wards were dirty; and the 'level' of service failed to match the expectations of patients or staff. In *The NHS Plan*, produced at the same date, messages from Mr. Blair and Mr. Milburn were suitably contrite about the same shortcomings.[10] Consistent with this new mood of humility, the 2001 general election manifesto was altogether more restrained than its 1997 predecessor. Even with the promised injection of additional resources that were a central feature of the government's new programme, it was accepted that modernisation was a long-term process. Consequently, immediate improvement was not regarded as a practicable possibility. On this occasion the government took care to spread out the target dates adopted for specific improvements, with many of them being conveniently located at fairly distant dates over the first decade of the new millennium. After the chastening experience of the first term of office, the government became more alert to the dangers of stimulating unrealistic public expectations about the capacities of its mission to restore the NHS. During the early stages of Labour's second administration, ministerial statements were noticeably more restrained than in the past. Much publicity was attracted by the admission of Charles Clarke, the Labour Party Chairman, that improvement in the NHS was a 'patchy story'; indeed he conceded that in some areas 'we have even gone backwards'. Instead of the customary obfuscations issued in response to the daily incidents of tragic deaths of patients subjected to humiliating conditions while waiting for treatment in hospitals, Mr. Clarke frankly admitted that the current situation was 'absolutely unacceptable'.[11]

The new level of realism about the scale of the difficulties facing the NHS was welcome to the public and helpful for restoring confidence in the government's handling of the NHS. However, this positive development was undermined by the government's continuing use of its public relations machinery to vilify its critics and exaggerate the success of the modernisation programme. Such careless regard for fact has damaging consequences since it suggests that the government is deluding itself into thinking of the NHS as a problem solved, rather than one of its continuing policy challenges, as yet not fully understood or effectively confronted.

Fresh Starts in a New NHS

In 1997, the new administration was faced with a delicate balancing act. The government continued to scorn its unpopular and discredited Conservative predecessor. One the other hand, policies evolved by the Conservatives offered the most ready means to avoid wholesale disruption and to extract a greater volume of service from the NHS without incurring additional costs and thereby recourse to higher taxation. Continuity was also in the interests of the civil servants, for whom New Labour represented an attractive proposition since papers left over from the previous administration could easily be repackaged to look as if they were purpose designed for the new government. Reversion to the Conservative policy perspective was also symbolically important to the City since it underlined the extent to which New Labour had become emancipated from its Old Labour ancestry. Labour in effect guaranteed that its reconfiguration of the NHS would be consistent with the principles of the New Public Management. Reform would therefore conform to private sector principles and indeed it raised the prospect of substantial returns to the corporate economy.

The slightly unlikely figure of Mr. Dobson therefore picked up where Mr. Dorrell had left off. Indeed, as noted above, Mr. Dorrell's last important White Paper, *A Service with Ambitions*, could equally have served as the prospectus for New Labour. Mr. Dorrell's final legislative initiative, the NHS (Primary Care) Act 1997, became the basis for Labour's interventions in primary care; and PFI legislation, introduced by Labour shortly after its return to power, was a next logical step from Conservative PFI legislation dating from a few months earlier. Also, as already indicated, the new government fell into line with Conservative spending plans, and its policy towards the internal market involved nothing like the radical rejection that was suggested by Labour's political rhetoric.

Most of the other policies featured in Labour' s 1997 manifesto represented signals of continuity. For the most part Labour pursued lines of policy that had been subject to long gestation. Labour for instance took over from the previous administration the idea primary care-led health service, the further improvement of hospital performance indicators, the extension of clinical audit, and revision of the *Patient's Charter*.

As noted above, the Conservatives had long wrestled with the problem of long-term care and had come near to presenting a package of proposals for consultation. However, on this important problem, no agreed scheme was available for Labour to implement. In these circumstances, the new government evaded the issue by remitting the problem to a Royal Commission, which effectively kicked the issue into the long grass for most of the first term of its administration, conveniently postponing any spending implications until a much later date. Labour was pledged to just one token measure relating to older people, which involved removing tax relief on their private medical insurance premiums. This looked like a symbolic stab at private medicine, which was attractive to Labour opinion, but conveniently for the government, this tax concession was never favoured by the Treasury, which welcomed its removal as a small cut in public spending to offset the impact of any future expansionist plans.

It is therefore evident that continuity with Conservative policies represented the dominant pattern. Perhaps no other approach was feasible, given the fiscal propriety that was the government's higher priority. However, this made it difficult to convince the electorate that Labour's New NHS was superior to the Conservative internal market. Much ingenuity was required to persuade the public that the NHS under Labour represented a real improvement or indeed that it was in any essential respect different from its condition under the Conservatives. Labour's difficulties in restoring public confidence are well illustrated by the attempts made to implement its key manifesto pledges on public health, hospital waiting lists and hospital renewal.

Public Health

As noted in the previous chapter, confidence in the Conservative government's commitment to public health was undermined by a long series of scandals, culminating with BSE. Action to restore public confidence was unavoidable. Mr. Major's government appreciated that the Ministry of Agriculture, Food and Fisheries had lost its credibility, and it investigated the case for an independent agency to protect food standards. Labour went further by making a pledge to establish an independent Food Standards Agency. It also exceeded the Conservatives in the range of its associated proposals for the development of public health. Labour promised to address the problem of health inequalities, adopt more demanding targets for health improvement and to appoint for the first time a Minister of Public Health. Most of this reflected a logical extension of the Health of the Nation policies that had been developing during the 1990s. However, the Conservatives were handicapped by the consequences of their Black Report public relations disaster, which inhibited them from realistically confronting the continuing problem of health inequalities. Indeed the Conservative government was even loath to admit 'health inequalities' terminology into their public health vocabulary. Labour exploited this weakness and the new government was pledged to bold confrontation with the problem of continuing health inequalities.

Policies designed to restore confidence in public health have figured prominently in Labour's programme. However, continuing bitter experience reminded the government that incidents relating to food standards and public health were liable to generate public anxiety and entail massive costs to the economy. The Food Standards Agency initially made a good impression, but this has been offset by continuing evidence of food scandals, confirming that the surveillance mechanism remains fragmented, insufficiently expert, and inadequately resourced. Establishment of the Food Standards Agency and associated organisational changes have therefore not materially assisted in preventing contaminated food from entering the human foodchain. The devastating outbreak of Foot and Mouth Disease that caused postponement of the 2001 general election was not a direct threat to human health, but it reinforced fears about dangerous practices in farming. The epidemic also suggested a continuing culture of secrecy and incompetence in the government public health laboratory services.

The decline of public health represented a problem that had had been building up since the beginning of the health service. Spurred on by BSE, Foot and Mouth, and the horrific prospects opened up by the new wave of international terrorism begun on

11 September 2001, efforts have been made to bolster the authority of the Chief Medical Officer and the public health function within the Department of Health and the NHS. The ambitious Shifting the Balance reforms, to be implemented in 2002 onwards, might well have treated public health as a formality. Instead, reflecting the need for active intervention, the government has produced elaborate proposals for strengthening the public health hierarchy.

To demonstrate its awareness of the need for action across the whole field of public health, the government sponsored a variety of innovations in the fields of prevention and promotion. In the course of its history, the NHS witnessed a string of failed attempts to establish an effective and credible central agency responsible for health education and promotion. In 2000 Labour made a fresh effort, converting the Thatcher-inspired Health Education Authority into the Health Development Agency. This provided a fresh opportunity to develop multiprofessional partnership and it was a sign of greater acceptance of the WHO health promotion agenda. Sanctioning an entirely independent update of the Black Report from a retired Chief Medical Officer pointed to a more relaxed attitude to confronting the intractable problem of inequalities in health.[12] Localised schemes such as Health Action Zones, NHS Walk-in Centres, or Healthy Living Centres partly funded by the National Lottery, were designed to bring about tangible improvements in access to care in city centres or districts experiencing social deprivation. These were reinforced by schemes at a national level ranging from NHS Direct to plans for improving health in schools or workplaces. In 1999, the White Paper, *Saving Lives: Our Healthier Nation* summarised the government's objectives for updating the Conservative Health of the Nation targets for health improvement and disease management.

The above examples testify to the inexhaustible energy of the government in addressing the problems of prevention and promotion. Ministerial speeches have been reassuring. Shortly after the 11 September outrages, Lord Hunt reported that the UK's systems for public health surveillance and capacity for emergency planning were of world class and were admired for being exemplary by the US Secretary for Health.[13] The Chief Medical Officer was less confident. Sir Liam Donaldson acknowledged that in the field of infectious disease surveillance, 'the present system falls short of what is necessary fully to protect the public health'. He pointed to a list of terrifying deficiencies, conceding that 'there is no integrated approach to encompass all aspects of health protection from national, to regional, to local level'.[14] He accepted that the threats posed by international terrorism had highlighted deep-seated deficiencies within the system. Proposals for the future include establishment of a new National Infection Control and Health Protection Agency, to give more integrated and determined leadership from the centre. It remains to be seen how smoothly these urgent improvements are applied in the devolved system of government now in existence in the UK. With good reason the community remains fearful that the public health system is unequal to the task of confronting the formidable threats to health that are being generated by the global political and economic system.

The government's paper plans for improving health and addressing inequalities in health cover a wide range and they are designed to look impressive. On the ground the government's initiatives look less impressive. They tend to be subject to the common criticism that on account of their token scale and especially because they fail to address the problems of economic disadvantage that lie at the roots of ill-health, they are unlikely to achieve anything like the impact promised in the government's expensive publicity presentations.[15]

Waiting for Treatment

By hard experience, Labour has discovered that public health represents more treacherous territory than ever it thought likely. Consequently, restoration of damaged public confidence is not a feasible proposition in the short term. The government has not succeeded much better with some of its main bids to bring about improvements in the curative services, where it has also run up against deeply entrenched problems. In opposition, Labour made a serious error of judgement in adopting the hospital inpatient waiting list as the main yardstick of improvement. This indeed reflected an issue of public concern, but Labour's policy was confused and when put into practice it risked doing more harm than good. The inpatient waiting list had been inching up throughout the 1990s; it broke through the million mark in 1992. Reduction of this waiting list by 100,000 was adopted as the third of five 'key pledges' for the 1997 general election. The government's meritorious goal was to deflect resources squandered on bureaucracy into patient care. The 1997 manifesto estimated that £1.5bn a year was wasted in this way, but Labour's initial savings target was only £100m, which was thought sufficient to treat an extra 100,000 patients. The manifesto left doubt over the use of these savings. Cancer in general and more specifically breast cancer, or alternatively the general waiting list, were mentioned as possible uses for this small increment of spending.

In practice the government attempted to improve the situation on all of these fronts. It aimed to focus effort on the most serious clinical conditions, but its waiting list pledge undermined this objective by embodying the perverse incentive to neglect life-threatening conditions and concentrate on minor problems requiring routine treatment. The government's waiting list pledge therefore had the unintended consequence of introducing a wholesale distortion of clinical priorities. Also, to meet the government's targets, NHS Trusts resorted to the more dubious practice of manipulating their lists, called euphemistically by the auditors 'inappropriate adjustments', again with adverse implication for the patients affected.[16] The appearance of a 100,000 reduction in the inpatient waiting list during Labour's first term was achieved, but with the greatest difficulty and only by means that worsened the situation with respect to many of those in greatest clinical need.

Although the much-publicised waiting list pledge was met, the inpatient and important 13–26 week outpatient waiting lists have stubbornly remained at one million and 300,000 respectively. No further promises of waiting list reductions have been issued. Instead, in its second term, the government has concentrated on targets for waiting times for specified groups of patients. By 2004 it should be possible to see a GP within 48 hours; by the end of 2005 the government hopes to reduce outpatient-waiting times to three months and inpatient waiting times to six months. Even if these targets are met, waiting times of this length would be regarded as intolerable elsewhere in Europe.

Serious confrontation with waiting lists and waiting times has been handicapped by resource constraints. Even with impressive improvements in efficiency there was a limit to which a shrinking NHS was able take on mounting volumes of treatment. Over a long period, resource restrictions progressively inhibited the recruitment and retention of skilled staff. They also forced economies such as ward closures, so reducing the number of available beds. Some of the bed cuts are understandable in light of the changing character of the health service, which has for instance justified part of the massive reduction that has occurred in long-stay hospital provision. But there is no rational basis for the reduction of acute hospital beds by one-third that has taken place since 1970. The cumulative effect of this progressive shrinkage in NHS facilities has been disastrous. OECD statistics show that England has gravitated to the bottom of the league table with respect to such important criteria as levels of trained staff or provision of acute hospital beds per thousand population. For instance Germany supplies more than twice as many acute beds and employs more than twice the numbers of medical staff than England. The same adverse comparison applies throughout the system. England is accordingly notoriously backward in its provision of critical care beds; also its critical care units are smaller than those of its European partners, and the evidence suggests that it is less efficient in its use of the highly-trained nursing staff employed in these units.[17] It therefore comes as no surprise that tragic incidents occasioned by shortage of intensive care facilities feature prominently in the adverse media coverage of the NHS. The government is committed to reversing the erosion of hospital facilities. Particular priority has understandably been given to critical care, where beds have been increased by one-third since Labour assumed office, but England still compares unfavourably by European standards. The government is also pledged to reverse the loss of acute care beds, but the NHS Plan target for an increase of 2,000 by 2004, although much publicised, is derisory, and represents replacement of only one-quarter of the number of acute beds lost since 1990.

The government has also embarked on a much-publicised campaign to improve recruitment. Its target for 20,000 extra nurses by 2004 is especially emphasised as evidence of the government's bold ambitions. When this target is examined in detail, it implies an increase in qualified nurses of only 1 per cent each year. In recent years recruitment difficulties have infected the whole health service. Even the once popular GP specialty now experiences difficulties in attracting trainees. Given the necessary long period to train personnel, the government has resorted to much-publicised campaigns to recruit staff from elsewhere. Staff are drawn from the surplus existing in some European countries, such as nurses from Finland and Spain, or doctors from Germany, Italy and Spain. More controversial is the influx from South Africa and the developing world. This deprives the countries of origin of a precious skilled resource, drives them to recruit from even more deprived countries, and it frequently exposes the immigrant staff to exploitation.

Staff shortages have made the NHS increasingly dependent on agency nurses, which has driven up the cost of nursing services. In an effort to improve the situation long-term the government has annually conceded pay increases above the rate of inflation. Indeed, Mr. Milburn has even shown signs of irritation that the Nursing Pay Review Body has not been more generous in responding to the demands of nursing organisations. In December 2001 the relevant Pay Review Bodies recommended pay increases in the NHS at about twice the level of inflation, with individual shortage or special skill groups receiving more. Nurses and their leaders responded with outrage about the continuing 'miserly' level of pay, which was particularly insufficient to sustain existence in expensive areas such as the South East of England.[18] On the other hand, the medical profession is not too dissatisfied with levels of remuneration. The basic pay of fully-qualified doctors is set at three times the level of an experienced staff nurse. Also their contracts incorporate allowance for substantial augmentation of income from sources such as distinction awards and private work. Finally, new contracts that have taken many years to hammer out are promised to include generous financial inducements for adaptation to the working practices embodied in Labour's modernisation programme.

Making up for past deficiencies in pay of the non-medical workforce, generally improving conditions of employment, and purchasing more willing compliance from doctors, may be necessary for preventing the collapse of morale and supporting the greater numbers of skilled personnel required by the NHS. However, the higher pay bill inevitably drives up unit costs, so absorbing much of any new money promised to the health service. This unavoidable commitment, together with the cost of meeting the endless stream of central directives or financing new schemes such as NHS Direct, goes a long way to explaining why NHS Trusts are left with little discretionary funding to support much needed expansion or improvement of their front line services. When, in addition, the higher costs of privatised services are taken into account, it is easy to see how higher spending on the NHS could actually result in a diminution of services. New Labour has translated this hitherto unlikely scenario into a real possibility.

Private Partners

With increasing confidence, Mr. Blair's government has embraced and made central to its modernisation policies what in opposition Labour attacked as 'privatisation' of the NHS. As indicated above, adoption of the Private Finance Initiative was a crucial first step in this total reversal of policy. The new government defended PFI as the only realistic means to revive the moribund capital investment programme of the NHS. PFI offered the one chance for New Labour to generate spectacular improvement without delay. The Prime Minister habitually called on the public to count the success of his administration in terms of new hospitals and schools. On the basis of PFI, the government launched what it claimed was the biggest capital programme in the history of the NHS. By contrast with the faltering Hospital Plan began in the 1960s, Labour promised that under PFI there would be no delays in completion or reversion to phased implementation over many decades. The Princess Margaret Hospital, Swindon, mentioned for illustrative purposes in previous chapters, well illustrated the incapacities of the NHS in bringing hospital modernisation schemes to fruition. Swindon became one of the first PFI schemes agreed under New Labour.

The government expected the public to be ready converts to PFI on account of the practical advantages of new hospitals. However, any positive responses were in many cases offset by a great deal of negative experience in the catchment areas of the

PFI hospitals. Labour was powerfully reminded of the potential for a public backlash in the case of Kidderminster, where the proposal to close down the popular local hospital to make way for a PFI project in Worcester cost Labour a seat in the 2001 general election.

Undeterred by lack of enthusiasm for PFI within the Labour Party and TUC, or the reservations of many independent observers, the new government rushed through fresh legislation and signed its first PFI deal in July 1997. Since then, in England twenty-four major PFI projects have been completed with a total capital value of about £2.3bn. The full PFI programme currently envisages sixty-eight major schemes. One of the most ambitious of the first wave of PFI hospitals was the Norfolk and Norwich Hospital, an incipient teaching hospital, which has replaced a patchwork of old buildings in the Norwich city centre, the renewal of which has been under consideration ever since the beginning of the NHS. This rapidly completed new hospital was accorded the distinction of a double-page spread in the 2000 Annual Report.[19]

PFI is cited as evidence of the government's decisive success in modernising the hospital stock. The shortcomings of individual schemes are accepted as inevitable teething troubles, but it is claimed that these are less than the hazards encountered in the past with traditional means of capital procurement. PFI is defended as good value for money.

The PFI scheme looks at its best at the beginning, when gleaming new high technology facilities spring out of their green field sites, without any cost being evident on NHS balance sheets. However, the gilt has soon worn off the PFI gingerbread. Many of the flagship projects have become the objects of adverse media attention. The Cumberland Infirmary at Carlisle, the first scheme to be completed, has become a veritable museum of design and building failures. The Norfolk and Norwich Hospital attracted publicity on account of a windfall of £70m that the consortia stood to gain from the refinancing of its borrowing. Refinancing deals have emerged as a major source of gain for the consortia, with no obligation for sharing with their public partners. Typically the costs of PFI projects have become massively inflated. For instance, the scheme for the Princess Margaret Hospital, Swindon, commenced life as a £45m refurbishment exercise, which was rejected in favour of an entirely new hospital on a green field site at a cost of £145m. Controversially the new plan involved the demolition of the existing hospital, which could easily have been refurbished, and also happened to be Grade II* listed building, of outstanding merit as an example of modernist architecture. Such drastic changes of plan and costs give rise to the understandable suspicion that PFI is being motivated and shaped by need to generate healthy profits for the private partner, rather than because these schemes represent the only means to meet essential health objectives.[20]

Big returns guaranteed to the consortia over many years contrast with the situation of cash-strapped NHS authorities, which shoulder the long-term burden of their inflated yearly PFI bills. PFI has been subject to a great deal of scrutiny. Economic analysis of the scheme as a whole and reports on individual projects have suggested that the advantages of PFI are at best marginal, whereas the disadvantages are often profound.[21] Because of affordability pressures, PFI facilities are kept to a minimum. As a consequence, the new hospitals contain fewer beds than the ones that they supplant, which of course is subversive to the government's campaign to reverse the alarming decline in bed provision. The high cost of PFI schemes is already exercising a distorting impact on health service planning. The strain of meeting costs exercises pressures for 'efficiency savings', necessitating reductions in numbers of all categories of staff, not only those employed by the PFI consortia managing the facilities. Inevitably service provisions are being be redefined in minimal terms, with the consequence that the NHS is progressively narrowing the range of functions undertaken within its own hospitals. PFI cannot be regarded as merely an alternative vehicle for renewal of hospital infrastructure. It exercises widespread effects, in general driving the NHS into yet further dependency on the private sector.

PFI accordingly exacerbated fears about privatisation within the NHS and the Labour movement, which at first were met by government assurances that essential services would continue to be provided within 'the NHS family'. Under Mr. Milburn this family has been redefined to include the private sector. This redefinition was confirmed in *The NHS Plan*, which announced a new

'Concordat', promising a closer working relationship between the private sector and the NHS. Under the agreement concluded in October 2000, the private sector has greatly increased its profile in the NHS. From the central advisory apparatus to the planning of services at the local level, there is now the expectation of active private sector involvement. Services are provided as a matter of course in the private sector. NHS authorities are required to employ the surplus capacity of private hospitals, if necessarily away from the patient's home area, and from 2002 onwards, this extended to the use of private facilities abroad. This latter scheme brought great personal relief to the beneficiaries, but it also attracted substantial adverse comment on account of drawing further attention to basic shortcomings in the NHS. Resort to treatment abroad was widely portrayed as a national humiliation.[22] Working with the private sector is not confined to hospitals. For instance the improvement of primary care facilities in inner city areas is dependent on the NHS Local Improvement Finance Trust, known as LIFT, which is a joint venture vehicle between the health department and the powerful Partnerships UK plc, with an initial aim to raise £1bn for this purpose.

The biggest retreat of the NHS relates to chronic and elderly patients. With the progressive reduction of beds in NHS hospitals, these patients have been ejected, often inappropriately or prematurely, to nursing and residential homes, which are now almost entirely within the private sector. Patients hitherto treated free in NHS hospital beds, find themselves carrying the major part of the cost of nursing and residential home care. Current proposals for intermediate care, or for the fusion of primary health care and social care organisation, give rise to the suspicion that services of a kind previously free under the NHS will in future be provided as social care on the basis of payment.

In the early years of the Labour administration, health ministers silenced their Labour critics by habitually insisting that the private sector would be limited to a marginal role in the NHS as it is statutorily defined. Given Labour's political gains from its attacks on Tory privatisation by stealth, at first ministers proceeded cautiously in expanding opportunities for private sector involvement.

The government finally declared its hand in January 2002, when Mr. Milburn outlined radical proposals for 'redefining' the NHS. He rounded on the NHS as 'the last great nationalised industry', an obsolete relic of 'monolithic, centrally run, monopoly' provision of services. Mr. Milburn was vague about his future intentions, but he was emphatic that private sector involvement was central to his plans. The NHS of the future would engage a variety of 'different health care providers—in the public private and voluntary sectors'. Private sector involvement would be important, but not necessarily paramount. His dreams for the NHS are evidently shaped by Transport Secretary, Stephen Byers' thinking about the railways. The 'not-for-profit trust' proposed as a replacement for Railtrack seemed like the right model for the health service. By this means a 'mutual or public interest company within rather than outside public services' could replace state ownership.[23] Mr. Milburn argued that franchising out the health service will draw on the best of charitable, voluntary and private sector initiative. Frank Dobson, and David Hinchliffe, Chairman of the House of Commons Health Committee, warn that the NHS might incorporate the worst features of these alternatives. The critics cite the unresolved chaos of the railway system or other prominent examples of market failure as warnings about departing from the public service principle.[24] They fear that the NHS could easily slide back to the unsustainable situation existing in health care before World War II, which was only resolved by establishing the 'monolithic' NHS that Mr. Milburn now regards as untenable. By labelling the critics 'wreckers', the government revealed its vulnerabilities on this issue. The future course of events is uncertain, but if current trends continue, regardless of Mr. Milburn's claim that his plans do not represent 'privatisation in any way, shape or form', they are most likely in practice to yet further increase private sector involvement.[25] The private sector is well prepared for this extended role and it is able to market its wares more effectively than any amateur competitor. On the basis of experience with PFI, private sector partners will exact a high price for any transfer of risk that they accept, in which case Mr. Milburn is launching the NHS on a costly experiment, the benefits of which are entirely uncertain.

Paying for Health

Gordon Brown's commitment to fiscal prudence and control of public expenditure was an understandable defensive posture. However, by this action he exposed the public sector to resource constraints that imperilled the expectations of improvement promised as the central policy pledge of New Labour. This dangerous gamble risked undermining the credibility of the new administration. With respect to the NHS, this awkward issue was glossed over in just three sentences in the 1997 manifesto, which placed the emphasis on savings through elimination of waste and bureaucracy. Progress would therefore occur primarily through deflecting existing resources from bureaucracy to patient care. It was also promised that spending on the NHS in real terms would increase year upon year, but as Table 3.1 indicates, this condition could be met by increases as low as 0.1 per cent.

Labour was told about the dangers of subscription to unrealistically low spending plans. Before the general election Andrew Dilnot pointed out that the spending plans announced by the Major administration constituted 'an elephant trap and Labour has walked into it'. Labour had embarked on a course that would exacerbate the crisis created by underspending under the Conservatives and catching up at a later date was not likely to be possible. Labour's plans were incompatible with its commitment to a service that was 'universal, comprehensive health care, free at point of use'. Writing a few months later, I warned that the NHS faced 'an almost impossible task of providing a comparable level of service, involving similar costs, but with only half the resources available elsewhere' among leading western economies.[26]

The government made few concessions to its critics. On NHS spending the main decisions were deferred pending the results of the Comprehensive Spending Review, which was completed in July 1998. This resulted in what at the time seemed like a generous injection of additional funds. Much positive publicity was attracted by the promise of £21bn of additional funds for the health service and £19bn for education, covering the three-year period beginning April 1999. In the NHS this was sufficient to generate an annual real terms increase of 4.8 per cent; Labour could therefore claim that its record on health spending during its first term had matched the historic average increase, which is usually stated as being just above 3 per cent.

Events on the ground, such as the winter crisis of 1998/99, reminded the government that progress was being made too slowly. After a moment of euphoria, it became evident that Mr. Brown's £21bn would be swallowed up by the backlog of unavoidable commitments, with the consequence that the health service would show little evidence of improvement. Approach of a general election prompted reappraisal. It seems that in the autumn of 1999 Brown and Blair agreed that more dramatic action was needed to counteract the growing complaint that the UK was drifting into the Third World league of health care. The recently appointed Alan Milburn exploited this opportunity to ask for more, claiming that the positive economic situation merited granting the NHS 'the sustained increases in funding that it needs'.[27]

At this point there occurred a fundamental change in the government's perspective. Ever since the beginning of the health service, ministers had rejected the validity of international spending comparisons. The methodology of these comparative exercises was treacherous, but by the 1990s league tables were established as standard sources of reference in the international economic community; critics of the government's spending policy cited these with damaging effect. Especially if the UK wished to be regarded as part of Europe, further refusal to accept that there could be any valid comparisons in health spending seemed perverse, suspicious, and could not be continued without explicit justification. A little noticed hint of a change of policy is detectable from the Prime Minister's message for the first year of the new millennium. He pointed out that the government was making up ground on health spending, but he accepted that the UK 'still lags behind many similar nations abroad, which is why I am determined for there to be sustained increases in investment in the health service'.[28] Mr. Blair's remarks could be interpreted as accepting that health spending needed to rise in order to close the gap between the UK and its western partners.

A stinging criticism of the government's health service record by Lord Winston, the infertility expert and respected Labour supporter, duly backed up by the Presidents of the Royal Colleges, reinforced the sense of crisis.[29] This situation was reminiscent of the representations made by the Presidents of the Royal Colleges in December 1987. It will be recalled that this demand for an increase in funding set off a chain of events that ended with the internal market reforms. Eventually, additional resources were forthcoming from the Thatcher government, but only momentarily, to support implementation of the market system. Under New Labour, the promise of additional funds came first, after which the NHS Plan was devised to specify the groundrules for the use of these extra resources.

Announcement of higher funding for the health service emanated from the Prime Minister rather than Chancellor of the Exchequer, and it was made in the unlikely environment of a David Frost BBC TV programme, rather than in parliament. Mr. Blair made the striking promise that, subject to the general economic situation, the UK would, over a period of five years, increase the level of health spending to reach the European average, as measured by the share of GDP.[30] This concession was such a radical departure that its interpretation has been a matter of continual debate. Both the Prime Minster and Mr. Brown are often reported as reneging on this promise, but in broad terms it has been repeatedly confirmed.

Labour's new thinking on spending was reflected in the 2000 Budget, which laid down commitments for the period ending March 2004. For this period average spending was set to grow in real terms at 6.1 per cent, which was nearly twice the historic average and one of the highest rates of sustained growth in the entire history of the NHS. The government's seriousness about this target was underlined by fresh injections of resources in the 2001 and 2002 Budgets. Reflecting the depressed mood that has taken root in recent years, even with this substantial increment in funding, there remained a great deal of scepticism concerning the chances of meeting the European average, however this was defined. Preliminary discussion of European comparisons contained in the Wanless Interim Report, confirmed the extent of the gulf between the UK and its neighbours. On the basis of 1998 figures, with respect to GDP, only Luxembourg in the EU devoted a smaller share of GDP to health. The UK rate of 6.8 per cent GDP compared with an Unweighted EU average of 7.9 per cent and an Income Weighted EU average of 8.4 per cent. With respect to health spending per head of population, the UK in 1998 was inferior to any comparator country except New Zealand; by this estimate the gap between the UK and EU average was about 17 per cent. Even with the promised increases in spending, Wanless accepted that the EU average was unlikely to be reached. He also pointed out that the shortfall incurred by the UK was a long-term phenomenon that had been steadily getting worse. Consequently, the accumulated deficit in spending was so massive that it was out of the question to engage in any kind of catching up exercise.[31]

Acceptance that the government needed to radically adjust its horizons concerning total health spending introduced a new note of uncertainty concerning the future situation. Past thinking had been predicated on the assumption that adjustments would fluctuate, but would generate an aggregate annual increase in the UK of about 3.5 per cent. Total health spending as a proportion of GDP inched upwards, but in the 1990s it stood constant, just below 7 per cent. In the new millennium, total spending on health as a share of GDP might just rise to 8 per cent by about 2005. A jump by a whole percentage point of GDP over the course of five years, or even a decade, is an unprecedented prospect. It is anticipated that public rather than private sources will assume the burden of this increase. To achieve the 8 per cent GDP target, levels of public spending on health care must continue to increase at a rate of least 6 per cent a year. Meeting this new demand represents a formidable assignment for the Exchequer. Also, since EU spending is steadily increasing, meeting the EU average is becoming an ever more demanding target to reach.

To resolve uncertainty concerning future levels of funding, in March 2001 the Treasury instituted an enquiry under Derek Wanless, the former chief executive of NatWest Bank. The interim Wanless Report, issued in November 2001, was mainly concerned with assessment of the likely funding requirements over the next twenty years.[32] The Wanless study is an interesting political animal. It is the first investigation of its kind ever conducted under the NHS. It is also noteworthy that the study only came about as a panic measure, then instigated by the Treasury rather than by the health department, and in the manner of Mrs. Thatcher it was trusted to a captain of commerce rather than academic experts. The latter seemed the more obvious choice in the 1950s, when a retrospective study of NHS costs was commissioned from Abel-Smith and Titmuss. Their impressive work, mentioned above, is the only near equivalent to Wanless existing in the quasi-official NHS literature.

Pending the final Wanless Report, to be submitted by April 2002, Mr. Brown's Pre-budget Report was examined for clues about government thinking on meeting the cost of augmented NHS funding. Confused handling of this issue by government public relations agencies conveyed the impression of disarray among ministers. The press took this as a sign that a debate was raging behind the scenes over the merits of reverting to a hypothecated tax for the whole or part funding of the NHS. Mr. Brown left no ambiguity on this question. He favours continuation of the existing mechanism of funding, using general taxation. In this respect he reached a conclusion similar to all of his Labour and Conservative predecessors who had examined this issue in depth. The Treasury is formally welcoming a debate, but its own preferences are already evident, rendering it unlikely that there will be any departure from Mr. Brown's expressed preference. General taxation entails many benefits, but it is now more problematical than in the past on account of government pledges that have sealed off the possibility of increasing income tax or VAT. All other possibilities for increases in direct taxation are problematical. The government's difficulties are complicated by the current stagnation in the western economies, which has introduced uncertainty over prospects for attaining levels of economic growth that might facilitate expansion in public spending.

Periodically in the past, the contribution to the NHS from the National Insurance Fund has been expanded. The Conservatives have sometimes favoured this option, but it has always been criticised by Labour as a poll tax bearing heavily on the lowest paid workers. Labour has so far consistently opposed the funding of health care on any basis other than general taxation. Its policy documents consistently expose the difficulties in expanding the role of social insurance, private insurance, or out of pocket payments. The arguments were fully rehearsed in *The NHS Plan*, in the only chapter to be accorded the privilege of citations to the technical literature.[33] Its critique of insurance was specifically addressed to the 'continental' model, with Germany and France specifically in mind. The interim Wanless Report repeats the argument, but it is careful to distinguish continental sickness insurance from the UK's social insurance payment to the NHS included in National Insurance Contributions. The latter is now described as 'highly progressive (more so than general taxation overall) contributing significantly to the overall progressivity of publicly-financed health care in the UK'.[34]

In the interim Wanless Report, the insurance contribution stands out as the only taxation option not ruled out on policy grounds and judged to be free from serious disadvantage. The passing comment by Wanless should perhaps be taken as a sign that the government is signalling new-found enthusiasm for expanding the role of National Insurance in the funding of the NHS. Such an escape route would also have the attraction of providing a point of compromise with the advocates of hypothecation, among whom the media tend to count Alan Milburn and various other senior Cabinet colleagues. Wanless has presented a huge bill, which Labour is pledged to pay. For this purpose Labour has taken a brave political step and warned the public that higher taxation is inevitable to meet the government's obligations to the NHS. Having made this leap of faith, other public services, from education to the railways will now be clamouring for similar treatment. Finding the resources to meet all of these urgent obligations presents a problem of daunting proportions.

Modernisation

Government concessions concerning funding are welcomed with relief, but past experience has repeatedly shown that the NHS possesses the capacity to swallow up resources without yielding the advantages of improved services. As noted above, in opposition, New Labour estimated that £1.5bn a year was being wasted by the internal market reforms. Also it claimed that PFI and other forms of privatisation were wasteful. Labour promised that its own path towards modernisation would avoid these costly mistakes. However, New Labour's colonisation of Conservative policy territory entailed the risk that it would also replicate the alleged errors of the previous government. Accordingly there was a risk that New Labour's modernisation cures would be little improvement on the disease they were designed to treat.

Modernisation was a central theme for New Labour in opposition and it has maintained its importance throughout Mr. Blair's administration. Modernisation rested on two lines of attack, which have been pursued in tandem. First, a programme of major structural reform was designed to shift the balance of power towards the front line staff most in touch with the needs of communities and individual patients. Secondly, a system of national standards and a strong accountability framework were used as incentives for professionals to raise their performance up to the best available standards of practice. Labour called this approach to modernisation 'integrated care' or a 'third way', to emphasise differences from the ethos of the internal market.

As with the Conservatives and their internal market, Labour drove forward its plans for integrated care with the expectation that its success would relieve pressure for higher spending. This imperative for maximum economy accounts for the urgency with which modernisation was pursued. A White Paper, *The New NHS Modern Dependable*, was issued in December 1997, only a few months after Labour's return to office.[35] This document emanated from Mr. Dobson's department, but reminiscent of *Working for Patients*, the Preface was written by the Prime Minister. Mr. Dobson's scheme was hastily scrambled together from papers left behind by Mr. Dorrell. The new image cultivated somewhat artificially for Mr. Dobson's plan was geared to compensate for the disappointment that spending would scarcely cover the cost of maintaining services at their current levels. It was promised that New Labour's Third Way would involve 'no return to the old centralised command and control systems' associated in the public mind with Old Labour.[36]

Even the breakneck implementation of this reform package failed to generate an impression of improvement. As noted above, the government was forced to increase investment, but every pledge of extra spending was made conditional on a further measure of modernisation. It was repeatedly insisted that 'investment has to be tied to reform and modernisation'.[37] This association was indeed reflected in the title of the successor White Paper, *The NHS Plan. A plan for investment. A plan for reform*, which was issued in July 2000. *The NHS Plan* was a further hasty compilation, initiated in March 2000 and suitably adapted to the promise of higher spending sufficient to permit a small amount of expansion in services. Mr. Milburn's White Paper was much longer and superficially more impressive than Mr. Dobson's *New NHS*. However, the new document was less a plan that a portmanteau, or progress report, summarising the condition of the NHS as it stood at this date, and setting out targets for future expansion. *The NHS Plan* was described as yet a further break with the failed 'command-and-control' model of the past.

Before the ink was dry on *The NHS Plan*, Mr. Milburn initiated a further major overhaul under the banner of *Shifting the Balance*.[38] The latter admitted that the government had still failed to emancipate itself from the 'command and control' philosophy in its previous reforms. It was now promised that central interference would be reduced and that power would at last be returned to front line staff. Not inappropriately, the headlines characterised these new changes as 'a top-to-bottom reorganisation in a dramatically short period'.[39]

Predictably, before implementation of Shifting the Balance had commenced, in the autumn of 2001, Mr. Adair Turner was thrown into the breach to produce a further strategic plan for the NHS, taking account of the spending horizons implicit in the Wanless Report. Mr. Turner is described as Vice-Chairman of Merrill Lynch and former Director-General of the CBI. He is attached to the Forward Strategy Unit of the Cabinet Office, which has the remit to 'do blue skies policy thinking for the Prime Minister'. The Forward Strategy Team is directed by a specialist on broadcasting and telecommunications. In this team, an 'overarching role' is exercised by Lord Birt, former Director-General of the BBC, who has already advised the Prime Minister on crime and gone on to an assignment on transport strategy. Reminiscent of the Thatcher review of the NHS undertaken in 1988, the Forward

Strategy Team conducts its work in secrecy and its reports are confidential.

As discussed above in the context of privatisation, Mr. Turner was not left with the field to himself. Almost before he had started work, in January 2002, Mr. Milburn sprang forward with yet further proposals for redefinition and decentralisation of the NHS, which were duly described as the most radical scheme yet produced, likely to produce the biggest changes to be made in the NHS since its inception. The same claim had of course been made for the Conservatives' *Working for Patients* reforms, and for each of Labour's plans issued in 1997, 2000, and 2001.

The above situation is not calculated to instil confidence in the government's capacity for strategic planning. One hastily contrived plan is soon succeeded by another, sometimes involving a reversal of direction. As in the case of the internal market reforms, there is evidence of competition between the Number 10 Downing Street Policy Unit, the Treasury, and Health Department for command of the direction of policy. Mr. Milburn and his team find themselves in competition with captains of commerce, to whom Mr. Blair and Mr. Brown instinctively turn, rather in the way that Mrs. Thatcher relied on Sir Roy Griffiths a decade earlier.

The NHS workforce, already war weary from the continuous disruption occasioned by the market reforms, has needed to accustom itself to similar instability under Labour, seemingly with no end in sight. NHS personnel are now accustomed to being told every couple of years that they are about to face the biggest overhaul since the beginning of the health service, that the process of modernisation is only just entering its stride, and that they are about to face 'unsettling times'.[40] Actual experience therefore contrasts with New Labour's previous promises that the NHS would be spared from 'permanent revolution', and that change would be made incrementally, after full consultation and on the basis of tried experiment.

Structural Overhaul

Labour's structural overhaul of the health service has been even more rapid and dramatic than the internal market changes of the

Conservatives. An additional complication has been introduced by Labour's devolution policy.

Devolution

Although the internal market changes were in theory adapted to the specific conditions of Scotland and Wales, in practice these partners were kept closely in line with England. Under Labour, the Scottish Parliament and Welsh Assembly assumed unambiguous command of their health services. Consequently in 1997 and 2000, Scotland and Wales published their own planning documents. These indicated that both nations were straining to depart from the English model, but they also showed conclusively that the manacles to Whitehall had not been severed. In the past UK-wide consultations have preceded all important policy changes. It is quite possible that this practice is in process of dissolution. It would be interesting to know the extent to which Scotland and Wales were consulted over the commission now being undertaken by Mr. Adair Turner, and whether their agreement was sought to the fertile ideas springing from the mind of Mr. Milburn over redefining the NHS. As yet the politicians with responsibility for the health service in Scotland and Wales have not echoed Mr. Milburn's denunciations of the historic NHS, or supported his ideas for franchising out the system.

It is not always clear that benefits arise from mechanical adherence to the devolutionary principle. The Medical Research Council retains the UK remit that it has possessed since its establishment in 1919. The Audit Commission, the Commission for Health Improvement and the National Institute for Clinical Excellence relate to England and Wales, with parallel agencies being established for Scotland. Such examples suggest that devolution has been responsible for a certain amount of groundless duplication of effort, which contributes to costs and makes inefficient use of scarce professional expertise. Sir Liam Donaldson's important report, *Getting Ahead of the Curve*, shows that urgent action is needed to reform the public health system in light of the events of 11 September 2001 and many other serious threats that are on the horizon. This report relates only to England; it will now be necessary to generate parallel changes in Scotland and Wales, taking account of the increasing disharmony between the national administrative systems, which could well be subversive to the improvements of public health that are such an urgent requirement.

Scotland and Wales have consolidated existing distinguishing features of their systems and they are in process of introducing further alterations, mainly designed to simplify lines of accountability and erase vestiges of the internal market. Both Scotland and Wales look likely to revert to something like the organisational arrangements that existed in 1982. Just occasionally these distinctions have the potential to occasion friction. For instance, the contentious English proposals to abolish Community Health Councils looked even less defensible in light of the decision to retain these bodies or their equivalents in Scotland and Wales. An even greater source of tension was the decision in Scotland to implement the recommendation of the Royal Commission on Long-term Care that all personal care in residential and nursing homes should be publicly funded. The lesser powers of the Welsh Assembly prevented Wales from following this line. Consequently, in England and Wales this additional public support was limited to nursing care. Inevitably the Scottish precedent was prominently cited by pressure groups in their campaign to achieve further extension of public support for older people in nursing and residential homes. Instead of being regarded as a generous concession, the changes south of the border seemed miserly and illogical.

In England, underlining the continuity of policy with respect to fundamentals of administration and management, Labour at first preserved much of the structure inherited in 1997. Labour therefore retained the purchaser/provider split, the use of contractual agreements as a basis for commissioning services, the NHS Trusts, the Health Authority structure, the central NHS Executive and its Regional Offices. Although, as reflected by Figure 4.1, most of these elements have subsequently been subject to further rationalisation, much of the basic structure bequeathed by the Conservatives remains recognisably in tact.

Primary Care

The most important structural changes introduced by Labour relate to primary care. Labour has continued the Conservative drive to

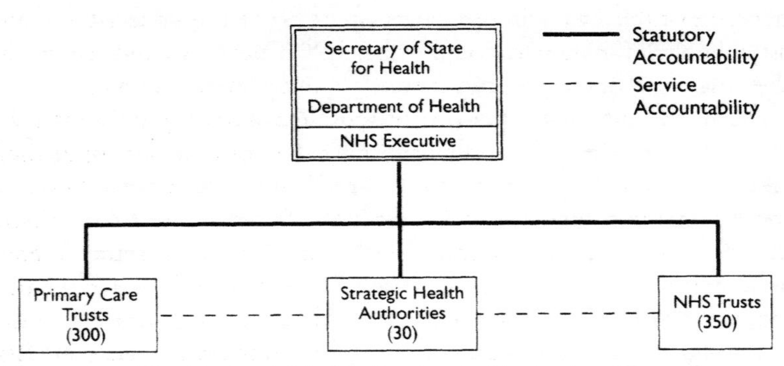

Figure 4.1. The National Health Service in England as Planned, 2002

Source: Based on *Shifting the Balance* (London: Department of Health, 2001) Numbers approximate; they describe the situation anticipated in 2004

make the NHS 'primary-care led', but it was pledged to remove fundholding. As already pointed out, the Conservative government had already modified its primary care policies to a substantial degree. Despite its adversarial rhetoric, Labour continued in essentially the same direction. The chapter on primary care in *The New NHS* therefore carried an appropriate subheading 'going with the grain' and its highlighted quotation stated that 'Primary Care Groups will grow out of the range of commissioning models that have developed in recent years'.[41] *The New NHS* conceded that fundholding had demonstrated the value of GP commissioning of services for their patients. Labour aimed to optimise the benefits of commissioning by GP practices. Its new policy might therefore be regarded as universalisation of fundholding rather than its abolition. Labour also used the previous government's NHS (Primary Care) Act 1997 as the basis for its experiments on variant forms of primary care.

The Primary Care Act allowed Labour to keep its pledges about experimentation, but in practice it concentrated on a single direction of change. All general practitioners were amalgamated into some 480 Primary Care Groups (PCCs). This was a temporary expedient, pending the evolutionary transformation of these groups into some 300 Primary Care Trusts (PCTs), a process which began in April 2000. At the beginning of Labour's second term, the transition to PCTs was half-complete. The change-over to PCTs is scheduled for completion in 2004. PCTs represent the end of the line for Labour's current policy commitments. However, the government anticipates that PCTs represent a staging post towards a further development involving even closer assimilation of health and social care, in which case, 'Care Trusts' will emerge as the model for the future. The legislative basis for this next step was set in place with the Health and Social Care Act 2001. Some fifteen areas are working on plans for Care Trusts, the first of which are expected to begin operation in April 2002.

The above changes represent the most rapid and wide-ranging overhaul ever undertaken in the field of primary care. The Shifting the Balance project launched in the autumn of 2001 further adds to the power of PCTs. These bodies are projected to control some 75 per cent of the NHS budget, either spent on directly provided primary care and community care services, or on commissioning from other providers such as NHS Trusts.

With the relocation of purchasing from Health Authorities to PCGs and PCTs, the government has undermined the purchaser/provider distinction to which it is committed. Under the internal market, Health Authorities were allocated the main secondary care purchasing role and intentionally excluded from service provision. The tendency begun with GP fundholding has now been carried to its logical conclusion with PCGs/PCTs. The purchasing of secondary care is being vested with the providers of primary care. It is likely that the purchaser/provider distinction will be further eroded in future, since PCTs are being encouraged to take over the provision of services and personnel currently the responsibility of NHS Trusts. The PCTs will also take on new activities in the spheres of prevention, promotion and public health. Their collaboration with local government agencies in the field of community care might well be extended to absorb functions currently within the orbit of local government social service departments. The role of PCTs will also be strengthened by the exercise of complete control over the new Personal Medical Services schemes, being developed under the 1997 primary care legislation. The Personal Medical Services have become one of government's favoured ways for encouraging new ways of working in deprived areas, where recruitment problems are at their worst. Some of these pilots have experimented with new approaches to care, giving opportunity for greater equality in multidisciplinary partnerships and offering incentives for greater initiative by groups such as nurses. It will be interesting to see whether PCTs prove capable of sustaining the diversity and radicalism that was promised for these Personal Medical Services schemes.

The drive towards PCTs is defended as a necessary step in the relocation of power to the front line of NHS primary care providers. The government has no doubt speeded up implementation of its primary care reforms in order to improve services, increase efficiency and facilitate cost savings. However the implications of this reform are even more radical. For the moment, PCTs are the favoured child of the system. PCTs are in effect incipient health authorities for their areas, something akin in size and number to the District Health Authorities established in 1982, but now operating from a primary care rather acute care platform. PCTs constitute a basis for further rationalisation that might parallel the privatisation already taking place in the hospital sector. The PCT system is well-placed for development in the direction of the American-style Health Maintenance Organisations or translation into the new entities specified by Mr. Milburn in his proposals for redefining the NHS. This would involve the greater injection of private finance and the franchising out of primary care services either to not-for-profit trusts, or to private sector interests, who are already extending their range of primary care activities and are clamouring on the sidelines for entry into this lucrative but hitherto protected market.

Reconfiguration

Concentrating power at the PCT level has exercised a domino effect on the rest of the system. It remains to be seen whether PCTs will establish harmonious working relations with NHS Trusts. The new arrangements place the GP at a position of advantage with respect to the consultant to an even greater extent than under the internal market. Since PCTs have taken over the commissioning role of Health Authorities, the latter have lost their main function. Therefore they are being reduced in number and reconstituted as Strategic Health Authorities. These are being accorded expanded functions in strategic planning and performance enhancement, which is being presented as an exciting future. In reality Strategic Health Authorities make little sense geographically or functionally; they are now the next obvious targets for abolition. For the moment the Strategic Health Authorities are preserved, not doubt to retain some kind of 'regional' presence in the system, especially because the Regional Offices of the NHS Executive have now been abolished. As noted in the previous chapter, these Offices dated back only a few years, and were themselves a token presence left over from the earlier Regional Health Authorities. The limited functions of Regional Offices have been redistributed, partly to the central department, which itself has undergone reorganisation in line with the Shifting the Balance programme. On the basis of the NHS Plan, the joint post of Permanent Secretary/Chief Executive was created to head the Department of Health and NHS Executive, a change that represents an admission of defeat for the troubled experiment of separating the policy and operational arms of the health service described in the previous chapter. The new post was intended to create unified direction to the entire range of NHS, public health, and social services functions of the Department of Health. Indicating the new level of importance attached to modernisation policies, a new central Modernisation Board was established to advise ministers on the implementation of *The NHS Plan*.

Community Health Councils

One further casualty of the new health service configuration is the Community Health Council. Because CHCs were designed to represent the voice of the patient at the district level, they were left behind during the evolution towards Strategic Health Authorities. In opposition Labour was a passionate advocate of the CHC, which was seen as the only statutory body on which the voice of the community was dominant in a health service that was increasingly management dominated. Under the internal market CHCs were frowned upon as a relic of collectivism; the government accordingly favoured the relocation of consumer protection to the individual. Abolition was periodically considered, but the CHCs were known to have a strong following; consequently, their lives were spared. Labour proposed to strengthen CHCs, an objective that was affirmed in the 1992 manifesto and in subsequent policy documents. Upon the basis of this policy Labour entered the 1997 general election. Ministerial statements and policy documents such as *Patient and Public Involvement in the New NHS* (September 1999) suggested high expectations for CHCs.

The decision to abolish CHCs was announced somewhat casually in *The NHS Plan* of July 2000. This reversal of policy was badly received in the labour movement and among consumer organisations. On the other hand abolition earned credit from dominant provider interests, who stood to rid themselves of a troublesome partner. NHS Trusts in particular had long regarded CHCs as an irritant owing to such monitoring activities as 'Casualty Watch'. The demand by CHCs for a central role in primary care, including the idea that they would act as the 'official bridge' between the public and the new PCTs was no doubt a last straw.[42] Expression of such insolent aspirations was taken as a sure sign that these consumer bodies had outlived their usefulness. Total abolition seemed the safest alternative, since it was especially important to avoid the risk of offending the powerful general practitioner lobby at a time when their co-operation was urgently required.

For the first time since their establishment in 1974, CHCs assumed centre stage; they took on a political importance out of all proportion to their scale. The proposal to abolish CHCs emerged as the most controversial aspect of the NHS Plan. Reminiscent of the controversies surrounding their establishment, abolition entailed a battle of similar magnitude, involving very much the same arguments. Whereas in 1974 the Conservatives conceded to demands to strengthen CHCs, New Labour persisted with abolition and the substitution of the inaptly titled PALS, the Patient Advocacy and Liaison Service. The government sought to palliate critics by introducing many elaborations to the local PALS machinery. This will now be reinforced by Patients Forums, the Independent Complaints Advocacy Service and the national Commission for Patient and Public Involvement in Health. The need for these concessions was taken by sceptics as a sign of the basic weakness of the PALS system as a whole. There persisted a suspicion that the new consumer bodies represent a vastly over-complicated and inferior substitute for CHCs.

CHCs will soon be forgotten, but the circumstances of their abolition are worthy of consideration for the light they throw on the government's attitude to patients, citizens, communities and local democratic accountability. Despite the government's earnest pretensions concerning openness to local consultation and expression of public concern, local communities and their representatives are likely to count for little when it comes to questions of appeasing corporate interests. This conclusion is reflected in a recent study of voluntary effort, which suggests that 'like its Conservative predecessor . . . the government wishes to encourage active citizenship, but very much on terms dictated by the state'.[43]

Quality Organisation

Quality assurance is the complement to Labour's structural reforms. As the balance of organisation is shifted to increase the empowerment of frontline staff, the government has undertaken to set in place machinery to ensure that services are redesigned to optimise performance.

Labour's attack on the record of the Conservatives revolved around accusations that inadmissible variations of standards were permitted and indeed encouraged by the internal market. Accusations that the NHS was being turned into a 'postcode lottery', or that fundholding had introduced a two-tier health service, were fundamental to Labour's electoral appeal in 1997. In fact, as noted above, the Conservatives were alert to these problems and many of their schemes to correct disparities were taken up by Labour. It is, however, unlikely that a Conservative government would have opted for anything like the system of central quality controls that Labour has introduced.

Dramatic action on the part of Labour was rendered unavoidable by the extent of professional misconduct uncovered in the course of the 1990s. The horrific career of Harold Shipman was a completely exceptional case, but it drew attention to the laxity of controls over standards of general medical practice in the NHS, as well as the inadequacy of professional regulation. The Bristol Royal

Infirmary paediatric cardio-vascular surgery scandal, which occasioned the biggest enquiry ever undertaken into malpractice in the NHS, as well as many other cases of blatant professional incompetence on the part of hospital consultants, revealed a similarly disquieting situation in acute hospital care. Indeed, unreliable doctors were likely to exercise tyrannous control and expect the recognition of distinction awards, while their critics were persecuted and driven from their jobs. Abuse of elderly patients at the North Lakeland NHS Trust in Cumbria showed that scandals in institutions for long-term care were not things of the past. The Alder Hey organ retention scandal exposed a particularly gruesome anomaly that came as a terrible surprise to the public and was found to be repeated elsewhere. Examples of cases of malpractice and fraud among senior hospital administrators that regularly came to public attention exposed a culture of sleaze that was difficult to penetrate, and where the culprits, when identified, tended to escape with trivial penalties. Experience during the last decade has confirmed that the NHS has failed to extinguish a masonic and secretive culture that possessed the potential to undermine the essential duty of public trust.

Labour inherited problems of misconduct and negligence that had been building up for decades and had been subject to cowardly evasion by previous governments. This situation was of course inimical to the goal of quality assurance that was central to the modernisation policy of New Labour. The tide of revelations about malpractice shook public confidence in the General Medical Council and Royal Colleges and it has caused them to radically reform their disciplinary, appraisal and revalidation procedures. In making these changes, they were forced into closer participation with the new quality assurance measures introduced by the government.

New Labour's main claim to originality lies in the employment of central regulatory bodies to further its quality agenda. Since 1997, a whole battery of agencies have been introduced with the idea of laying down national standards and establishing a strong accountability framework. An outline for the new structures was set out in 1997 in *The New NHS.* This provided for two main agencies, the National Institute for Clinical Excellence (NICE) and the Commission for Health Improvement (CHI). NICE began work in 1999; its remit extends to England and Wales. NICE is concerned with the evaluation of the clinical and cost effectiveness of new and existing technologies. NICE is the chosen vehicle for turning the analysis of evidence-based medicine into national policy and practice. It is faced with a massive agenda, which it is addressing at the rate of about 50 enquires each year. The work of NICE that attracts most interest is its production of guidelines relating to new and expensive drugs, where controversial postcode lottery issues tend to arise. NICE sets down guidelines, but as yet these are not mandatory. NICE has also extended its work into clinical audit. As the examples of Viagra and beta interferon indicate, NICE findings are widely criticised, and its judgements rarely attract unanimous support. While NICE is criticised for both its positive and negative recommendations, the latter attract the greatest attention. In general it is felt that political and economic criteria impinge on the decisions of NICE. Therefore it is seen less as an impartial assessor, and more as an ingenious blocking device, introduced to add yet further to already notorious delays in the introduction of new treatments that are know to be effective and are widely available elsewhere in Europe. Instead of introducing certitude and clarity into the process of innovation, NICE has become yet a further contributor to the fractious disputes that surround the continuing postcode lottery in the allocation of new treatments.

The Commission for Health Improvement started work in April 2000. It is responsible for monitoring clinical standards throughout the NHS in both England and Wales. Although purposely not called an inspectorate, it performs an inspectoral function throughout the NHS. CHI inspectors make periodic local visits to carry out clinical governance reviews. 'Clinical governance' was adopted as a concept in *The New NHS*. It is the favoured term for the framework adopted locally for the guarantee of best practice and promotion of quality improvement in clinical care. The government's aim was to make every NHS authority into a 'quality organisation'. An essential part of the work of the CHI relates to overseeing the implementation of NICE guidelines and National Service Frameworks. The latter have so far been produced for

Cancer, Coronary Heart Disease, Diabetes, Mental Health, and Older People. As noted in the second chapter, the model for these plans was the Calman-Hine report on cancer services produced under the Conservatives. To take forward the implementation of service redesign at the local level, the NHS Plan introduced the Modernisation Agency, which brought together a number of established bodies, as well as introducing some additions. The Modernisation Agency is overseeing the production of Local Modernisation Plans. Associated with the Modernisation Agency are Taskforces addressed to the implementation of individual National Service Frameworks. In some cases, national 'czars' have been appointed to give special leadership in problem areas such as cancer.

Particular attention has been attracted by the investigations of CHI undertaken at the behest of the Secretary of State for Health in England or the Welsh Assembly in Wales into examples of serious service failure. One of the early examples of such a report related to the North Lakeland NHS Trust, has been mentioned above. These special investigations are delicate assignments and might well elicit defensive responses from NHS authorities and the medical profession. So far, hard-hitting reports have been accepted without demur, largely because they were addressed at soft targets. Once the CHI offends more powerful interests, then it will risk the fate that befell Crossman's Hospital Advisory Service. Already the 'mounting burden of inspection and regulation' is being blamed for undermining the work of doctors, which is a sure sign that CHI will be regarded as the cause of the problems to which its inspections are addressed.[44]

In order to make the performance record more transparent, the government has introduced the Performance Assessment Framework. Initially this involved the production of annual tables indicating the performance of health authorities according to six areas where comparative data was available. Under the NHS Plan this scheme was refined and applied at the level of NHS Trusts. In order to instil confidence in the objectivity of performance assessment, it was placed under the CHI, working in association with the Audit Commission. Initially, application of the Performance Assessment Framework involved application of the traffic light system then in vogue among the performance panjandrums of Whitehall. Red Light designation indicated failure to meet core national targets, which set in motion sanctions and suitable remedial measures. By contrast, the Green classification was the trigger for rewards such as 'earned autonomy' or minor financial incentives. In the autumn of 2000, much media attention was attracted by the use of this method to classify NHS Trusts according to the degree of cleanliness of their hospitals. An alarming number of hospitals were classified as Red, but after a short campaign, a year later no hospitals were classified as Red. In its first annual report, in January 2002, the new Modernisation Board was able to declare victory over dirtiness in hospitals.

Both the government and independent agencies have begun the release of comparative performance data relating to trusts, specific hospitals, their constituent departments, or even specialist teams, and eventually this classification will extend to individuals. These findings suggest the existence of major differences in performance. Inevitably such assessments are contentious and subject to major difficulties of interpretation.

The public now has access to a range of information that was previously totally unavailable, which has created a new level of transparency regarding the comparative performance of their local hospitals and their professional teams. The government claims that this system provides an incentive for raising standards to the level of the best. The latter are now granted 'Beacon' status and expected to spread good practice in their vicinity with the help of the private partner, Status Ltd. Such hospitals are now in line for elevation to the status of 'foundation hospitals' under the plans announced in January 2002.

On the negative side, it is claimed that the system of rewards and punishments adds to the advantages of the privileged and serves to demoralise those working under adverse conditions and attending to the most intractable clinical conditions. In this respect the performance system might well further undermine staff morale, lead to undesirable clinical practices, including avoidance of high-risk cases, and exacerbate already serious problems of staff retention or inequality existing in areas of social deprivation.

The above short review of Labour's quality assurance machinery demonstrates seriousness of purpose in confronting problems of inexcusable poor performance. This complicated bureaucracy is likely to be remembered as New Labour's most distinctive contribution to the New Public Management reform. Quality assurance has come into the health service at a late date on account of its heavy IT demands, its general technical difficulties, and medico-political sensitivities. The new system will undoubtedly not survive long in its present form. In 2001, Professor Ian Kennedy's report on the Bristol Royal Infirmary made suggestions for substantial changes in the organisation of the central agencies, partly to bring about greater co-ordination, but also to increase their independence from the government. These proposals were almost entirely rejected by the government.

By hard experience the New Labour apostles of modernisation have discovered that there is no easy passage to their New Jerusalem. There is also likely to be some uncertainty when they arrive at Mount Zion, whether New Labour's works will look very much different from those of their despised Tory rivals. There would certainly have been difficulty in distinguishing between the policies of the two rivals, especially during the Labour's early stages of office. Even in its second term, Labour continues to pursue much of the Conservative policy agenda. With respect to the key issue of the privatisation of health and social care, Labour has emerged as an exemplary convert to the ideal of public-private partnership. On questions of organisation and management, Labour has hardly departed from the path of the New Public Management charted by the Conservatives. Its own special contribution has focussed on quality assurance, where its taste for central regulation is distinctive and would have been alien to the Conservatives.

On spending Labour also assumed a more distinct policy identity. After a shaky start, Labour confronted the problem of health spending in a more realistic manner than its Conservative predecessor. It is unlikely that the Conservatives would have accepted the European average of spending as a target, or commissioned anything like the Wanless Report on long-term spending requirements. Indeed, the Conservatives never embraced health policy with anything like this degree of commitment. The new spending plans provide some reassurance that Labour is honouring its promise to adopt the NHS as one of its highest policy priorities. It remains to be seen whether Labour will prove capable of sustaining this momentum. Mr. Blair's habitual and undiminishing expressions of utopian ambition for the NHS are positive signs, which should impose on his government a level of obligation that will be difficult to evade.

Labour's commitment to higher spending is an essential condition for progress, but the above review leaves it in doubt whether its policies will bring about improvements sufficient to reach standards of health care taken for granted elsewhere in the European Union. The public now expects European standards from the NHS and they have every right to be unforgiving if substantial changes for the better are not evident by the date of the next general election.

There is already a state of restiveness about the slow pace of improvement. The public is rightly sceptical about the excessive and sometimes ridiculous claims about the successes of the government's modernisation policies. Everyday experience suggests a different reality in which current policies have generated only marginal positive benefits. It is too soon to assess the impact of the more radical changes of policy, but the erratic course followed by the government is not calculated to inspire confidence. After five years in office, it is entirely unclear where the public-private amalgamation into which the NHS has been launched is heading. An authoritative voice has used an important platform to warn that inveterate taste for the fashionable panaceas of public management has built up a culture of self-deception entailing 'costs of massive gaps between what is claimed and what it true'.[45] There must be real risk that the transformations now taking place in the health service will fail to yield the promised rewards and also constitute a more expensive way of providing the same inferior service. This of course is reminiscent of the verdict passed by the Old Labour opposition on the Conservative internal market reforms. For the two political rivals it therefore seems that health policy has come to represent the 'Ditch into which the blind have led the blind in all Ages, and have both there miserably perished'.[46]

CONCLUSIONS

> We can save the NHS certainly. But the real task is to improve it, to build the same sense of excitement and enthusiasm about the NHS in the new Millennium as there was when it was created in the difficult years following World War II.[i]

Political leaders and thinkers, from Beveridge and Bevan to Blair, have appreciated the awesome magnitude of the challenge taken on when the state assumes responsibility for providing a comprehensive health service. They have nevertheless accepted this as one of their main priorities. Indeed they framed their aspirations for the National Health Service in the boldest terms. This book has examined the manner in which politicians have exercised this daunting task of stewardship over health care.

In the UK, as elsewhere, realistic engagement with the modernisation of health care came about only after World War II. The National Health Service was a very specific UK response to the problem of post-war reconstruction. Each of the western economies evolved a solution in line with the characteristics of its own political institutions, in most cases following a different course of funding and administration from that adopted in the UK.

In some important respects the national health systems have developed in unison. After World War II all western governments actively modernised their health care arrangements, in the course of which the state intervened to a greater degree than ever before. Health care assumed importance in the welfare state plans that were introduced everywhere and sometimes at lavish cost. For a time health care seemed like a problem that would solve itself. Technical advance held the promise of assured success. As noted above, this confidence was rapidly dispelled in the course of the 1970s. As the realities of health care became increasingly understood, health services became redesignated as one of the most intractable problems of the modern state, destined to absorb escalating resources without any assurance that basic requirements of health were being met.

For every western state, health care metamorphosed from a virtuous prize into an incubus with the potential to wreck the economy. With increasing urgency, governments embarked on campaigns of retrenchment, cost containment, and management reform. Every panacea in turn has been shown to have indifferent results. Uwe Rheinhardt points to the existence of a cyclical process characterised by periodic calls for bold reforms that are followed by incompetent implementation of change, prompting yet further calls for reform. He concludes that this demonstrates that health care resolutely refuses to be ordered according to the formulae applied with success in other parts of the economy.[2] Consequently, throughout the western world, governments have experienced acute difficulty in meeting the mounting costs of health care. No mode of organisation or level of spending seems capable of meeting the tide of legitimate public expectations. In panic, governments turn elsewhere for models to imitate, only to discover that these are infected by chronic weaknesses. The USA looks enviously at Canada, but Canadians are so alarmed about defects in their system that it has been necessary to establish a Royal Commission to locate an escape from their difficulties. The media and politicians in the UK contrast their dilapidated system with the lavish level of amenity available in France and Germany. On the other hand finance ministers in France and Germany gaze enviously at the UK record of comparable outcomes from half the spending. Throughout Western Europe there is more than a sneaking admiration for Cuba, where highly favourable outcomes are generated from minimal expenditure. Then of course Cuba relies on emergency aid from its well-wishers and international relief organisations to bolster its modest technical facilities.

The above negotiations between nations on questions of health are not merely a matter of friendly rivalry. Countless public health issues provide reminders of the importance of a unified effort, but the pressure for uniformity permeates the system considerably more deeply. Realities of federal structures, economic unions and the global economy impose pressures for uniform approaches to social provision. Nations like the UK, and many poorer countries, stand out as anomalies on account of the higher level of socialisation of their systems. Everywhere, constraints of the economic system and corporate interests exert pressure for reductions in public expenditure and provision of all services according to the norms of the market. In this situation non-conformity becomes intolerable. International good citizens like the UK are under particular pressure to set an example by bringing their welfare provision into line with the expectations of economic liberalisation. This ever more menacing global imperative provides a relevant context for evaluation of the whole recent development of the NHS.

The UK's unorthodoxy in opting for a system of health care financed by general taxation and provided in public sector institutions is understandable in the light of the historical circumstances. Failure effectively to confront health and related social welfare issues throughout the interwar Depression was deeply resented. Programmes of social reconstruction, promised as compensation for the huge sacrifice of life during World War I, turned into miserable tokenism. This betrayal by interwar administrations was fresh in the public consciousness when Labour was rewarded with its landslide victory after World War II. Social reconstruction was Labour's first priority; central to its welfare state was the new health service. Labour responded to public demand by decisively breaking with the gradgrind health policies of the past. The NHS was recognised as the most radical experiment in health care in the western world. The UK's unorthodox system of socialised medicine succeeded as well as could be expected in the circumstances of the times in lifting the burden of anxiety about ill-health. By its actions Labour benefited from a tide of positive sentiment that has been communicated to later generations and still persists as more than a distant memory. This idea of natural Labour proprietorship of the NHS, together with the difficulty experienced by the Conservatives in persuading the public that they are trustworthy in their handling of health care, are reminders that the politics of health care connects with deeply rooted and tenaciously held convictions.

The final years of the recent long period of Conservative

government were marked by deepening public concern about the deterioration of public services and the tawdry state of the physical environment. The condition of the NHS was central to these anxieties. By the date of the 1997 general election the dereliction that was overtaking the health service was a prime focus of media attention. The crisis in public health and health care in the NHS established health issues at the head of the domestic policy agenda. The public at last realised that the trust they had placed in generations of politicians had been misplaced. It was evident that the habitual posturing of governments towards the NHS and their ceaseless preoccupation with 'reform' were a smokescreen, calculated to detract attention from a long history of neglect.

This moment of revelation in 1997 was reminiscent of 1945. New Labour gained credit from its frank acknowledgement of failures in the NHS, which Mr. Blair declared was on the verge of collapse. Labour staked its reputation on its high level of commitment to the public services and this duly contributed to its immense electoral success. Mr. Blair's pledges to restore the NHS to a position of world leadership represented one of these main electoral assets.

Labour's record in office has not matched its stated ambitions. The public detects little improvement and much evidence of persistence of all the defects that Labour highlighted when it was in opposition. Labour seemed to fall into the same errors as its predecessors. Indeed the reputation of Labour looks worse on account of the evident gulf between its grandiose rhetoric and the dismal realities on the ground. The credibility of the government also suffered from the exaggerations of its public relations machinery, which attached altogether undue significance to the fulfilment of trivial pledges. At first New Labour seemed not to appreciate the mountainous scale of the problem that it had taken on. Its whole approach was undermined by self-satisfaction. As with previous administrations, its responses were insufficient to the magnitude of the problem. The government also repeated the mistake of its Conservative predecessors by vesting unwarranted confidence in structural overhaul and modernisation policies. The result was continuing crisis, which has occasioned a loss of public confidence to a greater degree than the 2001 electoral situation indicates.

As indicated in the previous chapter, the government belatedly awoke to the realities of a deteriorating situation. This realisation became unavoidable in the light of the UK's dismal and humiliating situation according to a wide range of international comparisons of performance. The government was more committed than any of its predecessors to performance indicators, evidence-based decisions and the need to raise standards to the level of the best. In this case the evidence suggested the inescapable conclusion that the NHS was approaching what the NHS Plan would label as a Red Light condition, indicating requirement for urgent remedial action.

After a slow and painful learning exercise, it was recognised that the making of bricks required the presence of straw. Consequently, in the new millennium a UK government, for the first time, conceded the need to bring its health service spending up to the European average. As a logical corollary, the Wanless Report has estimated the likely cost of meeting the future needs of the health service. There is no guarantee that funds will be available on a sustained basis required to bring UK standards up to the European average, but at least the government is now examining ways of meeting the cost of meeting minimum acceptable standards. This problem of increased costs of meeting basic obligations is faced by all health services, but it is particularly acute in the UK because New Labour is picking up the bill for decades of past neglect.

As the government recognises, real improvement depends on the effective use of resources. This constitutes a test for the government's modernisation programme, which is the latest packaging adopted for the New Public Management reforms that have been gathering pace for some twenty years. In this respect the UK is adhering to the general pattern of the western economies. The government now has to allay the suspicions of IMF and OECD that augmented spending plans imply a return to tax and spend polices that the international economic community finds alien. Labour's precipitate conversion to public/private partnership represents a response to this global economic imperative. As a consequence, strides taken by Mr. Blair towards what Labour previously stigmatised as 'privatisation' far exceeded anything attempted by Mrs. Thatcher. In the case of PFI, the private alternative is attractive in the short term, but it is expensive thereafter. In other examples (like the use of agency staff) the cost of private service is high from the outset. The escalating cost of private provision, together with other factors that serve to increase unit costs, will be expensive to the NHS and indeed might well absorb the greater part of the promised additional funding. It is therefore quite likely that the public will see little benefit from the additional resources that are now promised. In that case the real benefits from the sacrifices now expected from the taxpayer will accrue to the private sector balance sheets rather than the NHS patient.

Given the many uncertainties concerning the future, it is natural that the Prime Minster is now cautious in his estimates about the future and his New Year message for 2002 speaks of 'unsettling' times ahead for the public sector. The government already faces pressure from powerful economic interests to introduce further radical change with respect to both the funding and provision of services. Many of these ideas would take the NHS a long way from the founding principles that the government is pledged to uphold. Before bending to corporate pressures to further depart from the public service conception of the NHS, Mr. Blair should pay heed to the outstanding successes achieved under the 'New NHS' introduced by the Attlee government. As this book indicates, it is entirely misleading to caricature Bevan's health service as some kind of obsolete soviet-style command and control system.[4] Indeed it is arguable the early NHS succeeded better than any of market-orientated models introduced under later governments in meeting basic health care objectives. In the light of this history, the best chances for New Labour may well lie in continuing to uphold the conception of the NHS as a 'triumphant example of the superiority of collective action and public initiative applied to a segment of society where commercial principles are seen at their worst'.[3] It is doubtful whether any other basis for policy is capable of recapturing the 'sense of excitement and enthusiasm' that the Prime Minster regards as fundamental for the revival of the NHS in the new millennium.

APPENDIX

General Elections, Prime Ministers, and Health Ministers from 1945

In Scotland health functions are exercised by the Secretary of State for Scotland; and in Wales since 1969 they have been exercised by the Secretary of State for Wales. These arrangements are subject to change under the Labour devolution proposals of July 1997.

26 July 1945	General election: Labour majority 200. Prime Minister, Clement Attlee; Minister of Health, Aneurin Bevan.
23 February 1950	General election: Labour majority 6. Prime Minister, Clement Attlee; Minister of Health, Aneurin Bevan.
January 1951	Replacement of Bevan, by Hilary Marquand as Minister of Health. Bevan appointed Minister of Labour.
25 October 1951	General election: Conservative majority 17. Prime Minister, Winston Churchill; Minister of Health, Harry Crookshank.
May 1952	Replacement of Crookshank by Iain Macleod as Minister of Health.
26 May 1955	General election: Conservative majority 58. Prime Minister, Sir Anthony Eden; Minister of Health, Iain Macleod.
December 1955	Replacement of Macleod by Robert Turton as Minister of Health.
10 January 1957	Resignation of Eden following Suez Invasion and replacement as Prime Minister by Harold Macmillan; Minister of Health, Dennis Vosper.
September 1957	Replacement of Vosper by Derek Walker-Smith as Minister of Health.
8 October 1959	General election: Conservative majority 100. Prime Minister, Harold Macmillan; Minister of Health, Derek Walker-Smith.

July 1960	Replacement of Walker-Smith by Enoch Powell as Minister of Health.
October 1963	Resignation of Harold Macmillan owing to ill health. Prime Minister, Sir Alec Douglas-Home; Minister of Health, Anthony Barber.
15 October 1964	General election: Labour majority 5. Prime Minister, Harold Wilson; Minister of Health, Kenneth Robinson.
31 March 1966	General election: Labour majority 95. Prime Minister, Harold Wilson; Minister of Health, Kenneth Robinson.
November 1968	Robinson stands down as Minister of Health; Richard Crossman Secretary of State for Social Services of the combined Department of Health and Social Security.
18 June 1970	General election: Conservative majority 33. Prime Minister, Edward Heath; Secretary of State for Social Services, Sir Keith Joseph.
28 February 1974	General election: Labour minority government, 301 seats out of 635. Prime Minister, Harold Wilson; Secretary of State for Social Services, Barbara Castle.
10 October 1974	General election: Labour majority 4. Prime Minister Harold Wilson; Secretary of State for Social Services, Barbara Castle
April 1976	Retirement of Harold Wilson. Prime Minister, James Callaghan; Secretary of State for Social Services, David Ennals.
3 May 1979	General election: Conservative majority 43. Prime Minister, Margaret Thatcher; Secretary of State for Social Services, Patrick Jenkin.
September 1981	Replacement of Jenkin by Norman Fowler as Secretary of State for Social Services.
9 June 1983	General election: Conservative majority 144. Prime Minister, Margaret Thatcher; Secretary of State for Social Services, Norman Fowler.
11 June 1987	General election: Conservative majority 102. Prime Minister, Margaret Thatcher; Secretary of State for Social Services, John Moore.
July 1988	Split of Departments of Health and Social Security. Secretary of State for Health, Kenneth Clarke.

28 November 1990	Replacement of Thatcher by John Major as Prime Minister; Secretary of State for Health, William Waldegrave.
9 April 1992	General election: Conservative majority 21. Prime Minister, John Major; Secretary of State for Health, Virginia Bottomley.
July 1995	Replacement of Bottomley by Stephen Dorrell as Secretary of State for Health.
1 May 1997	General election: Labour majority 179. Prime Minister, Anthony (Tony) Blair; Secretary of State for Health, Frank Dobson.
October 1999	Replacement of Dobson by Alan Milburn as Secretary of State for Health.
7 June 2001	General election: Labour majority 167. Prime Minister, Tony Blair; Secretary of State for Health, Alan Milburn.

NOTES

Chapter 1. Creation and Consolidation

1. Aneurin Bevan, HC Debates, vol. 447, col. 50, 9 February 1948.
2. W. A. Robson, *The Development of Local Government* (London: Allen & Unwin, 1931). 296, 333.
3. Speeches by Lord Dawson of Penn, *The Times*, 19 Oct. and 13 Nov. 1937.
4. PEP, *Planning*, No. 177, 16 Sept. 1941, 1. See also PEP, *The British Health Services* (London: PEP, 1937).
5. Welsh Board of Health, *Hospital Survey: The Hospital Services of South Wales and Monmouthshire* (London: HMSO, 1945), 48.
6. PEP, *Planning*, No. 177, 16 Sept. 1941, 3.
7. Director General Emergency Medical Service memorandum, Aug. 1939, PRO MH 76/67.
8. PEP, *Planning*, No. 177, 16 Sept. 1941, 13.
9. R. M. Titmuss, *Problems of Social Policy* (London: HMSO, 1950), 474.
10. Ernest Brown, HC Debates, vol. 374, cols. 1116–20, 9 Oct. 1941.
11. Beveridge, SIC(42)100, 10 July 1942, PRO PIN 8/87. Repeated in an extended form in *Social Insurance and Allied Services*, Cmd. 6404 (London: HMSO, 1942), paras. 19 (xii), and 427.
12. Robson (ed.), *Social Security*.
13. NSRS, 'National Health Insurance', typescript, 1942, NSRS Archive, Nuffield College, especially 68–9.
14. The state medical schemes introduced in the present century have not affected the self-employed or 'independent-contractor' status of general medical practitioners, general dental practitioners, pharmacists, and opticians, who in effect run small businesses, deriving income from various sources. That part of income derived from the state through services rendered to NHI/NHS patients has been determined by the terms of contracts negotiated by their representatives.
15. Ministry of Health, Department of Health for Scotland, *A National Health Service*, Cmd. 6502 (London: HMSO, 1944).
16. Ministry of Health, Department of Health for Scotland, *Progress with the Proposals for a National Health Service*, draft Command Paper, June

1945, appendix to Lord Woolton, CP(45)13, 4 June 1945, PRO CAB 66/66.

17. J. E. Pater, *The Making of the National Health Service* (London: King's Fund, 1981), 104.
18. Enid Russell-Smith to R. A. Russell-Smith, 21 Aug. 1945, Durham University Library.
19. Sir William Scott Douglas to Bevan, 22 Sept. 1945, PRO MH 80/28.
20. Ministry of Health, *National Health Service Bill: Summary of the Proposed New Service*, Cmd. 6761 (London: HMSO, 1946).
21. R. C. Wofinden, *Health Services in England* (Bristol: J. Wright, 1947), 168–9.
22. 'Local Government in England and Wales', *The Economist*, 6 Jan. 1945, 3–4.
23. Bevan, 'National Health Service. The Future of the Hospital Services', CP(45)205, 5 Oct. 1945, PRO CAB 129/3.
24. Ibid.
25. Bevan, 'Proposals for a National Health Service', CP(45)339, 13 Dec. 1945, PRO CAB 129/5.
26. Ministry of Health, Department of Health for Scotland, *A National Health Service*, Cmd. 6502, 12.
27. Bevan, CP(45)339, 13 Dec. 1945, PRO CAB 129/5, paras. 52–3.
28. Bevan, CP(45)205, 5 Oct. 1945, PRO CAB 129/3, paras. 12–13.
29. Sir George Godber, *The Health Service: Past, Present and Future* (London: Athlone Press, 1975), 22.
30. Bevan, HC Debates, vol. 422, cols. 43–63, 30 Apr. 1946.
31. Editorial, *The Times*, 22 Mar. 1946; editorial, *The Economist*, 30 Mar. 1946.
32. Bevan, CP(45)205, 5 Oct. 1945, PRO CAB 129/3.
33. Godber, *The Health Service: Past, Present and Future*, 22.
34. Ibid.
35. Ffrangcon Roberts, *The Cost of Health* (London: Turnstile, 1952).
36. *The Times*, 6 July 1948.
37. *Report of the Committee of Enquiry into the Cost of the National Health Service*, Cmd. 9663 (London: HMSO, 1956); B. Abel-Smith and R. M. Titmuss, *The Cost of the National Health Service in England and Wales* (Cambridge: Cambridge University Press, 1956).
38. In the general reorganization of the Scottish Office in 1962, the Department of Health became the Scottish Home and Health Department.
39. Webster, ii. 77–8.

40. Ministry of Health, *Hospital Survey: The Hospital Services of Berkshire, Buckinghamshire, and Oxfordshire* (London: HMSO, 1945), 50.
41. Godber, *The Health Service: Past, Present and Future*, 27.
42. North West Metropolitan RHB, *Survey 1954–1958* (London: North West Metropolitan RHB, 1958), 37.
43. Russell Brock, *The Times*, 26 May 1956.
44. Ministry of Health, *A Hospital Plan for England and Wales*, Cmnd. 1604 (London: HMSO, 1962).
45. Sir Theodore Fox, *The Medical Journal of Australia*, 19 June 1971, 1346.
46. G. Forsyth, *Doctors and State Medicine: A Study of the British Health Service* (London: Pitman, 1966), 86; G. Forsyth and R. F. L. Logan, 'Studies in Medical Care', in G. McLachlan (ed.), *Towards a Measure of Medical Care* (London: NPHT, 1962).
47. D. Walker-Smith, 'Proposals in the Health Sphere', Feb. 1958, Treasury, SS 267/491/01D.
48. G. E Godber, 'Health Services Past, Present and Future', *Lancet* (1958), ii. 1–6, 5 July 1958.
49. Minister of Health, *Health & Welfare: The Development of Community Care: Plans for the Health and Welfare Services of the Local Authorities in England and Wales*, Cmnd. 1973 (London: HMSO, 1963).
50. Central Health Services Council, Standing Medical Advisory Committee, *The Field of Work of the Family Doctor: Report of a Sub-Committee* (London: HMSO, 1963).
51. *Report of the Committee of Enquiry into the Cost of the NHS*, Cmd. 9663, 274–86.
52. Bevan, CP(45) 205, 5 Oct. 1945, PRO CAB 129/3. Bevan, 'Local Government Management of Hospitals', *Municipal Journal*, 12 Mar. 1954, 544–5.
53. Medical Services Review Committee, *A Review of the Medical Services in Great Britain* (London: Social Assay, 1962).
54. John Revans, letter to Wessex General Practitioners, Nov. 1962, PRO MH 133/259.

Chapter 2. Planning and Reorganization

1. A. Lindsay, *Socialized Medicine in England and Wales: The National Health Service, 1948–1961* (Chapel Hill, NC: University of North Carolina Press, 1962), 453.
2. The others were Christopher Addison and Walter Elliot, who were Ministers of Health in 1919–21 and 1938–40, respectively.
3. D. Paige and K. Jones, *Health and Welfare Services in Britain in 1975* (Cambridge: Cambridge University Press, 1966), 116–26.

4. *Royal Commission on the National Health Service. Chairman: Sir Alec Merrison. Report*, Cmnd. 7615 (London: HMSO, 1979).
5. Webster, ii. 385–90.
6. DHSS, *Priorities for the Health and Personal Social Services in England: A Consultative Document* (London: HMSO, 1976).
7. DHSS, *Priorities in the Health and Social Services: The Way Forward* (London: HMSO, 1977).
8. DHSS, *The Future Structure of the National Health Service* (London: HMSO, 1970), para. 79.
9. M. H. Cooper and A. J. Culyer, 'Equality in the National Health Service: Intentions, Performance and Problems of Evaluation', in M. M. Hauser (ed.), *The Economics of Medical Care* (London: Allen & Unwin, 1972), 47–57; J. Noyce, A. H. Snaith, and A. J. Trickey, 'Regional Variations in the Allocation of Financial Resources to the Community Health Services', *Lancet* (1974), i. 554–7, 30 Mar. 1974; M. J. Buxton and R. E. Klein, 'Distribution of Hospital Provision: Policy Themes and Resource Variations', *British Medical Journal* (1975), i. 345–9, 8 Feb. 1975; P. Willmott, 'Health and Welfare', in M. Young (ed.), *Poverty Report 1974* (London: Temple Smith, 1974), 194–217.
10 *Sharing Resources for Health in England: Report of the Resource Allocation Working Party* (London: HMSO, 1976).
11. 'Problems of the Health Service', in Central Office of Information, *Health Services in Britain* (London: COI, 1959), 27–8.
12. National Board for Prices and Incomes, *Report No. 29*, Mar. 1967, paras. 71–2; *Report No. 60*, 1968, para. 90.
13. Paige and Jones, *Health and Welfare Services in Britain in 1975*, 27, 35–6, 130.
14. Scottish Home and Health Department, *Administrative Reorganisation of the Scottish Health Services* (Edinburgh: HMSO, 1968).
15. SHHD, *Reorganisation of the Scottish Health Services*, Cmnd. 4734 (Edinburgh: HMSO, 1971).
16. Ministry of Health, *First Report of the Joint Working Party on the Organisation of Medical Work in Hospitals* (London: HMSO, 1967), para. 16. This working party conducted most of its work in 1966. A cog-wheel device was employed on the cover of this and subsequent English reports on managing medical work.
17. For instance, R. H. S. Crossman, *A Politician's View of Health Service Planning*, The Maurice Block Lecture, 13 (Glasgow: University of Glasgow, 1972); Crossman, 'Personal View', *The Times*, 9 Aug. 1972.

18. DHSS, *National Health Service: The Future Structure of the National Health Service* (London: HMSO, 1972).
19. Welsh Office, *The Reorganisation of the Health Service in Wales* (Cardiff: HMSO, 1970).
20. DHSS, *National Health Service Reorganisation: Consultative Document* (London: DHSS, 1971).
21. Ibid., para. 6.
22. Crossman, HC Debates, vol. 820, col. 611, 1 July 1971.
23. Meyjes to Joseph, 9 Mar. 1972, quoted in Webster, ii. 504.
24. DHSS, *Management Arrangements for the Reorganised National Health Service* (London: HMSO, 1972).
25. Welsh Office, *National Health Service Reorganisation in Wales: Consultative Document* (Cardiff: Welsh Office, 1971); *National Health Service Reorganisation: Wales*, Cmnd. 5057 (Cardiff: HMSO, 1972).
26. S. Haywood and A. Alaszewski, *Crisis in the Health Service: The Politics of Management* (London: Croom Helm, 1980), 41.
27. D. Widgery, *Health in Danger: The Crisis in the National Health Service* (London: Archon Books, 1979), 144.
28. Imperial Cancer Research Fund, *Our Vision for Cancer* (London: ICRF, 1995), 23.
29. *Report of the Committee of Inquiry into Allegations of Ill-Treatment of Patients and other Irregularities at the Ely Hospital Cardiff*, Cmnd. 3975 (London: HMSO, 1969).
30. T. McKeown and C. R. Lowe, *An Introduction to Social Medicine* (2nd edn., Oxford: Blackwell, 1974), 213.
31. *Royal Commission on the NHS*, para. 972.
32. Ibid., ch. 9.
33. Ibid., para. 7.37.
34. Noyce, Snaith, and Trickey, 'Regional Variations in the Allocation of Financial Resources'.
35. W. J. H. Butterfield, Foreword, in Office of Health Economics, *New Frontiers in Health* (London: OHE, 1964).
36. *Royal Commission on the NHS*, para. 7.4.
37. A. Macfarlane and R. Mitchell, 'Health Services for Children and their Relationship to the Education and Social Services', in J. O. Forfar (ed.), *Child Health in a Changing Society* (Oxford: Oxford University Press, 1988), 185.
38. *Inequalities in Health: Report of a Working Party* (London: DHSS, 1980); chairman Sir Douglas Black.
39. B. Abel-Smith, *National Health Service: The First Thirty Years* (London: HMSO, 1978), 56.

Chapter 3. Continuous Revolution

1. P. Riddel, *The Thatcher Government* (Oxford: Martin Robertson, 1983), 138.
2. *The Economist*, 4 June 1988, 30–2.
3. Margaret Thatcher, *The Downing Street Years* (London: HarperCollins, 1963), 606.
4. Margaret Thatcher, HC Debates, vol. 42, col. 730, 10 May 1983; Thatcher, BBC TV, *Panorama*, 31 May 1983.
5. Nicholas Ridley, *My Style of Government* (London: Fontana, 1992), 86. For Conservative health service plans, *The Times*, 25 Feb. 1986.
6. National Association of Health Authorities and Trusts, *Health Care Economic Review* (Birmingham: NAHAT, 1990).
7. *House of Commons, Session 1988/89, Social Services Committee, Eighth Report. Resourcing the National Health Service: The Government's Plans for the Future of the National Health Service*, HC 214-III (London: HMSO, 1989).
8. For a representative estimate, *The Economist*, 5 Dec. 1981.
9. *The Times*, 28 Jan. and 31 July 1982.
10. The CPRS Report was discussed by the Cabinet on 9 Sept. 1982; for press leaks and analysis, *The Economist*, 18 Sept. 1982, 25–6; *The Times*, 18 Sept. 1982; *Observer*, 19 Sept. and 10 Oct. 1982.
11. See, for instance, Conservative Political Centre, *A New Deal for Health Care* (London: CPC, 1988).
12. Secretaries of State for Health, Wales, Northern Ireland and Scotland, *Working for Patients*, Cm. 555 (London: HMSO, 1989), Foreword.
13. CPRS, Report on Health Service Charges, *The Economist*, 12 Nov. 1983, 22–3.
14. To all intents and purposes the subsidy on spectacle lenses had ended in 1971.
15. P. Townsend and N. Davidson (eds.), *Inequalities in Health: The Black Report* (Harmondsworth: Penguin, 1982).
16. DHSS, *Care in Action: A Handbook of Policies and Priorities for the Health and Personal Social Services in England* (London: HMSO, 1981).
17. DHSS, Welsh Office, *Patients First: Consultative Paper on the Structure and Management of the National Health Service in England and Wales* (London: HMSO, 1979).
18. In Wales the eight AHAs were converted into nine DHAs; after some hesitation, in both Scotland and Wales the 1974 district arrangements were abandoned and replaced by management units.
19. DHSS, Welsh Office, *Patients First*, Foreword, para. 9.

20. Ibid., para. 11
21. *The Economist*, 26 July 1980, 57.
22. Howe to Conservative MPs, 28 July 1982, *The Times*, 29 July 1982.
23. For early criticism of Ministers' approach to consensus management, *The Economist*, 13 Oct. 1979
24. G. Forsyth, 'Background to Management', in D. Allen and J. A. Hughes (eds.), *Management for Health Service Administrators* (London: Pitman, 1983), 14.
25. DHSS, *Health Care and its Costs* (London: HMSO, 1983); DHSS, *The Health Service in England: Annual Report 1984* (London: HMSO, 1985). This revival of an annual report intended for public consumption lasted until 1987.
26. *The Economist*, 17 Sept. 1983, 35; *House of Commons. Fourth Report from the Social Services Committee, Session 1985–86*, HC 387-I (London: HMSO, 1986) pp. xii–xix.
27. Michael Forsyth, *Reservicing Health* (London: Adam Smith Institute, 1982).
28. Interview with Patrick Jenkin, *Director*, Dec. 1979. Similarly, Sir Patrick Nairne to Sir A. Rawlinson, 26 Mar. 1979, Treasury, T SS10/01E.
29. *NHS Management Inquiry*, DHSS 1983, General Observations, para. 5.
30. A. Maynard and A. Walker, *Doctor Manpower 1975–2000: Alternative Forecasts and their Resource Implications*, Royal Commission on the National Health Service, Research Paper No. 4 (London: HMSO, 1978).
31. DHSS, *Nurse Manpower: Maintaining the Balance* (London: HMSO, 1982).
32. S. Harrison, *National Health Service Management in the 1980s* (Aldershot: Avebury, 1994).
33. DHSS, *Health Care and its Costs*, para. 3.13, emphasis added.
34. *The Guardian*, 16 Dec. 1987.
35. *Social Services Committee, Eighth Report. Resourcing the National Health Service*, HC 214-III.
36. N. Timmins, *Five Giants: A Biography of the Welfare State* (London: Fontana, 1996), 434.
37. *The Times*, 27 July and 19 Dec. 1987.
38. *Spectator*, 9 Jan. 1988, 8.
39. *The Economist*, 23 Jan. 1988, 28.
40. *Spectator*, 23 Jan. 1988, 5.
41. J. Redwood and O. Letwin, *Britain's Biggest Enterprise: Ideas for Radical Reform of the NHS* (London: Centre for Policy Studies, 1988); L. Brittan, *A New Deal for Health Care* (London: Conservative Political

Centre, 1988); D. G. Green, *Everyone a Private Patient* (London: Institute for Econonic Affairs, 1988).

42. N. Macrae, 'Health Care International', *The Economist*, 28 Apr. 1984, 23–36.
43. A. Enthoven, 'National Health Service', *The Economist*, 22 June 1985; Enthoven, *Reflections on the Management of the National Health Service*, (London: NPHT, 1985).
44. Social Democratic Party, *Changing and Renewing the Health Services* (London: SDP, Aug. 1986); David Owen, *Our NHS* (London: Pan, 1988).
45. NHS Management Board, *Review of the Resource Allocation Working Party Formula* (London: DHSS, 1986).
46. G. Bevan, 'Organising Hospital Finance by Simulated Markets', *Fiscal Studies*, 5 (1984) 44–63; M. Marinker, 'Developments in Primary Health Care', in G. Teeling-Smith (ed.), *A New NHS Act for 1996?* (London: Office of Health Economics, 1984); A. Maynard, 'Performance Incentives in General Practice', in G. Teeling-Smith (ed.), *Health Education and General Practice* (London: Office of Health Economics, 1986); A. Maynard, M. Marinker, and D. Pereira Gray, 'The Doctor, the Patient and their Contract, iii. Alternative Contracts; are they viable?', *British Medical Journal*, 292 (1986), 1438–40.
47. 'Set the Hospitals Free', *The Economist*, 30 Apr. 1988, 13–16.
48. M. Goldsmith and D. Willetts, *Managed Health Care* (London: Centre for Policy Studies, 1988); R. Whitney, *National Health Service Crisis* (London: Shepheard-Walwyn, 1988); M. Pirie and E. Butler, *Health Management Units, the Operation of an Internal Market within the National Health Service* (London: Adam Smith Institute, 1988); Institute of Health Services Management, *Working Party on Alternative Delivery and Funding of Health Services* (London: IHSM, 1988).
49. See, for instance, *The Economist*, 19 Nov. 1988, 37–8.
50. Secretaries of State for Health, Wales, Northern Ireland and Scotland, *Working for Patients*, Cm. 555 (London: HMSO, 1989).
51. Ibid., Foreword. Similarly, Kenneth Clarke, HC Debates, vol. 146, col. 169, 31 Jan. 1989.
52. Kenneth Clarke, HC Debates, vol. 146, col. 165, 31 Jan. 1989.
53. Secretaries of State, *Working for Patients*, para. 3.3.
54. David Owen, HC Debates, vol. 146, col. 163, 31 Jan. 1989.
55. Klein, *The New Politics of the NHS* (3rd edn., London: Longman, 1995), 131.
56. *Social Services Committee, Eighth Report. Resourcing the National Health Service*, HC 214-III.

57. *Caring for People*, Cm. 849 (London: HMSO, 1989).
58 In Scotland there were in 1997 forty-seven Trusts, and in Wales twenty-nine. Direct-managed units were more common in Scotland than elsewhere.
59. In Scotland fundholding was noticeably less developed than in England, but in Wales the level was similar to England.
60. In Wales, the nine DHAs and eight FHSAs were amalgamated into five Health Authorities. No comparable change was made in Scotland.
61. NHS Executive, *The Operation of the NHS Internal Market*, HSG(94)55 (London: Department of Health, 1994). Department of Health, *The Purpose, Organisation, Management and Funding of the National Health Service. A Guide for the Private Sector* (London: Department of Health, 1997), 6
62. *Report of the Inquiry into London's Health Service, Medical Education and Research* (London: HMSO, 1992); chairman, Sir Bernard Tomlinson.
63. Klein, *New Politics of Health*, 237.
64. C. H. Smee, 'Self-Governing Trusts and GP Fundholders: The British Experience', in R. B. Saltmann and C. von Otter (eds.), *Implementing Planned Markets in Health Care: Balancing Social and Economic Responsibility* (Buckingham: Open University Press, 1995), 177–208, 204.
65. Stephen Dorrell, 'NHS 2000. The Millennium lecture'. Manchester Business School, 8 January 1996; *The National Health Service: A Service with Ambitions*, Cm. 3425, (London: The Stationery Office, 1996).
66. 'NHS White Paper', *The Independent*, 14 November 1996.

Chapter 4. New Age of Labour

1. Tony Blair, Foreword to *The NHS Plan. A Plan for investment. A plan for reform*, Cm. 4818-I (London: The Stationery Office, 2000), 9.
2. Margaret Beckett, 'Safe in whose hands?', *The Independent*, 12 June 1995.
3. Christopher Ham, *The Independent*, 30 June 1995.
4. Chris Smith, *Labour Party Conference Report 1996* (London: Labour Party, 1996), 76; idem, HC Debates, vol. 284, cols. 247–53, 25 October 1996.
5. Steve Richards (ed.), *Preparing for Power. Interviews 1996–1997* (London: New Statesman, 1997), 83–4.
6. 'A One Nation NHS', speech to the Annual Conference of the National Association of Health Authorities and Trusts, 20 June 1996.
7. *The NHS Plan*, para 2.26. *Securing our Future Health: Taking a Long-Term View. Interim Report* (London: HM Treasury, November 2001), 1.

8. 'The State of the Nation', *The Independent*, 27 July 1999.
9. *The Sun*, 15 July 2000.
10. *The government's annual report 99/00* (London: The Stationery Office, July 2000), 24. *The NHS Plan*, 1, 8, 15.
11. Charles Clarke, interview by Andrew Rawnsley, BBC Radio 4, The Westminster Hour, 25 November 2001.
12. Sir Donald Acheson, *Independent Inquiry into inequalities in health report* (London: The Stationery Office, 1998).
13. Lord Hunt, speech to Faculty of Public Health Medicine, 13 November 2001.
14. Chief Medical Officer, *Getting Ahead of the Curve. A Strategy for combatting infectious diseases* (London: Department of Health, 2002), 12–14.
15. Christina Pantazis and David Gordon (eds.), *Tackling inequalities* (Bristol: The Policy Press, 2000).
16. National Audit Office, *Inpatient and outpatient waiting in the NHS* (London: The Stationery Office, July 2001); National Audit Office, *Inappropriate adjustments to NHS waiting lists* (London: The Stationery Office, December 2001).
17. *Shaping the Future: Long Term Planning for Hospitals and Related Services* (London: Department of Health, February 2000); D. Adbrooke, C. Hilbert and M. Corcoran, *Adult Critical Care Services: an International Perspective* (Sheffield: Medical Economics and Research Centre, August 1999).
18. Mike Edwards, 'Nurses' fury at 3.6% rise' (indicating 96.3 per cent dissatisfaction, according to a *Nursing Times* survey), *Sunday Mirror*, 20 January 2002; John Carvel, 'Public Sector Mutiny', *The Guardian*, 21 February 2002.
19. *The government's annual report 99/00*, 26–7
20. D. Gaffney and A. Pollock, *Can the NHS afford the Private Finance Initiative?* (London: BMA, 1997); George Monbiot, *Captive State. The Corporate Takeover of Britain* (London: Macmillan, 2000), 62–82.
21. Jon Sussex, *The Economics of the Private Finance Initiative in the NHS* (London: OHE, 2001); A. Pollock, J. Shaoul, D. Rowland and S. Player, *Public services and the private sector. A response to the IPPR* (London: Catalyst, 2001). Reports favourable to PFI: *Building Better Partnerships: the final Report of the Commission on Public Private Partnerships* (London: IPPR, 2001); Arthur Anderson and Enterprise LSE, *Value for Money Drivers in the PFI* (London: HM Treasury, 2000).
22. Jane Mulkerrins, 'Britain's Best New Hospital (Its in France)', *Sunday Times*, 20 January 2002.
23. Alan Milburn, speech to the New Health Network, 'Redefining the

National Health Service', 15 January 2002; 10 Downing Street Newsroom, 'Radical decentralisation of NHS control', 15 January 2002; Tom Baldwin and Alice Miles, 'Firms to run hospitals. in Milburn plan', *The Times*, 15 January 2002; Alice Miles and Tom Baldwin, 'Milburn prescribes bitter pill for NHS', *The Times*, 15 January 2002; Alan Milburn, HC Debates, vol. 378, cols. 156–7, 15 January 2002; John Carvel and Michael White, 'Milburn's "Railtrack of the NHS"', *The Guardian*, 16 January 2002; David Charter. 'Private Firms are key to policy rethink', *The Times*, 11 February 2002.

24. Frank Dobson, HC Debates, vol. 378, col. 158, 15 January 2002; David Hinchliffe, HC Debates, vol. 378, cols. 160–1, 15 January 2002; Paul Waugh, 'Labour planning break-up of NHS', *The Independent*, 16 January 2002; Frank Dobson, 'The last thing the NHS needs is another edose of the private sector', *The Independent*, 28 January 2002; John Carvel, 'Public Sector Mutiny', *The Guardian*, 21 February 2002.
25. Lorna Duckworth, 'Failing hospitals to be run by outside managers', *The Independent*, 16 January 2002; Rosemary Bennett, 'Opponents of public/private partnership', *Financial Times*, 4 February 2002; idem, 'Accused Men: are these Blair's "wreckers"?', *Financial Times*, 5 February 2002.
26. Andrew Dilnot, 'Magic Required', *The Guardian*, 23 January 1997. Webster, *The NHS. A Political History*, 1998 edn., 216 (contained in Conclusions, now replaced in present edition).
27. Alan Milburn, speech to Institute for Public Policy Research, *The Guardian*, 21 December 1999; David Charter and Nigel Hawkes, 'NHS decline points to big tax increase', *The Times*, 20 February 2002.
28. *The Guardian*, 30 December 2000.
29. *New Statesman*, 12 January 2000.
30. Tony Blair, interview by David Frost, BBC TV, 16 January 2000.
31. *Securing our Future Health: Taking a Long-Term View. Interim Report* (London: HM Treasury, November 2001), 59–64. Note that the figures on p. 149 are one per cent less because they relate to NHS, rather than total health spending.
32. *Securing our Future Health.*
33. *The NHS Plan*, Chapter 3.
34. *Securing our Future Health*, para. 4.34.
35. *The New NHS Modern Dependable*, Cm. 3807 (London: The Stationery Office, December 1997).
36. *The New NHS Modern Dependable*, 10.

37. *The government's annual report 98/99* (London: The Stationery Office, July 1999).
38. These changes were first described in Mr. Milburn's speech to launch the Modernisation Agency on 25 April 2001. This was amplified in *Shifting the Balance of Power within the NHS* (London: Department of Health, July 2001).
39. Nicholas Timmins, 'NHS goes under the knife', *Financial Times*, 17 December 2001.
40. Prime Minister's New Year Message, 30 December 2001.
41. *The New NHS*, 32.
42. Association of Community Health Councils for England and Wales, *New Life for Health* (London: Vintage, 2000), 121–2.
43. J. Mohan and M. Gorsky, *Don't Look Back? Voluntary and Charitable Finance of Hospitals in Britain, Past and Present* (London: OHE, 2001), 112.
44. N. Timmins, 'Doctors' chiefs call for shake up in inspections of NHS Hospitals', *Financial Times*, 2 January 2002.
45. Professor Theodore Marmor, 'Fads in Medical Care Policy and Politics: the rhetoric and reality of managerialism', Rock Carling Lecture, 15 December 2001 (London: Nuffield Trust, in press).
46. John Bunyan, *The Pilgrim's Progress*, edited by N. H. Keeble (Oxford University Press, 1998), 51.

Conclusions

1. Tony Blair, 'My vision for the NHS of the future', Primary Care Conference, London, 13 April 1999.
2. Uwe E. Rheinhardt, *Accountable Health Care. Is it compatible with social solidarity?* (London: OHE, 1997), 5, 69.
3. Bevan, *In Place of Fear*, 85.
4. C. Webster, 'The Parable of the Incompetent Steward', *British Journal of Health Care Management*, 8 (2002), 107–8.

FURTHER READING

The following list is necessarily selective, especially concerning the period since 1989. Berridge provides a full survey of the recent historical literature. In most cases it will repay the reader to consult earlier editions of books cited below in their most recent editions.

ALLSOP, J., *Health Policy and the National Health Service: Towards 2000* (London: Longman, 1995).

BAGGOTT, R., *Health and Health Care in Britain* (2nd edn., Basingstoke: Macmillan, 1998).

BALY, M. E., *Nursing and Social Change* (3rd edn., London: Routledge, 1995).

BERRIDGE, V., *Health and Society in Britain since 1939* (Economic History Society Studies in Economic and Social History, Cambridge: Cambridge University Press, 1999).

BROWN, R. G. S., *Reorganising the National Health Service: A Case Study of Administrative Change* (Oxford: Blackwell/Robertson, 1979).

DEAKIN, N., *The Politics of Welfare: Continuities and Change* (London: Harvester/Wheatsheaf, 1994)

DINGWALL, R., RAFFERTY, A. M., and WEBSTER, C., *An Introduction to the Social History of Nursing* (London: Routledge, 1988).

HAM, C., *Health Policy in Britain* (4th edn., Basingstoke: Macmillan, 1999).

HARRIS, B., *The Health of the Schoolchild: A History of the School Medical Service in England and Wales* (Buckingham: Open University Press, 1995).

HARRISON, A., and DIXON, J., *The NHS Facing the Future* (London: King's Fund Publishing, 2000).

HARRISON, S., *National Health Service Management in the 1980s* (Aldershot: Avebury, 1994).

HONIGSBAUM, F., *The Division in British Medicine* (London: Kogan Page, 1979).

KLEIN, R., *The New Politics of the National Health Service* (4th edn., London: Prentice Hall, 2001).

LOWE, R., *The Welfare State in Britain since 1945* (2nd edn., Basingstoke: Macmillan, 1999).

MARTIN, J. P., *Hospitals in Trouble* (Oxford: Blackwell, 1984).

MOHAN, J., *A National Health Service? The Restructuring of Health Care in Britain since 1979* (London: Macmillan, 1995).

PATER, J., *The Making of the National Health Service* (London: King's Fund, 1981).

POWELL, M. A., *Evaluating the National Health Service* (Buckingham: Open University Press, 1997)

RANADE, W., *A Future for the National Health Service: Health Care in the 1990s* (2nd edn , Harlow: Longman, 1997).

RIVETT, G., *From Cradle to Grave. Fifty Years of the NHS* (London: King's Fund Publishing, 1998).

ROBINSON, R., and GRAND, J. Le (eds), *Evaluating the NHS Reforms* (London: King's Fund Institute, 1994).

STEVENS, R., *Medical Practice in Modern England* (New Haven, Conn.: Yale University Press, 1966).

TIMMINS, N., *The Five Giants: A Biography of the Welfare State* (Revised edn., London: HarperCollins, 2001).

WEBSTER, C., *The Health Services since the War*, i. *Problems of Health Care: The National Health Service before 1957* (London: HMSO, 1988).

—— *The Health Services since the War*, ii. *Government and Health Care: The British National Health Service 1958–1979* (London: The Stationery Office, 1996).

INDEX